AT THE FOUNTAIN OF YOUTH

Photograph by Fabian Bachrach

At the Fountain of Youth

Memories of a College President

WILLIAM PEARSON TOLLEY

SYRACUSE UNIVERSITY

Library of Congress Cataloging-in-Publication Data

Tolley, William Pearson, 1900–
    At the fountain of youth : memories of a college president /
    William Pearson Tolley.—1st ed.
    p.   cm.
    ISBN 0-8156-8114-3 (alk. paper)
    1. Tolley, William Pearson, 1900– . 2. College presidents—New
York (State)—Syracuse—Biography. 3. Syracuse University—
Presidents—Biography. I. Title.
LD5232.7 1942.A3   1989
378'.111—dc 19   88-27548
[B]   CIP

To R.C.T.

1900 – 1988

Let the heart keep memory bright

CONTENTS

PREFACE

*T*his book grew out of my efforts to assist Vice-Chancellor Michael O. Sawyer in the writing of another volume of the history of Syracuse University. Using a tape recorder, Vice-Chancellor Sawyer would question me about various aspects of the University and I would rely on my memory to reply. As we accumulated more and more material for his history, I also drew more and more on memories of personal experiences. Since so many of these had no part in the history of the University, I decided to tell the story of my life in a volume of my own. With Vice-Chancellor Sawyer's permission, I have made use of the material dictated to him.

Having been born in 1900, my life has spanned most of the twentieth century and a large share of that has been spent either as a student, teacher, dean, president, or chancellor. I have had the opportunity to observe the transformation of American higher education from elite institutions serving 3 or 4 percent of the youth of college age to a time when higher education is available to more than 50 percent of our youth. We have also seen an explosive expansion of graduate work and research leading to revolutionary changes in science and technology and our standards of living.

In the dictation and transcription of much of the material I was fortunate to have the assistance of Alexandra Mitchell Eyle. She is a writer of talent and experience. It was comforting to know that in the event of a failure in my health, she had the ability to bring the book to completion. I am also indebted to Mary Harmand for her devoted service in the final editing and rewriting. Finally, I am most grateful to Arpena Mesrobian for her counsel and help. She has made many useful suggestions.

Ponce de Leon came to America looking for the fountain of youth. He did not find it. He should have looked for it on the campuses of our schools and colleges. It is on the campuses of our colleges that our outlook is full of promise and hope.

Syracuse   WILLIAM PEARSON TOLLEY
July 1988

AT THE FOUNTAIN OF YOUTH

1

GROWING UP

I did not come from a family of educators. My father, Adolphus Charles Tolley, was the owner of shoe stores, first in Honesdale and Carbondale, Pennsylvania, and then in Binghamton, New York. His father, the Reverend Samuel Tolley, was a Wesleyan preacher in Cornwall before bringing his family to America when in his mid-forties. My mother, Emma Grace Sumner, traced her family history through Senator Charles Sumner of Massachusetts to ancestors who arrived in 1620 on the Mayflower. She was a high honors graduate of Wyoming Seminary in Kingston, Pennsylvania. Her father, the Reverend John Bunnell Sumner, was a leading minister in the Wyoming Conference of the Methodist Episcopal Church. He sang in the Wyoming Conference trio and wrote a number of hymns, of which the best known was "I'm a Child of the King." Grandfather Sumner had five daughters, two of whom inherited his exceptional voice. One was my mother, who was highly regarded in musical circles in New York's southern tier.

Mother was a bright, gracious, well-organized person who found time to raise five children, constantly entertain relatives and friends, teach a large Bible class for women, sing at weddings and funerals, and serve as soprano soloist on Sundays.

My father taught the Oxford class, a large Bible class for men. He was president of the Board of Trustees of the Centenary Methodist Church in Binghamton, New York, which we attended regularly as a family.

Our life was built around the church. In addition to going to Sunday school, we attended two church services on Sunday. We also went to prayer meeting on Wednesday night. At home, we

1

had regular family prayers, at which each of us learned to read the Bible aloud and with expression.

We had no tobacco, liquor, or cards in our house. We played games like Parcheesi, checkers, and dominoes, innocent card games like flinch and old maid, as well as croquet and tennis. Much of our leisure time was spent around the piano. Father had a fine bass voice, my brother Harold sang an excellent baritone, my brother Earl was an outstanding first tenor, and I sang second tenor. Mother and my sister Marjorie sang soprano, and my sister Dorothy alto. Both Mother and Father played the piano, and Earl played the mandolin like a professional. We were a closely knit family, and we made our own entertainment.

Father was fifteen when he left Cornwall and came to America. To help his family financially, he picked coal out of slag piles in Scranton, Pennsylvania. His formal schooling had ended when he left Cornwall, but he taught himself to read German. He knew a little French and Latin, read Shakespeare and the Bible, had a special interest in history, and was an excellent public speaker. Father also had superior penmanship. His writing had the flowing beauty and grace of an engraver, and this made his letters a delight to read. The lines were straight, the paragraphs neatly indented with a capital letter, and his name was signed with a flourish. Unfortunately, I did not inherit this talent. Few people can decipher what I write.

I was born in Honesdale, Wayne County, Pennsylvania, on September 13, 1900. Had I arrived a day later, it would have been on my brother Earl's second birthday. Another older brother, Harold, was born on January 16, 1894. To my mother's surprise and dismay, a sister, Marjorie, arrived on July 6, 1909, and then three years later, a second sister, Dorothy, was born on July 22, 1912. I remember that Father had a hangdog look as he awaited the arrival of the girls. Mother cried a good deal during the time she carried them, and Father felt sorry and ashamed. Neither knew anything about birth control, and Mother lived in constant fear of another pregnancy.

At the time I was born, Father had a shoe store in Honesdale and a second store in Carbondale. We lived in Honesdale the first three years of my life, and my memories of that time are pleasant and varied. On Sunday afternoons we went driving across the countryside with Father and his horse Prince. My older brothers enjoyed splashing in the stream in our backyard, and I loved to stare at the glittering trays of rings, watches, bracelets, and necklaces displayed in the jewelry store owned by our close friends the Butlers. My mother's grief when President McKinley was shot made an impression on me. His death on September 14, 1901, was on my brother Earl's third birthday. I was a year and a day old. It is my earliest memory.

Our days in Honesdale were full and satisfying, but Father's shoe stores were only modestly profitable. He knew his future was limited, and he was easily persuaded by his brother-in-law Clarence Willey to sell his Honesdale and Carbondale stores and open a shoe store under the name of Willey and Tolley at 31 Court Street in Binghamton, New York. We moved to Binghamton in the spring of 1903.

I learned one of my first lessons in diplomacy at Father's Binghamton store. Some of Father's Irish customers called the business Wiley and Toley, but father never corrected them. "Never disagree with customers," he told me: "Don't embarrass them."

The Court Street store was a success, but my uncle Clarence felt he could make a greater fortune in the building and contracting business, and so he sold his interest in the shoe store to Father. Father's rent rose steadily over the years, and this eventually led him to purchase a building at 157 Washington Street, just off Court Street, and move his business there. He also operated a second shoe store for several years, on the south side of Washington Street. This, however, was only marginally successful, and he soon traded it for several new homes near Floral Avenue in Johnson City. It was not a good year for real estate, and he had a hard time finding buyers.

The depression of the 1930s brought another disappointment to Father. While his customers had always been loyal to him, he depleted his working capital by paying off his mortgage too rapidly. At the bottom of the depression he lost both his Washington Street property and his store.

Fortunately by this time, we were able to help him, and he kept his home and his pride until he died at the age of eighty-nine. He had supported his father in his declining years, and when

Father grew older, his children did the same for him. We were glad we could do it.

Mother was not so fortunate. She contracted diabetes during her fifties, and, despite the daily use of insulin, she had one setback after another. She had one leg amputated when she was in her early sixties, and then the other leg had to go. She next suffered a stroke which left her bedridden and paralyzed. Finally, she had a second stroke, which left her blind. Yet whenever I called on her, she was writing hymns of praise and thanksgiving. Her only comment on her physical condition was, "Pray that I may be taken."

Mother was the most saintlike person I shall ever meet. She was completely unselfish. She was always serving others. She was full of compassion and love. We admired and loved our father, but we adored our mother. If any of the five children made his or her mark in life, it was because of her influence. None of us has been her equal.

During our years in Binghamton, Grandfather and Grandmother Tolley sometimes came to live with us. Grandfather Tolley had served in a succession of small Wesleyan chapels in Cornwall, but his lack of formal education and his age prevented his admission to the Wyoming Conference of the Methodist Episcopal Church. He was, however, given the status of local preacher. This permitted him to serve, on a year-to-year basis, small churches that no member of the Conference desired to serve. These were churches in hamlets like Shinhopple and Equinunk, Pennsylvania. Grandfather was not a great preacher, but he was well liked by his congregations. They especially enjoyed communion until a presiding elder discovered that Grandfather was serving wine instead of grape juice. There were years, however, when Grandfather had no congregation to serve—or presiding elders to offend. When this happened, he and Grandmother Tolley would live with us.

It did not make life any easier for Mother to care for my grandparents as well as my father and three lively boys. Yet Mother appeared to enjoy having them, and so did I.

Grandfather Tolley was patience itself with small children. Before I entered kindergarten, he taught me the alphabet and then how to spell, count, tell time, and read. I learned everything quickly, perhaps because it was such a delight to settle on his lap and learn from this wise, patient, and lovable man.

I remember asking him whether he believed in heaven. "I certainly do," he replied.

"Are you anxious to see it?" I asked.

Grandfather looked down at me and said, "Have I ever lied to you?"

"No, you haven't," I replied.

"Well," he confessed, "the truth is that I want to stay here as long as I can."

My childhood was simple and delightful. The only difficulties I encountered were with the educational system. In looking back I wonder whether the silly rules I did not like as a boy made me more tolerant when I myself became a dean and college president.

Thanks to the patience and forethought of Grandfather Tolley, I was well ahead of my peers in my learning skills. Because of this, I went to kindergarten at the age of four. According to school regulations, however, I could not enter the first grade until I reached the age of six. Thus, I stayed in kindergarten a second year, learning nothing. My sense of boredom continued until the fourth grade when, for the first time, I began studying things I did not already know.

In the ennui of waiting for the educational system to catch up with my grandfather's training, I encountered another problem. I am left-handed, and in that unenlightened time, one was not permitted to write with one's left hand. Again and again my teachers punished me, often with a heavy ruler, again with a good spanking, and at least twice with a note to my mother. The punishments, however, were to no avail. I continued to write with my left hand. Finally I was sent to see the school superintendent, Edward J. Banta. Mr. Banta put me on his knee, and asked me what my problem was. I explained that my teachers were stupid, but perhaps it was not their fault, since they were required to enforce a silly rule.

"You see, sir," I said, "I was born left-handed. It is as natural for me to use my left hand as it is for right-handed people to use their right hands. I shall always be left-handed."

"Isn't it interesting that your teacher sent you to me?" Mr.

Banta said with a smile. "You're a lucky boy. I am left-handed, too, and we are changing that rule today. Go back to school and write with your left hand."

The Pine Street school I attended was not in the best part of the city. It was close to a rough section known as "the Patch," and our school also had its share of underprivileged children. Our recesses were spent in fighting as much as in playing. I soon found that being left-handed was as much to my advantage in the school yard as it had been to my disadvantage in the classroom. In street fights, my left hand helped to give me a string of victories that made me a school-yard champion. The day came, however, when I met a boy who was quicker and stronger than I. With that defeat firmly imprinted on both my body and my mind, I learned a sense of caution and did little boxing until I went to college.

When I was nine, Mother engaged a music teacher to give her three boys piano lessons. They were not expensive, but Mother had to pinch pennies to pay for them. Like most boys, we did not like to practice. Finally, Mother decided her financial sacrifice was in vain. Later, we were each sorry the lessons stopped. I was almost at the point where even my parents would have been pleased with my progress. Ever since, I have played the piano primarily by ear. I greatly enjoy playing for my own entertainment.

The piano lessons paid off later, when I spent the sum of $1.65 for a piccolo ordered from Sears, Roebuck and Company, and taught myself to play it. It opened a whole new world for me.

One day my grandfather Sumner heard me play. He asked me if I could play "Old Black Joe," and I said, "Of course." After I played a number of Stephen Foster songs, Grandfather told me he had a flute he had played in a Union army band during the Civil War. His playing did not always charm his southern listeners. Once while he was playing in the Deep South, a woman sympathetic to the Confederacy threw a green apple at point-blank range and broke his nose. Upon showing me the flute, Grandfather said, "You may have it. Anyone who can play the piccolo can play the flute." Armed with both, I immediately joined the school orchestra and played throughout grade school and high school.

Money was scarce during my childhood. We soon learned that if we wanted a dollar to spend, we should earn it ourselves.

The easiest way to earn money was by selling and delivering papers. I was eight years old when I first stood on a street corner selling papers, and a year or two later I had my own paper route. My two older brothers also worked. We had our own spending money and bought most of our own clothes. Once a year, however, a blue serge suit was purchased for my brother Earl, and the following year I inherited it.

One year my parents also bought me a new suit. It was the first I had owned. I was so proud of it that I wore it every day until I had the misfortune of tearing a sizable hole in the trousers while riding my sled. I wept bitterly, and Mother wept with me. After that, despite the visible patch, I wore the suit only on Sundays and special occasions. After that, Earl's hand-me-down blue serge was again good enough for me. I still have the scar on my right leg from the sled ride that tore my new trousers.

My older brothers and I had been sharing a sled for years. When I was nine years old, however, mother took me to a department store to select the sled I wanted as my Christmas present. The salesman tried to sell me a Flexible Flyer, which was just coming on the market. It was much higher than the sled I had been using, and you could steer it with your hands or feet. I thought it looked like a girl's sled and would have nothing to do with it. Instead, I insisted on buying a low sled with rigid runners. Imagine my surprise and chagrin when on Christmas day all my friends displayed their new Flexible Flyers. My new sled was out of style. I learned a lesson then about the importance of fashion. It made a lasting impression on me.

As in the case of the sled, I did not have my own bicycle for many years. Instead, I borrowed my brothers' bicycles when they were not in use. I was very proud of my skill in riding with no hands. Once when showing off by looking backwards and waving to my friends, the back of my head hit a steel light pole at the curbside. That, too, made an impression on me.

After living on the southside of Binghamton where the Susquehanna River flooded our cellar every spring, we moved to 47 Pine Street. Later, we moved to an apartment house at 76 Pine Street. While we were living in the apartment, Father contracted a severe case of typhoid fever. We were all terrified that he would die. Finally, the fever broke, and he was soon on the road to recovery, but temporarily without hair. The hair gradually grew back again, and as long as he lived, Father kept a full head of hair that never turned gray. He always claimed that this was related to his having survived typhoid fever.

It was at 76 Pine Street that Marjorie was born, when I was nine years old. My brothers and I acted as baby-sitters, and Marjorie made that quite a job. Once when I was alone with her, she put a broom into a gas flame on the stove and then ran merrily through the apartment setting fire to the curtains. It was touch and go for a few minutes as to whether I could get the fires under control, and I remember how thoroughly frightened I was.

Some of my fondest memories are of spending time on the farm of Grandfather and Grandmother Sumner, near Kirkwood, New York. One summer Grandfather let us help with the haying. We discovered then that there is no smell so delightful as that of newly mown hay. When we weren't busy haying, Grandfather Sumner would take us to the blacksmith's shop, where we watched the shoeing of horses; or he would let us play in his barn, which was a paradise for children.

When I was eleven, Grandfather Sumner gave Mother three lots on West End Avenue, and Father decided to build a house on them. Two of the lots faced West End Avenue, and the third was directly in back of the two front lots on Sumner Avenue. They provided ample space for a house, garage, chicken house, and a large garden.

Both the Sumner farm at Kirkwood, and Grandfather's five acres on West End Avenue contained an abundance of chestnut trees. After a frosty night, the chestnuts were everywhere on the ground under the trees. We were allowed to gather them, and we loved this activity as much as we disliked picking raspberries from Grandmother Sumner's half acre of raspberry bushes at West End Avenue. Each of us was expected to help pick raspberries several times a week during the season.

The years at West End Avenue were happy and busy ones. Mother was a wonderful cook, and the table always had an abundance of food, much of it coming from our own garden. One or two week days, and every Sunday, we dined on chicken. Our flock usually numbered around one hundred, and it was my job to take care of them, along with some ducks. Needless to say, we had more eggs than we could eat. I particularly enjoyed taking care of the chickens and cleaning the coops, while my brothers would have no part of this. I did not like cutting off the heads of our chickens. I became adept at it, however, as well as at plucking and cleaning them. I believe we made at least a dollar per chicken, or more than a hundred dollars a year in addition to having all the eggs and chickens a family with five growing children could eat. Moreover, the chicken manure was better than any commerical fertilizer. It made everything grow.

The garden had lettuce, radishes, parsley, rutabaga, chard, parsnips, potatoes, peas, beans, squash, turnips, pumpkins, onions, rhubarb, cucumbers, cauliflower, tomatoes, strawberries, melons, grapes, and raspberries. We also had cherries, pears, peaches, and apples from our own fruit trees.

Father had a green thumb with both flowers and vegetables. No one on the street could match his dahlias or roses. Every morning he tended his garden for several hours before going to the shoe store. He had great pride in the quality of our fruits and vegetables, and he shared our surplus with neighbors and friends. We canned the extra produce for consumption during the long winter months. We had a huge fruit cellar in our basement, and we made jellies, jams, canned pears, beans, tomatoes, pickles, and stored our potatoes and apples.

Mother never let us eat any of the best apples. Instead, she sorted them carefully, giving us those with one or more small rotten spots. As a consequence, we ate rotten apples from November to March. We also had vast quantities of homemade applesauce and applesauce cake. I am sure those apples helped keep the doctor away. I still remember, however, the heavy doses of sulphur and molasses we all took before the last snows of winter. This ritual was one of the harbingers of spring.

I also recall mustard plasters, the daily use of Scott's Emulsion, and the frequent use of phthisopyrin. These medicines did what aspirin, Coricidin, Tylenol, and other cold tablets do today.

We were a healthy group of children, and we boys kept ourselves busy playing outdoors whenever the weather allowed. When we moved to our West End Avenue home, my brothers immediately decided to build a clay tennis court on the empty lot on the right side of the house. It was no small undertaking, and I was too young to be of much help. Finally, they succeeded in clearing and leveling the land, bringing in the clay, building the backstop, and setting the posts for the net. My assignment was to keep the lines fresh and the court well rolled. The tennis court was a great attraction to our friends, and it kept the boys busy, at home, and out of trouble. We had no tennis lessons, so our form was that of the self-taught. We learned, however, to keep the ball in play, and we were excellent retrievers.

I recall one city tournament when my brother Earl and I were in high school. Despite our lack of form, we defeated some of the best doubles teams in the city. Our opponents found it difficult to understand how we could have beaten them. They underestimated our ability to keep the ball in play. We were scramblers. We just kept returning the ball until our opponents hit it into the net or out of bounds. We were human backboards.

As much fun as we had in outdoor sports and activities, some of my happiest memories are of the hours we spent as a family.

Mother would serve our Sunday noon dinner, and afterward we would clear the table and do the dishes and then gather around the piano. Later, Father would keep Mother out of the kitchen while he made his delicious hash brown potatoes for our supper. I don't remember what else he cooked. I do recall that in the winter months we had lots of oyster stew, baked beans, baked ham, and homemade ice cream. What a joy it was to turn the crank of the freezer and then to lick the spoon!

Liquor never accompanied our meals and, as mentioned earlier, was never in the house. The closest thing to it was Dr. Kilmer's Swamp Root, a patent medicine that contained, among its ingredients, a high percentage of alcohol.

When Father was eighty-nine, and the doctor told us he had only a few hours to live, I went to the liquor store and bought a bottle of brandy. I put some in a tablespoon and tried to get Father to swallow it. He was unable to speak, but he wrote on a note pad, "Have lived eighty-nine years without it. Will go the rest of the way."

Before I left for college, we had a long talk about drinking. He said, "I have never discussed drinking with your older brothers, but I want to do so with you. You are different. You overdo everything. You play too hard, you work too hard, and if you begin to drink, you will drink too much. So I want you to stay away from it." I promised I would.

The care and respect my parents had for me and my brothers and sisters was not unique in my experience with adults. I found that my teachers also cared deeply for their students. In some ways our public school teachers were better than they are today. Every class was demanding. The attention given to public speaking and debates, the drills in parsing sentences, the exercises in mental arithmetic, the attention to grammar, spelling, composition, and reading meant that we all had the basic skills that are lacking among so many present-day students.

At a time when there were enormous differences in the level of education across the nation, it was a golden period for the bright students in the public schools of New York State. The Board of Regents made no compromise with quality in the statewide Regents examinations. Students went to school to learn, and good teachers were the rule and not the exception. The curriculum was designed to help students prepare for admission to college. There was little vocational training, and no subjects such as drivers' education were taught. Courses in physical education and social studies received minimal attention. Instead, the emphasis was placed on Latin, English, French, German, Spanish, biology, physics, chemistry, ancient history, modern history, algebra, geometry, intermediate algebra, and calculus. The goal was liberal education. Today we would call such a curriculum antiquated and designed for an elite few. In truth, it was designed for bright students who were college-bound.

Binghamton Central High School had many dedicated teachers. Belle F. Carver in geometry mothered and loved all of us. Amanda Frink was a superb teacher of algebra. Nellie B. Rogers, who taught German, marched us through our grammar again and again like a top drill sergeant. Alexander W. Miller was a demanding teacher of debate and English, whose students won many statewide oratorical contests. E. Corrine Lemon in English belied her name. She was sweet and lovable and we worshipped her. Our principal, John F. Hummer, was a firm, kindly, able principal for whom we had deep respect and admiration.

We also had one teacher who was a legend in her time, Caesar Brown of the Latin department. She looked like the cleaning lady in the Dutch Cleanser trademark. She ruled by fear. Her weakness was her toughness on girls. She was unfair to the members of her own sex. My best girl, Ruth Canfield, would meet me during the luncheon hours and share with me the fruits of several hours of study in translating Caesar, Cicero, or Virgil. I listened closely, looked at the text briefly, and tucked away the translation in my head. When Ruth recited, Caesar Brown would pounce on her like a hawk on a sparrow and destroy her confidence. She would then call on me. I would repeat Ruth's translation word for word, whereupon Caesar Brown would say, "Ruth, why can't you do your homework as well as Pearson Tolley?"

At the senior dance, Ruth and I, as vice-president and president of the senior class, respectively, sat with Principal and Mrs. Hummer. I remember him saying, "Someday I want you to invite Mrs. Hummer and me to dinner and let us meet three red-headed children."

Years later, Mr. Hummer became assistant superintendent of schools at Syracuse, a position he held while I was Chancellor of Syracuse University. One evening he and Mrs. Hummer were our guests for dinner. On that occasion they met our three children, Nelda, Bill, and Katryn. We shared many happy memories of Binghamton Central High School. We saw the Hummers often in the years that followed, and remained their friends until they died.

Mr. Hummer remembered me as a good student. Once I reached the fourth grade and discovered something I did not know, I quickly went to the head of my class. By the sixth grade, I was so far ahead of my classmates that my teachers urged my parents to let me skip a grade. It would have been good for me, I believe, but my parents were against it.

When I graduated from the elementary school at the end of the eighth grade, I was named valedictorian and had to give a speech at the graduation exercises. My brother Harold was sufficiently impressed to say that if I were also valedictorian of my high-school class he would give me a gold watch. I did not forget that promise, and four years later reminded him of it. He gave me an Elgin watch with seventeen jewels which I carried for some fifty years. I was happy to be at the head of my class, but much prouder to stand first in Broome County in the New York State Regents Examination. I was also happy that my scholastic standing entitled me to a Regents Scholarship.

In high school, I had four years of Latin, four years of English, three of mathematics, two of German, two of history, and one year each of physics and biology. My primary extracurricular activities were debating and public speaking, both of which served me well later. I won the Weeks Oratorial Contest, competed in the statewide oratorical contest at Hamilton College, played in the orchestra, was editor of the high school paper, and served as president of my class and of the student body.

Throughout the four years I was in high school, I was also working for Father, clerking in the shoe store, and delivering packages for a well-known men's clothing store, Grube and Dutcher, located on Court Street. Harold, my oldest brother, was in college, and Earl was the star quarterback on the team that won the New York State championship. That meant that Father needed me to clerk after school until the store closed at six o'clock. Then I would deliver packages for Grube and Dutcher as well as for my father's store. I received ten cents a package and put much of the money into a savings account for college.

In my sophomore year of high school, a lovely young lady with beautiful auburn hair sat directly in front of me in geometry class. She wore the same outfit every year: a white middy blouse and a navy-blue serge skirt. Her name was Ruth Canfield.

Ruth was an excellent student, a fine public speaker, vice-president of her class, vice-president of the student body, president of the Literary Society, and in my mind, the prettiest girl in high school.

Her older brother, Gordon Canfield, was an outstanding debater and public speaker who won first prize in a statewide oratorical contest at Columbia University. Later he served for more than twenty years in the House of Representatives in Washington, and was the senior congressman from New Jersey. Among other distinctions, he was widely known as the Father of the Coast Guard.

When I met Ruth we did not have much time for dating. Once a week I would take the street car from the west end of Binghamton to the north end of the city where she lived. No matter where we went, we had to be at her home by eleven o'clock so that I would not miss the last trolley, which left the north side at around eleven-thirty.

I had not known many girls before Ruth. As a boy, I worshipped from a distance a lovely girl named Dorothy Rogers. During my freshman year in high school, I finally had a date with her. I still recall with embarrassment how I slipped on an oriental rug in her home as I was being presented to her parents. I was even more ashamed and chagrined when, upon leaving the trolley car, I got off at the rear end, as she was about to leave from the front. I don't think I made a very favorable impression on her.

It is difficult for the present generation to appreciate that one could go steadily with one girl for three or four years before kissing her, and that even after a ten-year courtship, neither boy nor girl had experimented with sex. It just wasn't done in the circles in which we traveled. If one respected a girl, one made no improper advances. From my sophomore year in high school until I had completed seven years of college and postgraduate study, I had but one girl, and for much of that period I was the only boy in whom she was seriously interested.

While I was dreaming of Ruth, I was also dreaming of going to college. I wanted to go to Harvard, although at that time, I knew no Harvard graduate, and no one from Harvard was recruiting students in the New York southern tier. As far as my parents were concerned, however, there was only one university, and that was the institution founded by Methodists, Syracuse University.

At Syracuse, Harold had studied Bible under Dr. Ismar J. Peritz, and during these studies he encountered what was called higher criticism of the scriptures. This theory strengthened rather than upset Harold's faith. When, however, he returned home for the Christmas holidays, he shocked and outraged my parents. The ensuing debates over religion were endless, and Earl and I listened to both sides without taking part. Soon we found Harold's arguments convincing. After a time my parents agreed not to discuss the question, and the two generations remained poles apart in their views of the Bible's inspiration and meaning.

Nevertheless, my parents continued to view Syracuse University as the only place for the sons of good Methodist parents. Our Centenary Church offered me a scholarship to go to Syracuse, and between that and my Regents Scholarship, the matter was settled.

As I set off for college, I was not interested in the ministry. My goal was to become a lawyer. Mother had a cousin who had a substantial law practice in New York City. He encouraged me to study law and promised me a place in his law firm after admission to the bar.

2

AN UNDERGRADUATE AT
SYRACUSE UNIVERSITY

I had four of the best years of my life as an undergraduate at Syracuse University. Each of my teachers influenced me, many of them deeply. I also learned from diverse experiences outside of the classroom. These included serving in the Student Army Training Corps (SATC); working in a shoe store; acting in Boar's Head, the University's dramatic club, and the Tambourine and Bones Musicals; joining the University Chorus and Glee Club; serving on the debate teams; playing saxophone in my own band, the Synful Syncopaters; directing the Instrumental Club; editing the *Onondagan;* and serving on the senior council and as president and acting general secretary of the YMCA.

Before entering the university in 1918, I declared that I was older than I was in order to register for the draft. I was assigned to Company F of the Student Army Training Corps at Syracuse University. Our headquarters were in the Phi Kappa Psi house at 113 College Place, but our company also occupied the Psi Upsilon house, the Delta Kappa Upsilon house, and the Phi Gamma Delta house.

I was a poor soldier. I contracted Spanish influenza that had reached epidemic proportions shortly after my induction and spent several weeks in an emergency infirmary in Winchell Hall. Several of my roommates died from it, and I remember hearing a nurse say one morning, "Are you still here? We thought we were going to lose you last night." Even though none of us saw active duty, the members of the SATC had a heavy death toll from the influenza that swept the nation. Today, with penicillin, this would no longer be the case.

When I was at last strong enough to take part in daily drills, I was far behind my friends in military instruction, as well as in classwork. I was, however, made supply sergent. My job was to issue all military equipment, such as shoes, hats, stockings, underwear, uniforms, rifles, overcoats, pillows and blankets, and all cleaning materials, light bulbs, and toilet tissue.

My days as a supply sergeant brought about a change in my name. Throughout my childhood, I was known to everyone as Pearson Tolley, so as supply sergeant, I signed my requisitions: W. Pearson Tolley.

"What does the 'W' stand for?" asked my company commander. "William, sir," I replied.

"Where the hell do you think you are?" was his curt response. "In the Boy Scouts of America? Hereafter, you sign everything William P. Tolley."

"Yes, sir," was the response of this shaken boy. I have been Bill Tolley ever since to all but my immediate family. I recall a telephone call to Binghamton from George Coughlin of the Class of 1922 who asked, "Is Bill home?"

"There is no Bill here," said my mother. "We have Harold, Earl, Pearson, Marjorie, and Dorothy. Take your choice—but no Bill!"

We had a false armistice a few days in advance of November 11, 1918. When the news came, I was on guard duty. I remember that I wept for shame that I had not succeeded in getting to Europe, had not been shot at by Germans, and had no heroic tales to tell my children or grandchildren. Actually, I could tell them that I had an injured finger—the little finger on my right hand still shows a scar below the fingernail. We never had live ammunition in our rifles, but I pulled the trigger one day and my little finger got caught in the rifle. The scar is very visible. I have sometimes wondered whether I could have received a Purple Heart had I applied for one.

As supply sergeant, I had to stay in uniform and account for my company's supplies before I could be discharged. I was dismayed to find that while we had a surplus of blankets, we were short some twenty pairs of shoes. I had a sleepless night before I encountered the officer in charge. He put me at ease immediately, saying "Sergeant, Company F has the best record of any of our companies, and you've been scrupulously honest. No other supply sergeant has reported any surpluses, and they all had shortages. Let me thank you for a good job, and we'll expedite your honorable discharge."

When it finally came, the official discharge was a disappointment. It listed me at the rank of private, not as a sergeant. However, as I told a major general in introducing him at Chapel one day, "Like the general, I have had a distinguished record in the army. I enlisted as a private, rose rapidly in the ranks, and retired from the army as a private."

As a civilian, my first dormitory room was in Sims Hall. Sims had been built in 1913, and was still a relatively new building. One would not know this, however, after the SATC moved out in November 1918. Many of the doors were off the hinges, the mattresses and beds had been abused, curtains were torn, and the floors needed refinishing. Evidence of vandalism was everywhere. As men returned from the war and filled the dormitory, they added to the damage.

Freshman hazing was a popular sport when I entered the University, and the sophomores, ecstatic at no longer being looked down on as freshmen themselves, were merciless. At any opportunity, we freshmen retaliated in kind. I still feel guilty about the treatment we dealt a fine sophomore named Blair Wormer. We hit his backside so hard with a board that he was hospitalized for a week or more. Eventually, some sophomores discovered that I had been involved in the attack on Wormer, and they came to my room about 1:00 A.M. in late December and took me out to the Oakwood Cemetery where there was a pond covered with a thin coating of ice. They threw me in the pond and left me to swim ashore. I had been blindfolded, so I didn't have the faintest idea of where I was. I wandered around in the freezing cold until suddenly I heard a friendly voice. It turned out to be that of Howard Hoople. Howard, or Tot, as he was known to everyone, was president of the student body. He was a great football star and was admired by all. He and a friend had heard that a freshman had been taken out and dumped in a pond, and he was concerned about the danger to the freshman's health. He took me back to Sims Hall. I remember being ill for several weeks with a high temperature and a case of influenza almost as severe as I had experienced in September.

Today, the rivalry between freshmen and sophomores has practically died out on college campuses. Even the class rushes are a thing of the past. The place of fraternities has seen a resurgence of late, but it, too, does not carry the importance or influence that it did when I was an undergraduate. Joining the right fraternity was a major decision, marking a singular rite of passage for a college boy.

I joined the fraternity of my two older brothers, Pi Kappa Alpha. It might, however, have been different. For about twenty minutes I was pledged to Delta Kappa Epsilon. When I left the DKE house with the pledge pin on my lapel, I ran into my brother Earl. He saw what had happened, marched me back to the fraternity house, and told the members of DKE that they could have their pin back; his brother was going to join Pi Kappa Alpha. And so I did.

DKE was a rich man's fraternity, as was Psi Upsilon. Fraternity peer pressure has the effect of raising or lowering moral and academic standards. A good fraternity does a great deal of leveling up; a poor one is equally influential in leveling down. The Dekes had a reputation for drinking, and they lived down to their reputation. The Psi U's were not as well known for their drinking as the Dekes, and on the whole they did more for their members than the Dekes did. Both, however, were very strong organizations at that time.

My fraternity had a rule against drinking, and it was enforced. My fraternity brothers went out on the town only on Saturday nights, and did no drinking in the house. However, they wasted a great deal of time playing cards.

In addition to joining a fraternity, I sang in both the Glee Club and the University Choir, as did my brother Earl. There was a great deal of group singing at that time, and Gordon and Tot Hoople, my brother Earl, and I spent many a spring evening serenading the sorority houses. Earl sang first tenor, and I sang second. Tot was our baritone, and Gordon sang a majestic bass. From time to time we had others join us. One substitute was Mark Love. He didn't enjoy the college songs we sang. He was stiff and ill at ease with popular music. Although his voice was glorious, he didn't last long as a substitute. Later, he became a leading operatic singer in Chicago, where he was widely acclaimed.

The yearbook became another interest of mine, and during my sophomore year I worked on the *Onondagan*. A few days before the editor was selected, I learned that the Dekes and Psi U's controlling the election had decided to name Monroe P. O'Donnell editor of the *Onondagan*. Three people constituted the election committee. I went to each and showed them, page by page, that 85 percent of the forthcoming yearbook was the work of one William P. Tolley, and less than 2 percent was the work of Monroe P. O'Donnell. I can remember few other times in my life when I was more angered or determined. I hung on like a puppy to a root until finally each of the three told me, "We were wrong. Would you be satisfied to have Monty as managing editor?" I said, "Of course."

Everyone should experience failure as well as success while young. In my case, a nationwide printers' strike brought to a halt all my hard work in producing the 1922 *Onondagan*. Because of the strike, we could not print the yearbook until late summer. When we delivered the books at last in September, we had a marketing problem not unlike that of selling last year's calendar. No one was interested. Only those people who had paid for their yearbooks in advance wanted copies.

Editing the yearbook was a learning experience. I also learned a great deal performing in the Tambourine and Bones Musical Society. At that time, it was an all-male organization, and the men played the women's parts as well. I recall borrowing a black velvet dress from Florence Blount, which I wore in one show. Suddenly, in the middle of my act, I was hit by a cowardly tomato that ran when it hit me. I feared the stain could not be removed by dry cleaning, but Florence was very understanding.

I was also president of Boar's Head and took part in several productions, including "The Tailor-Made Man." I was not a great actor, but I have many fond memories of each play.

In my senior year I was a member of Tau Theta Upsilon,

which, along with Phi Kappa Alpha, comprised the university's two senior honor societies for men. These two honorary fraternities alternated each year between giving the Block S Dinner for athletes and the Senior Ball. Both societies had lost money the year before, and the loss was paid for by the members. Having been burned by the *Onondagan* experience, I insisted on handling the financial arrangements of the Senior Ball. This decision did not make me popular with my Tau Theta Upsilon brothers until it was over. It was a success both socially and financially. We divided $1,500 among seven members after paying for our guests' hotel bills, a limousine trip to Ithaca, and a special celebration party.

My personal recollection of the Senior Ball includes the memory of a blackout that occurred while I was dancing with the Dean of Women, Jean Marie Richards. When, however, the lights came back on, the girl in my arms was Ruth Canfield. She had been dancing near me, and when we lost the lights I took advantage of the darkness to steal her from the arms of her partner. Later, I made amends to Dean Richards, who had a warm heart despite a formidable manner.

Of all my undergraduate activities, my experiences on the S.U. debate teams served me best in later years. I was a varsity debater for four years, during which time we were led by the incomparable Professor Sherman L. Kennedy. A superb teacher and coach, he was a quiet man who resembled Socrates. Thanks to him, we were one of the best debate teams in the nation. Professor Kennedy had a remarkable ability to point out weaknesses without destroying one's self-esteem. I count among my memories a superb victory over Harvard at Albany, where we had a distinguished board of judges, including Chancellor John Finlay, New York State Commissioner of Education, who later became editor of the *New York Times*.

The only debate I remember losing was at the University of Pennsylvania, where a witty Irishman used sarcasm to make up for what he lacked in logic.

Encouraged by Professor Kennedy, I competed in a number of oratorical contests. In my senior year I entered the Horace White contest, which was by far the most important speaking contest of that time. My subject was "A College Man's Religion." The judges rated the written speeches as well as the performances of the speakers. Before the contest began, I learned that of the six speeches, mine had been ranked sixth. Knowing this was good for my adrenaline, apparently, for when my turn to speak arrived, I gave it a special effort. I could not believe my good fortune when the judges awarded me first prize. My sense of arithmetic told me this was impossible if they gave equal weight to both the writing and speaking. The rest of that night I told myself, "Don't get excited, they'll call you in the morning and say it was a mistake." They didn't, however, and the $100 prize was mine.

Professor Kennedy formed close personal relationships with each of us, and we trusted him implicitly. I had never taken a drink in college until my senior year when we debated Columbia University—and had an unexpected win. After the debate, I took Ruth Canfield to a late evening musical starring Marilyn Miller and returned to the Columbia University Club, where we were staying, long after midnight. I had a very severe cough, and George Coughlin, also one of our debaters, said, "Bill, you're going to catch pneumonia unless we stop it right now. I have a glass of stuff here that will cure you if you drink it." I said, "Fine." He had a tumbler full of whiskey. He expected me to sip it. I had never tasted liquor. I simply turned the glass up, and gulped it down the way one would drink water. Then I made a serious mistake. I said, "I have to go to the bathroom." He said, "No, jump into your bed." Needless to say before I got back from the bathroom I was drunk as a lord. George said later that I sang all the songs that I'd heard at the musical.

I was awakened on Sunday morning by Professor Kennedy, and I quickly became aware that I had thrown up everything while asleep. Viewing the evidence, I was sure Professor Kennedy knew exactly what had happened. Nonetheless, I confessed nothing—nor did anyone else. I sheepishly got dressed and went to church hoping the Lord would forgive me. Later, I was pleasantly surprised to learn Professor Kennedy never reported the incident.

We never spoke of this experience in the years that followed, but I always felt indebted to Professor Kennedy for keeping whatever he knew in confidence. When I returned to Syracuse in 1942 as Chancellor, my secretary said "There is a young man who wants to see you. His name is Kennedy." He came in, and said, "Sir, you've probably never heard of him, but my father was Sherman L. Kennedy, and he was a professor here." I looked at him and said, "Are you ready for college?" "Yes, sir." "Are you coming here as a freshman in the fall?" "Yes, sir." I said, "It gives me great pleasure to tell you that you have a scholarship covering your tuition for your four years here. It is one way I can say 'thank you' to your father."

I met Chancellor James Roscoe Day only twice during my undergraduate years. When registering at the University, I explained to Mr. Bassett, the treasurer, that I had both a Regents Scholarship for $100, and a church scholarship for $50. The tuition at the time was $120. Mr. Bassett said that I could have the Regents Scholarship, but not the scholarship from Centenary Church, in Binghamton. When I observed that one was state money and the other a fund controlled by the donor, he suggested that I see the Chancellor.

Chancellor Day was a majestic, overpowering figure. After I stated my case to him, he rose slowly to his full height, looked down at this timid, freshman boy, and said, "Young man, you may be right, but you lose!" That ended the matter.

Often when, as Chancellor, I was compelled to deny requests from students I remembered this experience—and tried to temper student disappointment by saying how sorry I was that I could not find a way to say yes.

Contrary to my experience with Chancellor Day, I had a close rapport with my teachers. My respect and admiration deepened as I came to know them better.

Dr. Mark A. May, professor of psychology, and one of the nation's best known psychologists, was determined that I, too, would be a psychology professor. Whenever he went away on a lecture tour, Professor May would ask me to teach his classes. Once he came back unexpectedly in the middle of a lecture, and at its close said, "I told you you would be a fine teacher."

I was a frequent guest in his home, as were many other students. Later Professor May became a professor at Columbia Uni-

versity Teacher's College and then at Yale. When I was a graduate
student of philosophy at Columbia, I met him on campus several
times, and each time he said, "You are in the wrong discipline.
Come study with me. I'll see that you get your doctorate in a
hurry!"

One of the most influential teachers at Syracuse University
was George Albert Wilson, chairman of the philosophy department. He made it a habit to take long walks with his philosophy
majors, and he took many walks with me. I can still remember
some of the things we talked about. Often our discussions centered around philosophers about whom we usually disagreed. At
the time, I was interested in Henri Bergson, the French philosopher, about whom Professor Wilson had very pronounced ideas. I
disagreed with many of his views, but he enjoyed our lively conversations.

Wilson was not an inspiring lecturer. In an 8:00 A.M. class
in the Hall of Languages, with radiators so hot that we slept if we
sat near them, or froze if we didn't, it was hard to concentrate on
his lectures. Yet despite the limited impact of his lectures, Wilson
was the teacher to whom I owe the most. Once I wrote a paper for
him on George Galloway's *Philosophy of Religion*. Back came my
paper with Wilson's succinct comment: "Excellent on Galloway;
what about Tolley?" Many of our best graduates were students of
Professor Wilson. He made us think for ourselves.

Ismar J. Peritz was another professor with great influence.
He was the man whose modernist approach to the Bible had
caused a rift between my parents and my eldest brother, Harold.

Professor Peritz converted to Christianity from Judaism. A
nationally known scholar, he taught the Bible in what was then a
very advanced way: Instead of insisting that the Bible was infal-
lible, as had been taught in my Sunday school, Peritz introduced
his students to the Old Testament sources of *J, E, D*, and *P*. The *J*
stood for the Jahweh tradition, the *E* for the Elohim material, the
D for the Deuteronomic tradition, and the *P* for the contribution
of the prophets. I read the Bible from Genesis to Revelations twice
as an undergraduate. His views changed the way in which I and
other students at Syracuse viewed the Bible.

Equally outstanding as a teacher was Perley Oakland Place,
professor of Latin. His impressive appearance, polished speech,

and courtly demeanor made him look like an ancient Roman. An outstanding scholar and teacher, he had been offered professorships at Dartmouth and Princeton, but chose to remain at Syracuse. Learning from him, we never thought of Latin as a dead language.

One of the most demanding teachers I encountered at Syracuse University was an eccentric professor of economics by the name of Frederick Roman. At the beginning of every class he gave a one-question quiz. Our textbook was the two-volume work *Principles of Economics,* by Frederick W. Taussig. Professor Roman would give either a mark of 100 or 0, and we had five minutes to complete the quiz. Needless to say, we were always prepared. Each semester I had a final grade of 96.

What most impressed me about Roman was not his teaching—which was outstanding—but the fact that he was a disciple of Henry George and was a single taxer, free trader, pacifist, and Socialist. He also waged a one-man war on tobacco. We disagreed with his views, yet Roman welcomed disagreement. He never penalized us for it. Because he was thought to be a dangerous radical, Professor Roman was fired by Chancellor Day during my junior year. This taught me a lesson I did not forget. Professor Roman was not a radical. Like so many professors, he was simply one who thought otherwise. He had his own ideas, and he loved to advocate them. He especially enjoyed a debate with students who disagreed with him. Because he invited tough, intellectual discussions, he was a great teacher. He should have been promoted, not fired.

In the history department, I remember Harry Carman and Alexander Flick. Both were outstanding teachers and scholars. Carman got his start at Syracuse, then he went to Columbia University where he was considered the greatest teacher on campus. Later he became Dean of Columbia College. He could do no wrong there. Flick became New York State historian. He was a magnificent lecturer who often was loudly applauded at the end of a lecture. His house on Ostrom Avenue was always open to students.

One teacher I had was so gifted that I was almost persuaded to major in accounting. Harry Guthman was professor of accounting, and he later went to Northwestern University. After taking his course, I decided that this subject would be my life's work.

It was like duck soup for me, and I loved it. I tutored all my fraternity brothers through the accounting class, and they received excellent grades. The following year, however, I realized that accounting was just too simple and easy. In fact, most of my subjects were easy for me. The notable exception was philosophy. Philosophy was abstract and conceptual rather than concrete and practical. Because I liked the challenge it offered, I decided to major in it. As it turned out, I would also earn a doctorate in philosophy.

Another faculty member I remember with affection was Minnie Mason Beebe. She had a large Sunday school class for men at the University Methodist Church, called "The Kollege Klan." I was president of the Klan during my senior year. Professor Beebe taught this Bible class so well that it regularly attracted between one and two hundred students.

While I have mentioned professors at Syracuse who stood out for their fine teaching skills, there is one I must mention because of his thoughtfulness: Professor Raymond A. Piper, of the philosophy department. He was a pedantic teacher, but very observant and concerned for his students. I discovered this one day when I was called downstairs at my fraternity house. Dressed only in my shirt and trousers, with no tie or jacket, I found to my dismay that the person who had come to call was none other than Professor Piper. He said, "I have come to talk to you about some words you mispronounce. I have a list of them here." I could have kissed him. Imagine a full professor coming over to an undergraduate's home to talk about something as personal as this! He did such things with many of his students, listening very closely to them, making little notes on a piece of paper, and talking to each one privately.

Despite my debt of gratitude to Professor Piper, we had our differences. Once I wrote a paper for him which involved translating Descartes's treatise *Discourse on Method* from French to English. He lost the paper and told me he would have to give me a zero because of this. I said, "Dr. Piper, I didn't lose the paper, you did. Furthermore, it was a good paper. Since I didn't lose it, you're going to have to give me the average I had prior to it. You teach a course in logic, and this seems to me only logical." At last he agreed, and although my paper was lost, I saved my grade.

There is one more teacher who is remembered by all who took his courses. The school of oratory had as its dean Hugh Massey Tilroe. Behind his back, students called him Huge Massey Tilroe, for he stood well over six feet and was a massive person. My recollection is that public speaking was a requirement of the freshman year. In some respects, the course was a joke. In other respects, it was a very useful course of instruction. He made us aware of the importance of diction and pronunciation. We all learned to say, repeating after him, "MAYRY had a little lamb, its fleece was WHYTE as snow, and every where that MAYRY went, the lamb was sure to go." I have a suspicion that every member of my class can still say that exactly as Dean Tilroe taught it.

This teaching method of Dean Tilroe's was not unlike the story of the boy who stuttered and after six months of training was able to recite the same lines. When complimented on how well he could recite them, he replied, "Y-y-y-eess, bbut hhow oofften dddoo yoyou gget a ch-chance to w-w-o-oorrk it in-into the con-conversation?"

Throughout my school years, I never had trouble earning high marks, and I loved learning. I also enjoyed working, and always worked while I was in school.

I had saved about $400 from my high school days of delivering packages, but I wanted to add to this, not spend it. Earl, who was in Syracuse ahead of me, found me a job selling shoes where he worked, at the Endicott Johnson shoe store on South Salina Street. Working from 2:00 to 5:30 P.M. Monday through Friday, and from noon until 9:00 P.M. on Saturdays, I earned ten dollars a week. With room and board costing nine dollars a week, I had a dollar left for spending money. Walking the approximately three-mile round trip to and from work, I dipped into my savings infrequently—for my fraternity initiation fee, an overcoat, a suit, and an occasional trip home.

I worked in the store basement, where the lowest priced shoes were on sale. Selling was exhilarating, and I was happiest when waiting on several customers at once. I was good with people.

During my first month there, I found an answer to a delicate problem that had baffled other salesmen. At that time, the average size of a woman's shoe was 4B. A few women, however, had much larger feet—a size 10 or 11. Our ladies' stock contained nothing in their size, and it was humiliating for them to shop for shoes. Again and again they were told there were no shoes to fit them. Thinking about the problem, I examined the styles in men's shoes, and found there were usually two or three that had higher heels, and were more attractive than the others. Whenever I could not fit one of these women with a ladies' shoe, I would say, "Come with me, I think I know what you want." I then fitted them with comfortable men's shoes, which were also attractive. Able to buy shoes without loss of face, these women began asking for me by name. They knew I would treat them with respect.

Each Saturday, the store held a sales competition. I took special pride in it, and worked hard to win. There was a clerk named Katie Downes who was a fine saleswoman, and the race was usually between us. She was very competitive, but I was even more so. The competition was tough, but I would have been deeply disappointed if I did not win.

My brother Earl, who had found the job for me, worked on the main floor of the shoe store. He earned two dollars more than I, but I did not mind the difference in pay. At no point in my life have I ever asked for a raise in salary, and I did not think of doing so then. In fact, I never paid much attention to what I was earning. My interest was in doing my best.

I am proud of all of the jobs I held. When I was Chancellor of Syracuse University, a trustee, Crandall Melvin, who, for a time, had taken a dislike to me, once said, "You're nothing but a shoe salesman!" I replied, "That's not an insult, Crandall. I was a very good shoe salesman."

Despite my outstanding record, I was fired from my job with Endicott-Johnson. In my junior year, Philo Chambers, who worked under me on the *Onondagan* yearbook staff as business manager, had what he thought was a brilliant idea. I would supply him with two hundred pairs of galoshes using my father's credit, and he would sell them to the sorority and fraternity members. We would split the profits. Given Syracuse's history of heavy snow and ice, it seemed like a sure-fire business proposition.

My father was not enthusiastic about the idea, but he finally sent the two hundred pairs of galoshes we needed. We had our stock ready well before winter, but it turned out to be the winter with the least snow in the history of Syracuse. The first snow did not fall until late January and then only came to a few inches. The wholesale price dropped one dollar a pair, and Philo did not sell a single pair. After returning the galoshes to my father, I still owed him $200 because of the drop in price.

Father and I engaged in a spirited exchange of letters, wherein I vowed that not only would he be repaid every cent I owed him, I would never again accept financial help from him. The financial loss was serious, but that was not the worst of the story.

The crowning blow was my dismissal from my job. The order came directly from management in Johnson City, where word of our business had spread. I had not thought of a possible conflict of interest, but that was how they saw it. I, however, knew I more than earned my ten dollars a week, and failed to see that being a silent partner in the galoshes business would be in competition with Endicott-Johnson. My manager was a kind man, and he explained that my dismissal was not his doing. "I have no choice," he said.

At the time, it was a serious blow to my ego. Yet, it taught me an important lesson. After that, I was always sensitive to any conflict of interest. Never again could anyone say, "You're wearing two hats at the same time."

With about $200 left in my bank account, I withdrew $165 and bought a B-flat tenor saxophone. The fingering on the saxophone is the same as on the flute and piccolo, so all I had to learn was how to blow it. I learned that trick in less than a week. I then recruited an excellent drummer, a fine trumpeter, and an outstanding pianist, Suds Leslie. I also began phoning the social chairmen of the fraternities and sororities to tell them that the Synful Syncopators were now available to play at their dances.

I had lined up all the engagements we needed well before I mastered the "ill wind that no one blows good!" Soon, I had built my savings back up and was once more financially secure. When I graduated, I had $600 in the bank after paying back all that my father had advanced for my undergraduate years, including the loan on the galoshes.

I took Paul Whiteman as my model for my jazz career. It was

the day of "Whispering," "Alice Blue Gown," "Margie," and "The Dark Town Strutters Ball." There were many wonderful songs. Sometimes I sang the lyrics, but that was not so common a practice with jazz bands of the late teens and twenties. What was required was a steady beat and a great pianist. We had both. Suds Leslie was not just a good pianist; he was superb. And he got better the more beer he drank.

Suds loved to improvise. His fingers would fly up and down the keyboard while his feet worked the pedals, and he would come up with endless variations on any theme. I was not the greatest sax player, but I had a good ear. I needed no notes, and I, too, liked to improvise and do arpeggios. Every time we played together we had a jam session. How we loved it!

Soon, we had much more business than we could handle, and we were turning away engagements. At the time that I was revelling in my jazz sax, I was still faithful to the flute. I joined the University's instrumental club my junior year, when Al Diesseroth resigned and it looked as if the club would fold. In a rash moment I agreed to succeed Al as director, and I took the club on tour my junior and senior years. It was a case of fools rushing in where angels fear to tread, but we had a happy and successful time. It was another way to learn the skills of leadership that would serve me well in later life.

After graduating from college, I never again played for money. Suds Leslie, on the other hand, went on to become a professional jazz pianist, and a very good one indeed.

Perhaps my retirement from playing for dances had something to do with the influence my first music lesson had on me. I took this lesson the summer after I graduated from S.U. Even though I had been playing for two years, I felt it was high time I took my first sax lesson. It was a disaster. Like Harpo Marx, I knew nothing of theory or technique. "Why aren't you tonguing?" my appalled teacher asked of me. "I thought you just blew the thing," I replied. My ignorance exposed, my first lesson was my last.

In addition to sampling careers as a musician and salesman, I also had my first taste of administration during my undergraduate years at S.U. In my senior year, after my election as president of the YMCA, I also became the Y's acting general secretary. The YMCA and YWCA at Syracuse had nothing to do with physical education, athletics, or recreation. They were the voluntary religious organizations on the campus. They also helped in finding student employment; assisted in academic and social counseling; promoted religious conferences, such as those at Silver Bay on Lake George; organized Bible study and prayer groups; and brought religious leaders to the campus.

In September of 1921, the general secretary of the YMCA, Charles W. Carlton, left to teach at a business school in downtown Syracuse. Vice-Chancellor William Pratt Graham sent for me and said, "You're president of the YMCA. I want you to also serve as acting general secretary. We shall pay you $3,500 a year." I said, "No, Dr. Graham, I won't accept that. I'll accept $100 a month for nine months, if you will earmark the balance for program development. I can't develop an effective program without money."

I devoted myself fully to my duties at the Y. In order to get more students involved in its activities, we organized a number of Bible study groups that met once or twice a week. They were extraordinarily successful. While we continued to find undergraduates part-time jobs, our primary mission was to strengthen the place of religion on campus.

We brought dozens of outstanding speakers to campus, and held Sunday evening religious services in Crouse College. The most important religious leader brought to the campus was Bishop Theodore S. Henderson, from the Detroit area of the Methodist Episcopal Church. He was a magnificent speaker who was particularly successful in speaking to young people of college age. He spoke thirty-five times on the Syracuse campus. I heard thirty-one of those speeches. The crowds grew larger and larger each time he spoke. The climax came on the final Sunday at the University Methodist Church, when a specially organized University choir, the Henderson Hundred, supplied the music to a completely packed church.

My chief assistant in running the YMCA was a classmate named Harry Upperman, who later became President of Baxter Seminary and Chancellor of Nebraska Wesleyan University. He had been secretary to a congressman and was several years older than most of us. At my request Harry became chairman of our program of deputation teams. Sending out 120 of these teams, Harry made the program a great success. The teams were made up of three to five persons who went to a church each weekend to meet the young people. They held day-long programs on Saturdays, and on Sundays they would lead both the morning and the evening services. They returned to campus late each Sunday night.

These services were instructional as well as devotional. The students would discuss the importance of religion in their lives and talk to the young people about why they went to church, what they expected from religion, and what their faith meant to them. The last thing we did during the evening service was to invite all who wished to, to come forward and give their lives to Christ. When they did, it was a high point for all of us.

In leading the YMCA, I had gotten religion in a big way and this pleased my mother. She was determined that all three of her sons would be clergymen. She had the first two, and now she would get the third and last. As it turned out, however, only one of us would actually take a parish. Harold, the eldest, had one year at Drew Theological Seminary, and then the war broke out. He went to France, was a captain there, and saw some action. Before going to France, he had married Marguerite Germond, a classmate at Syracuse. His wife became pregnant, but the baby died soon after it was born. This was a great trauma to Harold and his wife, and he decided not to go back to Drew after the war. In retrospect, I believe this was a serious blunder. Harold was the orator of the family. He would have been a wonderful minister.

When he returned to America, there were few jobs available, and so he joined father in the shoe store. He was an excellent salesman, and the store did well. Nevertheless, it became clear to Harold that he would not make his fortune in the shoe business. He left to become Welfare Commissioner for Binghamton, then served in Congress, and later became Director of Welfare for western New York. But even with these accomplishments, I have always thought of him as a war casualty. Throughout his life, he excelled at what he did, and when he died the letters that poured in were evidence of the influence he had on other lives.

My second brother, Earl, was as gifted as Harold. He was president of his high school class and the student government. He was also president of the student body at Drew, where he was an outstanding student. He missed Phi Beta Kappa as an undergraduate only because he wasted too much time playing cards in the chapter house! After finishing at Drew, Earl went on to become a successful Methodist minister with large congregations in Endicott, Johnson City, and Oneonta, New York. He served as district superintendent of the Wyoming Conference, was a member of the national board of education of the Methodist Episcopal Church, and received an honorary doctorate from West Virginia Wesleyan.

With my background in religion and the influence of my mother and my brothers as role models, it was natural that I, too, should want to become a minister. I was considering going to Drew when, near the end of my senior year, Vice-Chancellor Graham sent for me and said, "We want you to stay on as general secretary of the YMCA." I said, "Let me sleep on it."

The next day, I took a long walk with Professor Wilson. As we strolled together, he looked at me and said, "There's something on your mind today." I said, "Yes, there is. Vice-Chancellor Graham wants me to stay on as general secretary of the YMCA next year."

"Well," Wilson said, "you're going to say no, aren't you?"

"I'm not sure," I replied. "Perhaps I should say yes."

"No, you're going to say no. At your age you don't take the short view. You must go on to graduate school."

"Do you think I can be a scholar?" I asked.

"Yes," he said, "you could be a scholar. I'm not sure that you'll spend your whole life as a professor. I think that you will manage something. In any case, however, you need a doctorate."

"If I'm going to graduate school," I said, "I shall go to Drew Theological Seminary."

"Good! You'll be only twenty-five miles from New York. Go over to Columbia while you're there and pick up a Ph.D.," he said.

I did just that. I have always been grateful to Professor Wilson for his perceptive advice and counsel. He knew me better than I knew myself.

3

DREW AND COLUMBIA

I entered Drew Theological Seminary at Madison, New Jersey, in the autumn of 1922. As all Drew students do, I immediately fell in love with the Drew campus. It is a university set in a forest of ancestral oaks punctuated with a few glorious copper beeches. In the spring, there are hundreds of white and pink dogwood trees in bloom. Everyone who has been a student at Drew remembers the month of May as a time of matchless beauty.

At the center of Drew was Mead Hall, a colonial mansion owned by the Gibbons family before the Seminary was founded in 1868. This grand building served as the center of hospitality for many of New York's Four Hundred in the early nineteenth century. In its academic use, it housed classrooms, the bookstore, and the offices of the president, registrar, and admissions director.

Drew had a faculty of exceptional excellence. It had the reputation of being conservative theologically, but I did not find it so. Its best-known scholar was Rabbi Robert William Rogers, professor of the Old Testament. A world famous Orientalist, he was a graduate of the University of Pennsylvania and of Johns Hopkins University, and he earned doctorates at Haverford College and the University of Leipzig. He was a life member of St. John's College at Oxford, where he received one of his many honorary degrees. He was also a visiting professor at Princeton. He had a deep, sonorous voice, beautiful diction, lectured without a note, and held everyone's attention from the first syllable. In one of his classes, I was having great difficulty in learning Hebrew, despite the many hours I spent studying, but with his inspiration I persisted. Shortly before the Christmas vacation, I stayed up most of the night reviewing what I had learned; and suddenly at about four o'clock in the morning, everything became clear. From that time on, learning Hebrew was a delight. I had some exceptional lecturers at Syracuse and Columbia, but none was the equal of Rabbi Rogers.

I also thrived under the tutelage of a native of Wales named J. Newton Davies, New Testament professor of Greek. A superb scholar, Professor Davies was patient with his students and very supportive. "Don't let yourself get discouraged," he would say. "New Testament Greek is much easier than classical Greek, and I want all of you to progress to the point where it will be a pleasure for you to read the Greek New Testament in your daily devotions."

Dr. Edwin Lewis, professor of systematic theology, was another outstanding teacher. He had read widely in the field of English literature as a boy, and he had a phenomenal memory. No matter what the subject was, Professor Lewis would draw on his memory to quote from Shakespeare, Chaucer, Byron, Keats, Shelley, Browning, Wordsworth, Kipling, Swinburne, or Tennyson to illustrate a point. The notes I took in his lectures were so full of insight and wisdom that they would require little revision to serve as a model textbook.

Professor Lewis was a demanding teacher, and many students complained about the amount of outside reading he required. I found him inspiring and greatly enjoyed working with him. He would aks me to take his classes when he went off on a protracted holiday. After I received my bachelor's of divinity degree, he engaged me to teach in his department.

I studied homiletics, the art of preaching, under the able Professor Frederic Watson Hannan. Professor Hannan felt each student should develop an individual style. "Don't try to make a lion out of a bear," he would say. "Build on your natural abilities, and on your personal strengths."

Dr. Hannan required each of us to give a public sermon in the Chapel. Dr. Hannan's outstanding teaching abilities not withstanding, I was not proud of my performance. Looking back, I see that I expected too much of myself. Good preaching is rare. It requires experience as well as a talent for public speaking.

One of the greatest scholars I have known at Drew was John

Alfred Faulkner, professor of church history. Faulkner was an omnivorous reader and, like Professor Lewis, had an extraordinary memory. Once I completed my thesis on St. Augustine, I asked Professor Faulkner to read it. He returned it to me within a few days, along with half a dozen pages of notes and a long bibliography listing the authors' full names, book titles, date of publication, and the name of the publisher, which he compiled from memory. Most of the books were German, French, and Italian.

Dr. Faulkner was the personification of the absentminded professor. He once attended a tea where he met Professor Lewis on the staircase and engaged him in a spirited conversation for fifteen minutes. He then left for home because he couldn't remember whether he was coming to the tea or going.

Once, having locked himself out of his house, Dr. Faulkner climbed up a ladder to enter through a window. After crawling inside, he went downstairs, unlocked the front door, and then went upstairs and climbed down the ladder.

Dr. Faulkner's students were continually amused by his habit of interrupting his own lectures on church history with irrelevant asides: "If any of you are students of Roland Walker of Ohio Wesleyan," he would say, "please come to my desk after the lecture is over." Then, five minutes later: "If there are any students of Ismar J. Peritz of Syracuse University, I should also like to talk with you."

Once Faulkner interrupted himself by asking: "Has anyone seen my wife's scissors?" We thought that was hysterically funny. Some months later, he suddenly exclaimed, as he turned the pages of his manuscript, "Martha, here are your scissors."

One morning during prayer at Chapel, Professor Faulkner said, "Lord, did you see that story in the *New York Times* this morning? Or was it the *Herald Tribune*, Lord?"

At another Chapel service he said in a prayer, "Lord, I have just reread *The Scarlet Letter*. Lord, that is a great book! Don't let any of the seniors graduate until they have read it!"

The stories about Faulkner are legion. I was with him one day when he was having furnace trouble. I wasn't much help, but was intrigued by his comment "I've looked closely at the furnace, but I can't find the publisher's name."

I received a rich social and academic education at Drew. Yet a crucial part of that education was received not on the Drew campus but on the streets of New York City.

In addition to studying at Drew on a full scholarship, I worked part-time at the People's Home Church and Settlement House on East Eleventh Street, in Manhattan. My work schedule took me to Columbia University for two graduate courses on Friday afternoon and to the Settlement House in New York on Friday evenings. I returned to Drew late Sunday night or early Monday morning.

The Settlement House was a Methodist home-missionary service for newly arrived immigrants and first-generation Americans. Most of our members were Italian or Russian, but we also served Polish, Hungarian, Czechoslovakian, French, German, Austrian, and South American immigrants. It was our job to minister to their religious needs and provide a church home that would help them adjust to life in America.

The Settlement House offered a full set of social and athletic activities. My task was to supervise basketball in the gymnasium, teach a Bible class, assist in the church services, lead the choir, as well as plan and supervise the dances and social programs for close to fifty young people ranging in age from fifteen to twenty-five.

I slept in the Settlement House in a fourth-floor room, where I shared a bunk bed with another staff member. I had the top berth. From there I could see the public bathhouse across the street on Eleventh Street. The men stood in an orderly line as they waited for the baths to open. The women, however, formed a mob, pushing, shouting, and fighting to get in. It was a study in contrasts.

These were the people we served. They lived in what were called "dumbbell apartments," so called because the doorbells did not ring. Tenants kept potatoes or coal in their bathtubs, and shared one toilet per floor among several families. All of the garbage and the contents of the chamber pots were thrown to the street from the windows on the upper floor, creating an unholy mess. Firemen came daily to hose down the sidewalks and streets. When men left for work in the morning, they locked their wives in and unlocked the door when they returned, thus "protecting" their wives' safety and virtue.

In the summertime, the firemen provided free showers from their fire hoses to keep the youngsters cool. In the winter, Tammany Hall provided free coal. It was easy to see why everyone voted the Democratic party ticket.

Policemen never stayed more than a month on the same beat. If they did, they were harassed until the precinct captain got the message. Minor crimes were often overlooked. Prostitutes were not bothered by police, so long as they made modest payments to them.

Courts found they could not be too severe. When some of my young people were arrested, I could quickly secure their release without bail by having them remanded to my care. My most serious case was a boy named Eddie Felber.

Eddie's mother and sister were prostitutes, and his father was an alcoholic. Eddie was a burglar and petty thief. He ransacked the rooms of the staff at the Settlement House, emptying the ladies' purses and stealing their jewelry. I came to know the precinct officers and city magistrate well, thanks to Eddie. Although I tried again and again, I failed to reform Eddie. I consoled myself by thinking that some people are beyond help.

Some ten years later, while on a trip to Manhattan, I stopped in to see the Settlement House staff. An attractive, well-dressed man greeted me. "Mr. Tolley," he said, "How nice to see you again!" It was Eddie Felber. "What are you doing here, Eddie?" I asked. "This is my avocation," he replied. "I am the treasurer of the church and Settlement House. Outside of my job, it is my chief interest in life." He then went on to tell me how Paul Dubois, who was the minister when I was there during 1922–23, never gave up on him. Finally, he turned Eddie around. It was a miracle. Eddie's rehabilitation made a deep impression on me. It was proof that nothing is impossible when one is dealing with people.

Each of the young people whom I served in the Settlement House had a unique story. One was informed by his parents on his sixteenth birthday that they were retiring from work and he was to support them. He did.

A husky Hungarian named Joe accompanied me to a Sunday morning service at St. Thomas' Protestant Episcopal Church at Fifty-third Street and Fifth Avenue. When we knelt at the altar for communion, the priest offered Joe the large silver communion goblet. Joe wrested it away from the priest, lifted it to his lips, slurped and swallowed, emptied the chalice, and returned it to the priest. Smacking his lips, he said in a voice that could be heard throughout the church, "Good!" I left as quickly as I could!

One Saturday morning, we were locked out of the gymnasium because Mr. Dubois had forgotten to leave me the keys. When I explained this to the disappointed boys, one of them, Frank Snappy, asked, "Is this on the level, Mr. Tolley?"

"Yes," I replied, "it is."

"Would you mind if I opened the lock?" he asked.

"Can you?" I asked.

He opened the door in a jiffy, saying "Locks are for honest men." He could unlock any door he ever saw.

I tried to educate my charges by taking them to the second-hand book shops on Fourth and lower Fifth Avenue and to the Labor Temple on Fourteenth Street to hear the lectures of Stuart Chase, Norman Thomas, Sherwood Eddy, and others. We also went to the Madison Avenue Presbyterian Church to hear Henry Sloan Coffin, to the Brick Presbyterian Church to hear William Pierson Merrill, and to the lower Fifth Avenue Church where Harry Emerson Fosdick was the preacher. It was a great experience for them and a greater one for me.

One of our boys, Willie Kohler, had been baptized by Mr. Dubois and finally was ready to be admitted to the church. When the hour came for the service to begin, Willie was not there. Finally, the processional started without him. We were in the second or third stanza of Charles Wesley's hymn "Christ the Lord Is Risen Today" when I spotted Willie entering the church. I raised my voice and sang out, "Willie Kohler just came in, Hallelujah, Hallelujah." To this day when I sing that great hymn, I hear myself singing, "Willie Kohler just came in, Hallelujah, Hallelujah."

The Lower East Side was a way station for immigrants. They arrived there with nothing, found jobs, rented small tenement apartments, and eventually bought new carpet for their living rooms. That was a major step. In time, they bought a piano. When I called on the families of my young people and found a piano as well as a rug, I knew what it meant. It was a clear sign that the third step, to move to Staten Island, was only months away.

About fifteen years after I left the People's Home Church and Settlement House, I received a visit from two of the young people who had been members of my group. They were happily married, had three beautiful children, and drove a new car. I learned that the young man had an excellent position and had moved from Staten Island to New Jersey. Before he left, he said, "Please, Mr. Tolley, don't tell anyone that we once lived on the Lower East Side. I don't want any of my friends to know." I promised but was puzzled. To me it was a success story to be told with pride. To him it was an embarrassment. He had made it up the ladder. He did not want to be reminded of how far he had come.

In addition to teaching me about people, my work at the Settlement House also gave me a chance to spend time with Ruth. There were many Saturday evenings when there was no program at the Settlement House, and I was free to go out on a date with Ruth, who had moved to New York to work for the Standard Oil Company. She had lived with her aunt, in exchange for house-keeping duties, while we were both studying at Syracuse, but had been forced to leave the University when her aunt decided she was not earning her room and board. Unable to pay full room and board costs, plus tuition, Ruth had had to end her education and go to work full-time.

She was living in the Nevins Street YWCA in Brooklyn while I was working at the Settlement House and studying at Drew. On the Saturday nights I had free, we would go to a restaurant named Joe's in Brooklyn for a sizzling steak and French fries. I would pay for it one Saturday, and she would pay the next. It cost $1.25 for each of us. Moreover, it was delicious. We would walk back to the YWCA after dinner, feeling as though we were on top of the world.

Full as my weekends in New York were, they did not interfere with my scholastic work. While commuting to and from the Settlement House, I put the time to good use by devouring the blue books of E. Haldeman Julius. I also read all the Greek comedies and tragedies, and much Roman and English literature. I had read little as a youth because my father's library had been thin. Having grown up on Horatio Alger, the *Bible,* and *The Water Babies,* I now began to quench a literary interest that had begun during my years at Syracuse. While commuting, I also studied Greek and Hebrew using two sets of flash cards—one with Greek letters on one side, and their English translations on the other; the other with Hebrew on one side, and English on the other. I memorized and reviewed these on the subways and trains as well as in church. Whenever the preacher failed to hold my attention, I would reach in my pocket for a pack of cards.

In addition to educating myself in this manner, I was also taking a full set of courses at Drew and Columbia. In my second year at Drew I carried twenty-seven semester credit hours my first semester and twenty-four the second semester. I earned nothing less than an A in all my years of graduate study. I completed a master's degree from Syracuse in 1924 and earned my bachelor's of divinity from Drew Theological Seminary in 1925. Because I had graduated from S.U. in 1922 just six credits short of my master's, I stayed in Syracuse to complete them in summer school. I wrote my master's thesis for Syracuse while at Drew. I also completed my master's from Columbia in 1927. In 1930, I received a doctorate in philosophy from Columbia.

It was a good time to be at Columbia. Without question the department of philosophy was the best in the nation. John Dewey's presence alone would have ensured that; but there were also many others, like Professors Frederick J. Woodbridge, William P. Montague, Irwin Edman, John Herman Randall, John Storck, and Richard P. McKeon.

Woodbridge was a towering figure. A magnificent lecturer, his course on the history of philosophy was already a legend by the time I was privileged to take it. No one in the twentieth century could match his lectures on Plato, although Edman was a close second. Woodbridge did not write a great deal, but he was the dominant figure in the philosophy department and the intellectual leader of the graduate faculty. His personal interest in students and his incisive judgment influenced hundreds of careers, including mine.

He served on my dissertation defense committee. He had the habit of saying *"Tolle et lege"*: "Take and read" to students in medieval philosophy. He did not do so with me, but during my defense he did ask me about a dissertation involving St. Augustine and St. Thomas Aquinas that had been written under his direction. I told him that the thesis was full of errors, and if he wanted me to take the time I could recite them one by one. At the time I thought that would end my quest for a doctorate. When, however, I demonstrated that I knew what I was talking about, he did not pursue his question.

The only disappointment in my experience with teachers at Columbia was with John Dewey. Here was a classic case of the great scholar—poor teacher so frequently cited by undergraduates. I was forewarned by other students, but that, of course, did not deter me. Dewey had a low voice. He never looked at his students. Most of the time he looked out of the window. His dress was careless with tie out of place. He appeared to be thinking rather than lecturing, and, in fact, he was. His method of teaching was ruminating. I took careful notes, and when I read them later I was deeply impressed by their insight. To listen to what he said, however, was to be put to sleep.

Paul Ward, one of my Syracuse professors, was a Dewey disciple. When I reported my estimate of Dewey's teaching skill he waved his hand and said, "He is a magnificent teacher. What is wrong with you?" About one year later Professor Ward entered one of the 2:00 P.M. classes I was taking with Professor Dewey. I saw him come in and began clocking him. In exactly twelve minutes he fell sound asleep. When the class was over at 3:40 P.M., I woke Professor Ward, saying, "Wasn't that wonderful?"

Dean Herbert Hawkes, who later became Dean of Columbia College, told me about a boy who transferred from Upper Iowa College to Columbia University. After a year of study in New York, Dean Hawkes asked the young man if he observed any difference between the teachers at Upper Iowa and Columbia.

"No," said the boy, "but to be honest, Dean Hawkes, when you are walking in a deep fog you can't tell whether the buildings are two stories high or twenty." That sums up my assessment of John Dewey's teaching skills. One needed to be a very serious, very bright student to appreciate John Dewey. To all but a few, he was hopeless. To a handful of students he was a genius. In my own case, I had to fight to stay awake, but I kept my notes for some forty years.

A great favorite with students was William P. Montague. In his course "Ways of Knowing," he discussed rationalism, empiricism, authoritarianism, pragmatism, mysticism, and nihilism. His thesis was that each of the six ways of knowing was right in what it affirmed and wrong in what it denied. For example, Christian Science is right in saying that the mind can play an important role in dealing with illness and wrong in saying that illness can be completely dominated by the mind.

At the time I was taking his course, Will Durant published his *Story of Philosophy*. The consensus among philosophers was that it was a cheap popularization. The students in Montague's class asked him what he thought of Durant's book.

"Do you want the truth?" he demanded. "If you do, let me say that I would gladly have given my right arm to have written it!" We all applauded.

Montague directed my dissertation on St. Anselm's ontological argument for the existence of God. Rereading it now, I recognize that I was wrong in my conclusions, but Montague was intrigued by my argument and he approved the thesis.

I thought I would write my doctoral dissertation on St. Anselm, but Richard McKeon said, "First read everything St. Augustine wrote. You will never understand St. Anselm until you have mastered St. Augustine." Later he told me, "Write about Anselm when you are ninety. For now, write about Augustine."

One of the most important lessons I learned while studying at Columbia was that it is crucial to set a time table for one's self. The year that I completed my doctorate at Columbia was an extraordinarily busy one. I was teaching a morning class six days a week at Drew and also taking a seminar at Columbia with Professor McKeon.

McKeon had the habit of translating Latin manuscripts during class for our benefit. There were four or five nuns in the class, all of whom dozed off for most of the afternoon. I, however, found the seminar and translations exciting and rewarding.

Everything McKeon said revealed the richness of his knowledge. At the close of the class, one afternoon, he took me aside and said, "I want the first chapter of your thesis by next Monday." I said, "I can't do it." "Yes, you can," he said. I worked from 7:00 P.M. until 4:00 A.M. every day of that week. The following Monday, I appeared for the seminar and handed him the chapter. He read it with a smile and said, "This is great! I want the second chapter next week." "I can't do it," I said. "Yes you can," was his answer, and so I repeated the previous week's experience and presented him with the second chapter on deadline.

When I delivered the manuscript to Professor McKeon, I said, "Did you ever hear of the farmer who didn't feed his horse? They got along just fine until suddenly the horse died." Despite my protests, Professor McKeon continued to drive me, and I continued to write chapter after chapter, although not one a week. When the manuscript was completed, I realized that its existence owed as much to his efforts as it did to mine. We all need time tables. We all need to be driven. We need to set goals and hold to them. Without goals, nothing is accomplished.

The person to whom I owe my greatest debt was Ezra Squier Tipple, who was President of Drew. At the start of my second year, Dr. Tipple asked me to work for him as a general assistant. I helped in alumni relations and the admission of students. I ran the mimeograph and multigraph machines, visited colleges to recruit students, and even tried my hand at fund raising. Because the unanswered letters on his desk were a problem, I volunteered to help him with his correspondence. He would read what I wrote before signing it, but rarely did he ask me to revise the letters. Soon, I was answering almost all of his correspondence, and then I began writing articles for him.

One day Dr. Tipple came to me and said, "For heaven's sake, tell me when I've written an article. Last night at dinner my hostess praised an article in the magazine published by the New Jersey Historical Society. I never even knew the magazine existed!"

I said, "Look, it's yours, Dr. Tipple. I used your language, I used your phrasing, I used your pet words. You saw it before I mailed it."

"Fine," he said, "just be sure I know before it is published."

Dr. Tipple was a kind, warmhearted, generous man. Somehow he always knew when a student was in trouble. Often he would hand me an envelope full of money and instruct me to give it to a particular student in need. He insisted that these gifts be anonymous. Whenever I was entrusted with one of these envelopes I would tell the student, "There is no need to thank your benefactor. Just thank the Lord." I never knew how much he gave, but the envelopes were thick.

The faculty, however, had a different view of Dr. Tipple's generosity. I remember one faculty meeting when Dr. Tipple announced an increase in the faculty salaries. At the close of the meeting Dr. Tipple proposed that the faculty join together in the singing of a hymn, whereupon Dr. Lewis suggested they sing the hymn, "After Many Years the Increase."

During my years as Dr. Tipple's assistant, there was a student uprising. A group of students charged into Dr. Tipple's office full of demands and angrier than wet hens. Dr. Tipple was a polite man, but he also had a quick temper, and their attitude put them on his wrong side immediately. He laid them out in lavender. Naturally, they got angrier. The bitter exchange continued until I finally asked Dr. Tipple to leave me alone with the students for half an hour.

"You don't know what kind of man he is," I told them. "You've caught him at his worst. Now, tell me. What's bothering you the most?"

They told me their main grievance, and I said, "Fine, now what if we did this?" They agreed, and I said, "Fine, now what's next on your list of grievances?" They told me their next problem, and again we arrived at a solution. So it went, down the line. When we were finished, I said, "May we call it quits now, and be friends again if we get Dr. Tipple to agree to this?" "Of course," they said.

I ushered Dr. Tipple back into his office. "What would you think if we agreed to settle these problems as follows?" I said. When I had finished explaining our proposed solutions, Dr. Tipple said, "That makes a lot of sense." We had a truce at last.

When the students were gone, he came over and put his arm around me. For some reason he always called me Peerie.

"Peerie," he said, "you don't know it, but you're going to be a college president."

"I don't want to be a college president, Dr. Tipple," I said. "I want to be a minister." I held onto that dream throughout my student years at Drew. I was ordained as a minister in the Methodist Episcopal Church in 1923, and near the close of my senior year I was offered a church near Coney Island, in Brooklyn. When I came back from my interview with the Methodist district superintendent, I told Dr. Tipple of the offer.

"I have news for you," he said. "You're not going to take a church in Brooklyn. You're going to work for me."

"If I work for you," I said, "I'll probably never be a minister."

"Look," he said, "I'll make a deal with you. You work for me for three years, and then I'll retire. I won't hold you beyond three years, but I need you. I really can't function without you." Reluctantly, I agreed.

This changed the direction of my life. I never served as pastor in a church. I stayed at Drew as alumni secretary and assistant to the president after I graduated in 1925. Ruth and I were married that year. I supported her in reasonable style by working for Dr. Tipple and teaching systematic theology.

In the winter of 1928, Leonard and Arthur Baldwin, two brothers who were successful New York lawyers, donated $1.5 million to Drew to establish Brothers College and change the name of Drew Theological Seminary to Drew University.

The Baldwin brothers had been poor as boys, but Leonard eventually saved enough to start his freshman year at Cornell and later paid the way for his brother, Arthur. The two had been very close. In their childhood, their primary interest had been trapping. At the end of the season when they sold their furs, the money went into a common checking account. All through their university years they had but one checking account between them. Both went into law school, and after graduation from law school, they each got married.

They had been so close that when they married their wives agreed that the two couples share a home together. All through married life there was but one checking account for the two families. One wife managed the household one month, and the next month the other wife would take her turn. The brothers were very successful. Leonard was a Republican who was very active on the national scene. Arthur was a Democrat and the personal attorney of the head of Tammany Hall.

Leonard made a fortune as a corporate lawyer, and Arthur made another fortune in companies dealing with ash and waste disposal. They made still another fortune in real estate. But they had only one checking account.

When it came time to draw up the check for Drew Theological Seminary, Leonard said to Arthur, "You sign the check." Arthur said, "No, you're the senior member of the family, you sign the check." That was the closest they ever came to a difference of opinion.

As donors, they made no demands. Although they did select the architect, they gave him complete freedom. They insisted on having reports on the progress of the college, but they never interfered in any way.

The relationship between the two brothers is one I can understand. What is most remarkable to me, however, is that the two wives accepted the situation, adjusted to it, and lived happily with it.

I have heard the sons speak of "our fathers." Arthur's son, Donald, was much like his father and his uncle. He had a remarkably successful business career. He became chairman of the board of Drew University and was most generous to Drew. Donald's wife, Winifred, now in her mid-eighties, is equally generous to Drew. She is an artist of exceptional talent and has been active in the leadership and support of New Jersey hospitals and nursing schools. She is a fine public speaker and a woman of great charm.

I became the Acting Dean of Brothers College in the spring of 1928 at the age of twenty-seven. I knew my appointment would be unpopular in the eyes of the faculty because I was so young. When the appointment was announced, no one congratulated me. This did not bother me. I realized that Dr. Tipple had appointed me because he trusted me, and saw things in me that I didn't see in myself. I knew, however, that it was up to me to prove to others that Dr. Tipple's faith in me was justified.

The first thing I did was make the rounds of the Theological Seminary faculty and explain the situation to them. "I feel exactly as you do about this appointment," I told each one of them. "But Dr. Tipple has confidence in me. He's asked me to take it, and I can't say no to him. I'm going to do the best I can, and I'll need your help along the way. I hope you'll be patient with me."

By the end of my first year as Acting Dean of Brothers College the seminary faculty was solidly behind me. Having been appointed as Acting Dean in 1928, I became Dean in 1929.

It was an interesting period in American higher education. Woodrow Wilson was making sizable changes as President of Princeton. Sarah Lawrence and Bennington—two newly established women's colleges—were making a central place for the fine arts and introducing independent study courses. Northeastern University and Antioch College were implementing work study programs. Reed College and Barnard and other institutions were trying new approaches to education and giving students much more freedom.

On the curricular side, Columbia University had organized its first and second years around two survey courses in contemporary civilization. The most exciting innovation of all was the experimental college at the University of Wisconsin, under the leadership of Alexander Meiklejohn.

I made it my business to learn as much as I could about all the new developments and particularly the programs at Sarah Lawrence and Bennington. I did not think Drew should attempt to implement the work study idea that was being successfully developed at Northeastern and Antioch, but I was greatly attracted by the new program at Wisconsin. After an exchange of correspondence with Dr. Meiklejohn, I spent several weeks at Madison, Wisconsin, studying the program in depth and getting acquainted with the bright young people running it. It was a most exciting intellectual adventure, and I learned a great deal. I borrowed many of the ideas, but not the program itself.

Dr. Meiklejohn was a fascinating teacher. He had been President of Amherst, where he displayed a shocking disregard for financial management. He did much for Amherst's intellectual life, but the trustees eventually decided to request his resignation. I still regard Dr. Meiklejohn as one of the foremost educators of the twentieth century and am grateful that I could see the famous experimental college at first hand.

Like so many experiments, the one at Wisconsin was killed by a conservative faculty, motivated in part by envy and in part by fear. The program was divided into two parts: The first year was devoted to the study of fifth-century Greece. The second year was devoted to the study of the thirteenth-century Renaissance. Both years were comprehensive studies that cut across departmental lines and required the use of primary sources. Disregard for departments and departmental boundaries caused the program's failure. Faculty members not involved in the experimental college saw the new program as a threat to their departmental structure.

I finally decided that we didn't need to make drastic changes in organizing our departments and courses at Brothers College. We did, however, have to establish priorities. I wanted to build a college where the sideshows were not important. I knew we should have organized sports, but I thought they should be completely amateur, organized largely by students to please participants and not to attract spectators. We had a basketball team, a baseball team, a tennis team, and a track team. We had no football. Nor did we have fraternities, having no need for them at such a small college.

The business of the college was liberal learning. We had no interest in vocational education. We did not have to worry about graduate education. We were an undergraduate college for men. We were strictly liberal arts. We gave special attention to fundamentals such as public speaking, vocabulary, grammar, written composition, developing good reading habits, and the stretching of the mind by extending intellectual interests. We encouraged debating and dramatics. We gave a great deal of attention to the building of personal libraries. We served tea to the student body every afternoon, five days a week. These gatherings served as intellectual as well as social experiences.

Less than six months after my appointment as Acting Dean of Brothers College, we admitted our first freshman class. Our faculty was drawn from local sources, including recent graduates and members of the faculty of the Theological Seminary. Our classes were held in the Seminary buildings while the new Brothers College building was under construction.

The first class numbered only fourteen, and we had nearly a dozen faculty members. Mortimer Powell Giffen, a gifted teacher in the Theological Seminary, taught our public speaking courses; Louise McCoy North, a Phi Beta Kappa Wellesley graduate and trustee, taught Greek; Fritz Pyen, later bishop of Korea, taught German; Sherman Plato Young, a brilliant Drew graduate, taught Latin; James McClintock, who later became Dean, taught psychology; Sarah Anne Davies, of the University of Wales, taught English; F. Taylor Jones, another fine Drew graduate, taught history; George W. Briggs, from the Seminary faculty, taught Bible; and I taught philosophy.

The following year we brought Louis Jordy from Syracuse to teach chemistry, Julian Carrington also from Syracuse to teach biology, Frank Glenn Lankard from Northwestern University to teach Bible, Earl Aldrich from Tufts University to teach English, and Norman Milligan Guy from Mount Allison University to teach economics and sociology. All proved to be outstanding teachers, and Lankard succeeded me as Dean.

At the end of three years we still had fewer than a hundred students. This number, however, did not trouble us. Our concern was the quality of the educational program. We were determined that the college would be an adventure in excellence. We gave a great deal of personal attention to each of our students. We wanted them to be highly motivated to learn and to assume responsibility for their education. We knew their strengths and weaknesses. The secret of good teaching is a caring faculty. That is what we had. We also had a one-on-one teaching relationship.

The members of that first class were not outstanding students in high school. All, however, graduated in four years, and all were successful in life after graduation. When they returned to Drew for the fiftieth anniversary of their graduation, they were an impressive group of lawyers, clergymen, university professors, theological seminary professors, and business executives. More than half of them had graduate degrees. It was a wonderful example of the unlimited potential of students.

Beginning the second year in 1929, we had an opportunity

to be more selective in our admissions policy. There was, however, one notable exception. I received a telephone call from a high school principal asking if he could bring a senior student to see me on a Saturday morning. When they appeared in my office, I learned that the boy, Harold "Cy" Seymeur ranked 299 in a class of 303. I told the principal the case was hopeless. He insisted, however, that the young man had the potential to succeed. "What do you know?" I asked "Cy." "Baseball," he answered. I borrowed a Spalding Guide on baseball from the college library and questioned him about the life and batting average of Ty Cobb, the pitching record of Christy Mathewson, and the records of Tinker Evers, Chance, and others. No matter what I asked, he had the correct answer.

Finally I said, "We are going to give you a chance to prove yourself, but our problem is to motivate you to learn other subjects as you have learned about baseball. You will take Latin under Sherman Plato Young, our coach of baseball, and he will be your faculty advisor."

Cy was not an easy student to handle. He transferred to Bucknell University for a year and then returned to Drew. He was a star first baseman and captain of the baseball team. He knew more about coaching than Professor Young.

Later, after I went to Allegheny, I lost track of Cy. When I became Chancellor of Syracuse, Cy wrote me. After graduation from Brothers College, he took a doctorate in history at Cornell, writing his dissertation on a history of baseball, and then he began a successful career as a college and university professor, completing his career at the Banks School in New York. At the time he wrote me, the University of Oxford Press had just published his *History of Baseball.* He is perhaps the nation's best known authority on baseball.

As Dean, I gave my full energies to Brothers College at Drew. We stepped up our recruitment of faculty and students. I gave innumerable speeches at high schools. We had a hard-working faculty, and I was happy in my association with both the faculty and the students. It was like a bolt from the blue when I learned that Allegheny College wanted to interview me for the presidency.

4

ALLEGHENY PRESIDENT

When in the fall of 1930 I learned that I was being considered for the presidency of Allegheny College, I thought the idea was out of the question. My work at Drew had only just begun.

As a matter of courtesy, however, I agreed to meet Clarence Frisbee Ross, Acting President of Allegheny, who was paying a visit to Drew. Professor Ross was a classics scholar, a person of high academic standards, and an excellent administrator. At the close of our meeting, I told him that if the trustees had any sense, they would make him president. I did not close the door on being considered for the presidency, but I said that I did not think I was ready to leave Drew.

A few days later I received a telephone call from the secretary of Andrew Wells Robertson, Chairman of the Board of Westinghouse Electric Company, and an Allegheny trustee. She said that Mr. Robertson wanted to see me in his office. We agreed on a time, and I appeared for the interview.

Mr. Robertson opened the conference by saying, "Why do you want to be President of Allegheny College?" "Mr. Robertson," I replied, "I don't want to be President of Allegheny College. I am not a candidate. Dr. Ross came to Madison to meet me, and then I received a summons to your office. I'm here. What do you have to say to me?"

Andy Robertson was a bear. He liked to bully people. With each attack I counter attacked. At the end of the interview I was convinced that whatever interest Allegheny had in me had been eliminated by this interview. I did not think I made a favorable impression on Mr. Robertson, but he did not show his hand. Later, he urged the committee to offer me the position.

If the interview with Mr. Robertson was disheartening, my meeting with Allegheny's Board of Trustees was even worse. It was a strong board. Andrew Culbertson, a utility president from Erie, Pennsylvania, was its chairman; and the journalist and Lincoln scholar Ida Minerva Tarbell was one of the active members. Paul Sturtevant, a partner in Harris Forbes and a trustee of both Drew and Allegheny, was an active board member, as were William Preston Beazell of the *New York Herald;* John W. Barclay, one of the outstanding lawyers of Cleveland; Charles K. Arter of Cleveland, donor of Arter Hall at Allegheny; and Colonel Lewis Walker, President of Hookless Fastener Company, which later became Talon, Incorporated. These among other trustees interviewed me.

William Ridge, a trustee from Long Island, played a role similar to that which Mr. Robertson had played in his interview. "Dr. Tolley," Mr. Ridge said, "I have no doubt you're a promising scholar and teacher. But we don't need another scholar at Allegheny. What we need is a fund raiser. We haven't had a successful president since William Henry Crawford retired eleven years ago. Nobody's raised any money since he left. Now we're in the midst of a depression, and we haven't reached the bottom of it yet. Under the direction of a scholar, this college could go broke. What do you say to that?"

"Mr. Ridge," I said, "of course a college president has to raise money. But where does the money come from? It comes first from the trustees. Second, it comes from the alumni. Leadership and fund raising have to start with the trustees, not the president. It has to start with you, Mr. Ridge. If I should come to Allegheny, how much would you give?"

After that meeting, I again felt I would no longer be considered for the presidency of Allegheny. What I did not know was that Paul Sturtevant had been watching my work at Drew and was convinced that I was ready for the job. It was largely on his recommendation that I was offered the position.

I had not bargained for this. I immediately went to the new

President of Drew, Arlo Ayres Brown, who knew I had been offered the job, and told him I didn't think I should take it.

"I ought to stay here and finish the job I started three years ago." I said, "I don't think it would be fair to leave Brothers College now."

"You'll do no such thing," Dr. Brown said. "You *must* take it. We're in a depression, and it's going to be a tough job, but they need you. You can do it."

I went home to Ruth and said, "Dr. Brown wants me to leave." And leave I did. Years later, I met Dr. Brown and said, "Arlo, you know you really upset me when you told me to go to Allegheny. I went home and told Ruth you wanted me to leave." Dr. Brown looked at me with a smile and said, "How could you have been so stupid? I didn't want you to leave. I've always believed that a college administrator should not stand in the way of a man's path upward. If some other college offers more than you can offer, you give your blessing and say, 'Go!' "

This was an important lesson for me to learn. I had a number of experiences later in my career as a college administrator that allowed me to apply this lesson. In one of these cases, I sent a young man to Harvard for his Ph.D., at Syracuse University's expense. Harvard offered him an attractive post when he received his degree. He wrote me saying he owed his loyalty to us and would come back to Syracuse. I told him to take the job, and he did. I did the same thing with Fritz Mosher, a Maxwell professor, when he was offered a distinguished professorship at Berkeley. We had financed his doctorate at Harvard, and he too would have stayed at Syracuse out of loyalty.

Allegheny College was founded in 1851 by an exceptional Presbyterian minister and Harvard graduate, Timothy Alden, a descendant of the American puritan colonist and statesman John Alden and his wife, Priscilla. President Alden built Bentley Hall to house the William Bentley Library. The library holds many important manuscripts and a wealth of Americana, including collections of Isaiah Thomas and rare first editions of Cotton Mather and George Washington. Even in its first years the library was so outstanding that when Thomas Jefferson was founding the University of Virginia, he wrote President Alden saying that he could not hope to match the treasures housed in Allegheny's library. He did hope, however, that the only emulation between the two institutions would be the worthy one of which could do the greater good. The letter is reproduced on a bronze tablet in the library.

Despite President Alden's success with Bentley Hall and the library, he became discouraged by the expense of running a college and closed Allegheny in 1831. It reopened in 1833 under the auspices of the Methodist Episcopal Church with the Reverend Martin Ruter as its President. Ruter later went to Texas as a missionary where he established Ruter College and was one of the important people in the early history of Texas.

In 1893, William Henry Crawford was elected President of Allegheny. He served in that role for twenty-seven years, and he made Allegheny a college of exceptional quality. When Crawford retired in 1920, he was replaced by Frederick W. Hixon, who would have done an outstanding job had he not become ill. He died in 1924. Little was accomplished during his four-year term. James A. Beebe took over in 1928. Like President Hixon, he too became ill. He retired in 1930. Dean Clarence Frisbee Ross, professor of Latin, was Acting President from 1930 through 1931. He should have been made President, but the board did not believe he could raise the funds that the college needed.

When I took over as Allegheny's President, I discovered that Dr. Ross was a fountain of knowledge. He knew everything about Allegheny and was also completely loyal and unselfish. There was not an ounce of jealousy in his makeup. I could not have had a finer associate.

Before coming to Allegheny, I sought the advice of Professor Floyd W. Reeves of the University of Chicago who was one of the leading authorities on American higher education. "You're a very young man," he told me, "and you're going to be in a hurry. Don't be. Be patient. Don't try to set the world on fire." Determined to follow Reeves's counsel, I went to Allegheny planning to play it safe.

Professor Lee D. McLean, however, threw that idea out of the window. He told me that for over a year he had headed a committee that had been developing a new curriculum for the college. "I don't know what to do now," he said. "I hate to scrap the work we've done." I asked him to tell me about it. When he had finished, I said, "It sounds fine. Are you sure the faculty is with you?" He said that there were some problems with Henry Ward Church, professor of French, and a few others; but that if they came over to his side, there would be unanimous support.

I met with Professor Church and the others several times and incorporated a number of their ideas into the plan. The new curriculum was adopted with no dissenting votes. A sound reform, it contained many new ideas, including well-planned survey courses not too different from those at Columbia University. They gave an overview of the humanities, the social sciences, and the natural sciences and were required courses for freshmen and sophomores.

The adoption of the new curriculum was a tremendous morale builder. It allowed me to start with a united faculty as well as an exciting new academic program. My presidency was not entirely smooth, however. One of my first decisions upon arriving at Allegheny antagonized alumni, but not the members of the faculty. I decided to discontinue athletic scholarships, which of course meant the deemphasis of football.

At the time, Allegheny was playing nationally ranked teams like Dartmouth and the University of Pittsburgh. Although we often lost and had a number of serious injuries, we were making a creditable showing. With cash, however, as tight as it was and with faculty salaries so low, I could not justify giving eleven football players $1,150 annual cash scholarships in addition to free room, board, and tuition. We were still far from the bottom of the depression. For a small college to spend so much for football at such a time seemed sinful.

I sent for each of the players and explained to them that we would honor their contracts, but that once they had graduated we would have no more football scholarships. In the meantime, I met with the football coach. In the course of our interview he said that he believed that the college President should earn as much money as the football coach.

"That's very generous of you," I said. "Unfortunately, I have bad news for you. Your contract expires this year, and will not be renewed."

Needless to say, all hell broke loose. Frank Labounty, an

alumnus and long-time supporter of Allegheny, who was paying much of the bill for the players' scholarships, was the leader of the opposition. When I met with him I said, "I appreciate your generosity, but this is not right. We are a small college with a reputation for scholastic excellence. Our ambition is to make the college famous for the quality of its faculty and students. Big-time football distorts this image. It is completely out of scale. Perhaps a case can be made for strong teams in large universities, but at Allegheny we have different priorities."

My intention was not to eliminate football, but to keep it free from professionalism. Of course, without scholarships to attract star players, the level of our team's performance fell like a stone. The first year we were without our professional players we had only five people in the freshman class who had earned letters in high school, and three of these were in tennis! Each fall I would tell the tallest and heaviest men in the freshmen class that they were going to play football. If they said they had never played before, which was often the case, I would answer: "You're going to learn!" I soon discovered, though, that it takes years to become a good football player.

We had an excellent coach in Karl Lawrence. He was a superb teacher. Nonetheless, our team was so weak that we came to regard a first down as a moral victory. Once, Washington and Jefferson College put up a sign in the locker room asking whether the final score against Allegheny would be 60-0 or 70-0. This stirred up our team so much that we won 14-0. For several years, however, our victories were few and far between. Given the importance Allegheny had previously placed on football, it was a wonder I survived.

That I did survive may be due to the fact that we had more pressing problems. Figuratively speaking, grass had grown in the streets of Allegheny, and the college was in desperate need of money. At one point in 1933, the Meadville banks refused to lend us money for our payroll. To pay our faculty, I borrowed funds from five individuals, including members of the oil rich Crary family in Warren, Pennsylvania, and George W. Olmsted of Ludlow, the owner of several leather tanning factories and a major stockholder in the Long Island Lighting Company.

The following month the banks gave me an equally hard

time. I then threatened to take all our banking to the Pittsburgh banks. I had spent several days in Pittsburgh exploring the matter, so I was on firm ground when I met with the officers of the Meadville banks. The First National Bank capitulated first and then the others surrendered. It was, however, a close call.

We were at the bottom of the depression, and almost everyone was pessimistic about the future. Frank P. Miller, Vice-Chairman of Allegheny's Board of Trustees, predicted that the annual budget of the nation would "never again reach the $100 billion mark in income and expenditures."

His mood was contagious. At the next board meeting, the trustees decided to sell all of the college's common stocks and put the money into bonds. By this time our $2 million endowment had shrunk to a market value of $200,000. I thought that the trustees had lost their minds. I finally managed a thirty-day delay. During that time, I made the rounds and pleaded with each of the trustees either to sell none of the common stocks or, in any case, not more than 50 percent. They eventually agreed to sell only half our stocks. As a consequence, when the market recovered, we had lost only $1 million instead of $2 million.

It was a difficult time for everyone. Mr. Andrew Culbertson, the chairman of the Board of Trustees, went bankrupt. About a year before he filed for bankruptcy, he had given us $100,000. I told him I felt bad about the gift, but he said that he was sorry it wasn't a $1 million. At least, he said, $100,000 was saved. Later we provided an annuity for his widow, and this gave the story of his gift a happy ending.

Given Allegheny's shaky financial status, I devoted much of my time to fund raising. For many years this was my most difficult task. I disliked it so much that it literally made me sick. One day, however, it dawned on me that "If you can't lick 'em, join 'em."

"This is part of my job," I thought. "It's a disagreeable job, but like washing dishes, making beds, or changing diapers, it needs to be done. Stop complaining about it. Stop getting sick about it. Just do it." After I made that decision, I took fund raising in my stride. It never made me sick again.

No matter how I warmed to my task, however, I never employed high-pressure fund-raising tactics. My slower, more methodical approach seemed to work, and we regularly received gifts of $25,000, $50,000, and $100,000, as well as bequests in wills for larger amounts. I was learning that the New Testament is right: "Ask and ye shall receive."

Salaries were, of course, much lower than they are now. My starting salary as President of Allegheny was $8,000. Today, that would not pay the bills for a family of four. On the other hand, a dollar went much further. I paid $1,010 for my first automobile, a 1931 Dodge. I received a $500 raise annually, until my salary reached $10,000. At that point I asked that the faculty's salaries continue to be raised, and that mine remain the same. In 1940, over my protest, the board insisted on raising my salary to $12,000, where it stayed for my last two years at Allegheny.

By that time, the college was moving forward in every way. In addition to balancing the budget, restoring the endowment, and paying for the addition to Reis Library, we added several dormitories, including Tarbell House, Brooks Hall, Walker Hall, and the John Scott Craig Room, the Lincoln Room, and the Arthur W. Thompson Rare Book Room in Reis Library. We also built Alumni Gardens, doubled the size of the heating plant, and added new science laboratories to Carnegie, Alden, and Wilcox Halls. We restored Cochran Hall, providing bowling alleys, a bookstore, and a student center. In addition, we built playing fields, tennis courts, and increased our book holdings in the library. We also received a $300,000 gift for the erection of Baldwin Hall. In order to break out of our landlocked campus, we purchased dozens of neighboring houses and bought vacant land to the east and more than a hundred acres to the north for the Robertson Playing Field. William Preston Beazell, one of my trustees, became so weary of our buying contiguous properties that he began calling me "Contiguous Property Tolley."

By this time, we were also writing many wills. For some twenty years after I left Allegheny, I kept my contacts with these alumni and friends to make sure they remained loyal to the College. As a result, Allegheny continued to receive a steady stream of bequests.

One of our important donors was Colonel Lewis Walker. Colonel Walker loved to have me ride with him in the back seat of his chauffeured Lincoln while he smoked a cigar and told stories. The number of his anecdotes, I soon discovered, was limited, and he told them in exactly the same way. All that was required of me was that I sit and listen. I came to know those stories so well that I could anticipate every pause and every sentence. At the end of the drive, Colonel Walker would always slip me a check for $1,000. In the course of a year his gifts exceeded $50,000. In my time, I think I was one of the highest-paid listeners in the Grove of Academe.

In 1933, the same year the banks were closing, I learned that some three hundred acres of farm land were for sale just outside of Meadville. I asked the executive committee of the Board of Trustees if I could make an offer. Money was so tight that they said, "No." Then I tried another tack. "If I can buy it for nothing, may I buy it?" They then gave their permission.

I made an offer of $1,200 to the Philadelphia bank that held the property. To my surprise they accepted it. Before the time came to pay, I had sold the farmhouse with five acres of land for $1,000, and the barns for $300, netting a $100 profit, and retaining 295 acres of land.

The property had originally been the home of the Bousson family, French emigres loyal to Napoleon. When political fortunes changed, they returned to France as suddenly as they had left. Their land included a fine ski hill, a small pond, and a beautiful trout stream running through the property. It was perfect acreage for a student, faculty, and alumni retreat.

I proposed the idea of a retreat to Colonel Walker, who immediately offered to donate the funds to build a lodge where the students could stay on weekends. It was situated on the edge of the lake that we later named Lake Siple after Paul Siple, a prize student. The lodge had a huge fireplace and was an ideal spot for students to gather socially or to change for swimming.

Later, Colonel Walker suggested we build a second cabin for Ruth and me. I thanked him for the thought, but suggested that instead we build a cabin for faculty use, which he did.

It is hard to put a value on the contribution the Bousson property made to the social life of students and faculty. In my own case, Bousson gave me an opportunity to go skiing, trout fishing, and swimming with students, and to have endless discussions with them on all sorts of topics around the fireplace in the lodge. Thanks to the Bousson property, I came to know the faculty and students much better. As I became a friend of the members of the faculty, I learned to appreciate their quality. They were exceptional teachers and scholars.

In Alice Huntington Spalding, professor of public speaking and dramatics, we had both a gifted teacher and an absentminded professor. Professor Spalding had a habit of driving her car to downtown Meadville, parking, and forgetting where she had left it. Once after leaving it in a no-parking zone, she spent two days fruitlessly searching for it. When she finally located it at the police station, she turned to the police chief and said, "You did this on purpose!"

After announcing that we would install a sprinkler system in Hulings Hall, a women's dormitory, I was paid a surprise visit by Professor Spalding. "Look, Dr. Tolley," she said, "this is a complete waste of money. You can't burn down Hulings Hall. I know. I've set fire to it three times myself. Once I left an iron on, and it burned a hole through the floor and dropped into the room below, but it didn't set fire to Hulings Hall." Despite her habitual absentmindedness, Professor Spalding performed wonders as director of Allegheny's dramatic productions. John Hulbert who succeeded her was also an outstanding teacher and director.

Hurst Robins Anderson, chairman of the speech department, was a dynamic teacher with exceptional administrative gifts. He later became President of Centenary Collegiate Institute in Hackettstown, New Jersey, President of Hamline University in St. Paul, Minnesota, and then President of American University in Washington, D.C.

Paul Henry Giddens, chairman of the history department, was a superb lecturer and a fine teacher. In addition to writing a first-class history of the oil industry, he wrote a history of the Standard Oil Company of Indiana. He also became President of Hamline University, which he served with distinction.

John Ritchie Schultz, professor of American literature, was a singularly talented teacher as well as a superb Dean of Men. He succeeded me as President of Allegheny.

At the time I became President, the two greatest teachers were Dean Clarence Ross, our professor of Latin, and William Arthur Elliott. Elliott was a nationally known Greek scholar who also became a magnificent teacher of art.

Other strong teachers included Henry Ward Church, professor of French; Chester A. Darling, an exciting teacher of biology, who succeeded Schultz as President of Allegheny; Oscar P. Akers in mathematics; and Richard Edwin Lee, a tremendously gifted lecturer in chemistry with a statewide reputation as a scholar. Warner Woodring, chairman of the history department, was a teacher of university quality whose only weakness was the frequent use of sarcasm with poor students. That is an unforgivable sin no matter how gifted one is in other respects as a teacher and scholar.

Professors Arman Kalfayan and Mildred Ludwig gave Allegheny a fine French department. One of our brightest students, Paul Cares, began his brilliant career as an instructor in history after his graduation.

In music, Morten J. Luvaas had enormous influence. He had served under the great choral director at St. Olaf's College, F. Melius Christiansen. In time, he came to rival Christiansen in national influence. Under the direction of Luvaas, the Allegheny Singers were one of the nation's best choral groups. Luvaas was also my doubles partner in tennis. Thanks to him, we were the doubles champions of Crawford County.

In English we had a delightful little man, Stanley Swartley, who when introduced to me said, "If you see a big Cadillac coming down North Main Street without a driver, that will be I." I never could understand how he saw over the wheel, even when sitting on a pillow. The Swartleys adopted a boy named David, and as he approached age three I was asked to baptize him. I waited for more than an hour at the Swartley home. Finally, Professor Swartley came downstairs and announced, "I am sorry, but David says he does not want to be baptized."

Professor Frederick Goodrich Henke in psychology was a fussy perfectionist and a campus character. Independently wealthy, he purchased a new Cadillac every year. He would walk rather than ride whenever it rained or snowed. He washed the car each day after driving and covered it with cheesecloth to protect it from dust. People stood in line to buy his car at the end of each year. Henke kept two pedigreed dogs, and they were his pride and joy. I remember when Professor Chester Darling bought a mongrel dog for $10. He took the dog to Professor Henke's office. Henke examined the dog closely and then asked, "How much did you pay for him?" "Ten dollars," said Darling. There was a long pause. Then Henke said, "a good dog for the money."

Ted Seeley was an outstanding teacher of English. The star among the younger English teachers, however, was Julian Ross, the son of Dean Ross. Julian had a problem with stammering which, when he lectured, only lasted through his first sentences. Once he was started, he held his students spellbound. In all my years at Columbia, Drew, Allegheny, and Syracuse, I would put Julian Ross close to the top of the list of great teachers I have known.

We had a weak philosophy department. Since the chairman was tenured in that position, it was difficult to improve the department. I finally had the idea that Julian Ross might be persuaded to teach a course on literature and philosophy. When I discussed the idea with him, he said, "If you will teach the history of philosophy next year, I will take the course. I will tell you at the end of the year whether I can develop a philosophy and literature curriculum." I gave Horace Lavely a year's sabbatical during which I taught his courses. In the front seat of every class on the "History of Philosophy" was the most brilliant member of the faculty, Julian Ross. The next year and each year until he retired, Ross taught what became Allegheny's most popular course, "Philosophy and Literature."

Not all members of the Allegheny staff were as strong as those I have mentioned. The chairman of the Bible department, Irwin Ross Beiler, was a superb human being and a fine scholar. He was not, however, a particularly gifted teacher. He had a habit of clearing his throat and of stopping at what we used to call the "er" junction. When lecturing he would interrupt himself in almost every sentence with "er, er, er." Shortly before I came to Allegheny, Professor Beiler was under fire from a trustee named Singleton for so-called radicalism. At a meeting of the board of trustees, Mr. Singleton made a motion that Professor Beiler be fired. After launching a blistering attack, he concluded his remarks by saying "he does not teach the religion I learned at my mother's knee." Ida Tarbell rose to Professor Beiler's defense and looking Mr. Singleton in the eye said, "You know, Mr. Singleton, that is exactly the trouble with you. You never learned anything about religion after you were two years old."

Our librarian, Edith Rowley, was a great favorite among alumni, and she was a sweet and lovely person. She was not, however, a well-trained librarian and on occasion she tested my patience. She called me one morning saying, "There is a nice young man in my office who would like to buy several books he found in the stacks. Will this be all right with you?" "Hold everything," I said. "I will be right up to see you." Reis Library was only about two hundred feet from my office in Bentley. I was in Miss Rowley's office almost immediately. There I found an undersized, insignificant looking young man holding about a dozen books. "What do you have there?" I asked. "I found these in the stacks," he said. "I will be glad to pay the college $10 for each of them." I looked quickly at the books and saw that each was a rare book from the Bentley Library. On the top was Eliot's Indian Bible worth several thousand dollars. As I looked at the young swindler, my blood began to boil. "Have you been doing this all across the state?" I asked. "Yes," he replied. I took a step toward him. "If you ever set foot on this campus again, I will strangle you with my two hands. Get out of here and never come back." I turned to Edith and said, "Do not ever sell any books, and let's build the rare book room as fast as we can."

Shortly after this experience, Andrew Robertson, our board chairman, asked me to fire Edith Rowley. "Andy," I said, "I know much better than you do that she is not a competent librarian. She is, however, a graduate of Allegheny, Class of 1905, and she has been a librarian here ever since. Over the years, Allegheny has had plenty of opportunity to find her another job, but it did not. She now has been here more than twenty-five years. Allegheny is a family. We do not fire people who have been here twenty-five years. You may fire me, Andy, but you cannot fire Edith Rowley."

It was not easy to recruit new faculty members. We worked hard, however, at the search for talent, and we were successful. One of the best teachers and scholars we brought to Allegheny was John Elmer Cavelti, professor of chemistry. We found him at Wesleyan, where he was the youngest and the best member of a large department.

In Latin, we recruited William Tongue, who had led his class at the University of Pennsylvania. Later, he became chairman of classics at Catholic University. We also employed John Heller, who later became chairman of the Latin department of the University of Minnesota. Charles Wilbur Ufford in physics came to us from Princeton University. Later, he became chairman at the University of Pennsylvania. We also had Albert Olivie in biology; Herbert Rhinesmith and Harold State in chemistry; Guy Emerson Buckingham and Charles S. Miller in education; Blair Hanson, a wonderful teacher of French; Julius Miller, a gifted teacher of art; and Louis Jefferson Long in economics. Long was not only a fine teacher but a superb administrator. He served as Allegheny's treasurer and business manager and taught a full load as chairman of economics. Later, he became president of Wells College.

Recruiting top faculty members was part of my strategy to improve Allegheny's already excellent academic standing. I also wanted the College to excel in the fields of guidance and academic tests and measurements, which were then in a tremendously exciting period. In 1932, Dr. Ben Wood of Teachers College at Columbia began what was known as the Pennsylvania Study, financed by the Carnegie Foundation. The study involved giving freshmen from all the colleges in the Commonwealth of Pennsylvania a series of comprehensive examinations to discover how much they knew in such different fields as mathematics, history, science, government, English, and foreign languages. The students took the comprehensive exams again in their sophomore year, and two years later took them for the third time in their senior year. The results were illuminating. The greatest gain in knowledge as measured by the test scores was at Lehigh University. Not surprising to those who knew the state teachers' colleges of Pennsylvania, the seniors at the teachers' colleges knew less than they had as freshmen, a negative growth in knowledge as measured by the examinations. Allegheny did very well; much better than its neighbors Thiel, Westminster, Grove City, Geneva, and Washington and Jefferson. Our test results were in the upper quarter of Pennsylvania colleges.

I decided that something like the Pennsylvania Study should continue at Allegheny. I brought in two exceptionally well-qualified testing experts: Henry S. Dyer and Henry Chauncey. Unable to get foundation support, we financed the project ourselves. We gave a series of comprehensive exams to freshmen each year for several years, repeating the exams in the sophomore year, and again in their senior year. The fact that the students knew they would take the tests again motivated them to learn more than they probably would have had there been no tests.

At the same time, we encouraged students to read widely, and we kept a record of their use of the library. The library records proved to be extremely useful. Students who were on probation and in danger of being expelled won a grace period because the records showed they were using the library extensively. They were failing their classwork, but they were getting their education in the library.

Our use of tests and measurements also taught us about academic failures. We would normally drop twenty-five to thirty students for poor scholarship at the end of the freshman year. One year, I decided to have our test-and-measurement staff select thirty-five of the least talented members of the freshman class. We provided them with special tutoring, and we had a required study hall from 7:00 to 9:00 P.M. four days a week. At the end of the year, all thirty-five survived, but the faculty still flunked some thirty students. All we had succeeded in doing was to flunk out brighter students than in previous years. It pointed up the need for better academic counseling for all our students.

Dyer left Allegheny to become director of tests and measurements at Harvard. Chauncey eventually became President of the College Entrance Examination Board and the Educational Testing Service. The Chauncey Testing Center at Princeton is a monument to the accomplishments of this outstanding man.

The 1930s were a time of ferment in the field of vocational guidance testing. The Stevens Institute of Technology had an educational guidance testing clinic which attracted attention throughout the East. There was nothing like it in Pennsylvania, and so we developed an educational guidance clinic at Allegheny. For several weeks each summer, high school juniors and seniors came to the clinic for testing. The center's outstanding faculty tested the students' vocational aptitudes, gave them I.Q. tests, and tested for special aptitudes. No attempt was made to influence students to enter Allegheny. The educational guidance clinic was a great success. We learned a great deal about counseling as well as the value of tests and measurements.

Our plan to improve Allegheny's standing included raising the caliber of its students. When I came to Allegheny in 1931, its student body ranked 144th out of 500 colleges in admissions aptitude testing sponsored by the American Council on Education. I knew we could do better. It was simply a matter of changing our recruitment strategy.

I appointed Paul Younger, a recent graduate of Allegheny, as our new director of admissions. He later became President of Martz and Lundy, one of the best of the national fund-raising organizations.

"Paul," I told him, "I'm giving you a car, unlimited travel money, and a list of the top high schools in Pennsylvania and Ohio. Meet the teachers of these schools and tell them you want as many of their top ten students as possible to come to Allegheny. We will offer them scholarships. This first generation of top students will attract others of similar quality."

Younger's first year was so successful that our students' aptitude testing jumped from 144th to 72d in the nation. Paul was jubilant. I shared his enthusiasm, but told him we could do better. The next year our students' aptitude standing ranked 64th, then 32d, and then 17th. We ranked sixth during the last year the national tests were given.

Allegheny was small enough for me to know most of its students. With only about six hundred students in all four classes, I was able to interview every member of the freshman class. I kept notes on what I learned from the interviews. Many lived up to their promise and made their dreams come true.

One such student was a brash young man named Paul Siple. Siple told me he wished to take a doctorate at Clark University, revisit the South Pole with Admiral Byrd, and become a college professor, then a college president, and finally a United States senator. He did achieve some of his goals. He took his doctorate at Clark and went to the South Pole with Byrd. He did not, however, become a college professor, a college president, or United States senator. He served his country well, not only through his Arctic explorations, but by inventing equipment of inestimable value to explorers of the Arctic and Antarctic. He also wrote some of the best books about the Arctic and the Antarctic.

In another interview with an Allegheny freshman, I encountered a boy who was certain of what he would *not* be when he grew up. Seymour Smith opened our interview by saying, "I presume my Methodist minister told you to send for me."

"No," I said, "he didn't. But tell me what the problem is."

"Well, sir," he said, "He wants me to be a Methodist minister, and I don't want to do that."

"Fine," I said. "No one should be a minister unless he can't help himself. It's a miserable job."

During his senior year, Smith came to see me. "You may have forgotten what you told me when I was a freshman, but I haven't," he said. "I've decided to go to Yale Divinity School next year and become a minister."

"Fine," I said, "But in addition, I want you to take a Ph.D. from Yale."

"Do you think I can?" he said.

"For you," I said, "it will be a lead-pipe cinch."

Seymour Smith took his doctorate, became a professor at Yale, and then served with great success as president of Stephens College in Columbia, Missouri.

Another boy who impressed me was Raymond Philip Shafer. Ray was a fine, talented boy with an exceptional gift for leadership. I nominated Ray for a Rhodes scholarship in his senior year. He did not win the Rhodes, but he became Governor of Pennsylvania, a senior partner in Coopers and Lybrand, chairman of the Allegheny board of trustees, and, as he approached the age of seventy, President of Allegheny.

Bob Appleyard was a handsome boy who made his mark in the Protestant Episcopal Church in Florida before becoming bishop of the diocese of Pittsburgh. His distinguished career was no surprise to those of us who knew him as an undergraduate.

Among the scores of others who had exceptional success after graduation was Jim Gettamy, one of the great preachers of our time, who served as President of the Hartford Theological Seminary. Gettamy seemed to have been born for the pulpit. When he was a student his classmates regarded him in a class by himself as a public speaker.

Still another was Bruce Dearing, who became Dean at the University of Delaware, then President of the State University of New York at Binghamton, the successor of Triple Cities College, which I started.

One of my favorite students was Sam Ziskind. Sam had to earn his way through school and, for a time, was the night telephone operator at the Catholic hospital run by nuns. Sam had one of the deepest bass voices I have ever heard. He greeted each call with sepulchral tones, "Sister Sam Ziskind speaking!"

Another was Dick Horne. Dick was a member of the Allegheny singers as well as captain of the football team. After a Bach concert by the singers, fellow students found Dick overcome with emotion. "What's the trouble?" they asked. "Nothing," said Dick, "but Jesus Christ how I love that Bach!"

Henry Merritt Wriston, President of Lawrence College, and later of Brown University, was chairman of the Committee on Academic Freedom and Tenure of the Association of American Colleges (AAC). He and John L. Seaton of Albion College were my mentors while I was President of Allegheny. Wriston put me on the Academic Freedom and Tenure committee and then saw to it that I became chairman. In 1940, the Association of American Colleges and the American Association of University Professors (AAUP) joined forces to produce the famous statement on academic freedom and tenure, which is still the bible on that subject in American higher education. As chairman of the Committee on Academic Freedom and Tenure, I drafted most of that document.

Generally speaking, tenure is regarded with suspicion by those not in the academic world. I knew, however, from my having observed the dismissal of Frederick Roman at Syracuse and a number of so-called radicals at Columbia that teachers need special protection in their search for truth. I remember a professor from the University of Chicago who said, "President Robert Maynard Hutchins says he is opposed to tenure for professors because he wants to keep them on their toes. What he really means is that he wants to keep them on their knees!"

The 1940 statement provides for the job security of academic tenure after a trial period not to exceed seven years. This gives administrative officers an adequate opportunity to make a judgment about the qualifications of newly appointed teachers and scholars. Those who attain tenure may then pursue their scholarly investigations without fear of witch hunts and the loss of jobs.

I served as President of the College Presidents of Pennsylvania, an active and useful organization, and in 1940 became chairman of the Cooperative Study in General Education of the American Council on Education. For some six years, this study produced major changes in undergraduate curricula in American higher education. The study's director, Professor Ralph W. Tyler of the University of Chicago, gave it inspired leadership. Using this study for background, teachers from scores of colleges initiated experimental methods and approaches to teaching that revolutionized language study and greatly improved undergraduate courses in the humanities, social studies, and the sciences. It was a landmark undertaking and lifted the quality of undergraduate instruction in all the participating colleges. The introduction of foreign language laboratories, the use of radio and television in classrooms, new approaches to reading and mathematics, and the place of research in methods of teaching are but a few of the contributions of the Cooperative Study.

In my final year at Allegheny, I was elected President of the Association of American Colleges, and served in that capacity both in 1942 and 1943. As President of the association and in the years that followed, one particularly rewarding experience was working with Congress in drafting the Servicemen's Readjust-

ment Act of 1944, now known as the G.I. Bill of Rights, for returning veterans. We worked hard to promote its passage and I remember how happy we were when we were successful. We
underestimated, however, the revolutionary impact on higher education the G.I. Bill would have. Not in our time has there been
more important government action to promote equality of opportunity.

In 1932, I was appointed to the University Senate of the
Methodist Episcopal Church. The senate was the accrediting
body to more than one hundred colleges, preparatory schools,
and universities associated with the Methodist Church. Except for
a four-year period from 1936 to 1940, I was very active in the senate. I served as its President from 1960 to 1970. As a senate member and President, I visited most of the Methodist related colleges
and universities. I had a hand in the selection of the presidents of
many of the colleges, as well as the upgrading of academic standards within these institutions. It was a unique organization with
enormous influence. I doubt if any accrediting organization has
done more to improve the quality of higher education in America.

In the years I was at Allegheny, it was still considered to be
a Methodist college, and the Methodist Episcopal Church had a
strong influence on it. Most of the trustees were Methodists, and
the trustees appointed by the Pittsburgh and Erie Methodist Conferences were very active. The Methodist Bishop, Adna Wright
Leonard, was a strong and able man who insisted on having his
own way in both important and unimportant matters. In this respect he was more like a Catholic cardinal than a Methodist
bishop. Nevertheless, Ruth and I became dear friends with
Bishop Leonard and entertained him often in our home. Many
times he played with our children using a handkerchief for a
make-believe rabbit.

Bishop Leonard believed Stuart Chase, the well-known
writer on economics and public affairs, to be a dangerous radical,
although Chase's beliefs were really very much in the center.
When the Bishop learned that Chase had been invited to speak at
the Old Stone Church in Meadville, he telephoned the minister
and ordered him to withdraw the invitation, saying, "Chase will
not be given a forum in any Methodist church in my jurisdiction."

The minister of Old Stone Church came to me and asked if Chase could give his lecture in Ford Chapel in Allegheny. I said, "of course." Within a day or two, Bishop Leonard telephoned me and asked that I withdraw the invitation. When I declined to do so, he said, "If you let this man speak at Ford Chapel, I will have to ask for your resignation."

"That," I said, "is for you to decide, Bishop Leonard."

I knew he would call the leading layman of the Methodist church in Pittsburgh, Mr. W. Stuart Horner, Vice-President of Armco Steel and a trustee of Allegheny. I spent the better part of a day working with the Meadville Housing Commission on a $5 million steel contract that we decided to award to Armco Steel. When Mr. Horner called, I immediately gave him the good news about the contract. This disarmed him, and he did not raise the issue of Stuart Chase again.

The next call came from the chairman of the Allegheny Board of Trustees, Andrew Robertson. He came directly to the point. "The Bishop called me," he said, "and he wants your scalp."

"I know," I said. "He has been on the war path in each area he has served as Bishop. He has told me with great pride about the radical speakers he has kept off the campuses of the College of Puget Sound, Willamette University, and Syracuse University."

Then Andy surprised me. He said, "I think you are wrong, but I don't believe we should let a Methodist bishop push the College around." Mr. Chase spoke, and the speech was as harmless as tap water.

Bishop Leonard turned from friend to enemy. He was relentless. He summoned the Conference trustees of Allegheny and demanded my resignation. When that failed, he began traveling up and down western Pennsylvania using the pulpits of the leading churches to preach against William P. Tolley at Allegheny College and to tell people not to give money to that godless institution. The attack went on until he moved from Pittsburgh to the Washington area.

It was a good experience for me. When McCarthyism was on the rise during my tenure at Syracuse, I did not need to be converted to the cause of academic freedom.

In 1940, I was approached by Pomona College at Claremont, California, to see if I would consider taking its presidency. I
was in the middle of a capital funds campaign at Allegheny at the
time and said, "Come back later." The financial campaign was a
success, and shortly after its completion the Pomono offer was renewed. In January of 1941, Ruth and I visited Claremont. The
trustees announced that I had already been elected. "Strike the
motion from the minutes of the trustees," I said. "Pomona is a
wonderful college. I have not yet talked to Mrs. Tolley about your
offer. If she should withhold her consent, I would not want the action you have taken to appear on the college records."

As it happened, Ruth took a dim view of my leaving Allegheny. "Both are small colleges," she said; "Pomona may be somewhat stronger, but if you stay at Allegheny you can make it the
equal of any small college in the country."

In October of 1941, Allegheny held a tenth anniversary convocation celebrating a decade of my service as President. On the
morning of that day a beautiful baby girl was delivered by Ruth
in the Meadville Memorial Hospital. Two breathless coeds burst
into my office shortly after the news came. "We have a name for
the baby," they said: "Constance Anne, for the convocation anniversary."

"How wonderful!" I said. "But for a girl the initials C. A. T.
are wrong. Moreover, my wife has just proposed the name Constance for her sister-in-law's baby. How about letting Ruth choose
the baby's first name, but using Diane as a middle name. We
would always have Dee Anniversary Baby."

The girls, although disappointed, agreed to my proposal. I
asked Ruth what name she wanted to give the baby. "Katryn," she
said, "after Katryn Brown," our dear friend.

"What about a middle name?" I asked.

"I don't care," she said.

I waited a minute and finally said, "What about Katryn Diane?" "That's all right," she said. "I don't really care what her middle name is."

That is how Katryn, who is such a delight to us, got her middle name. She will always be "Dee Anniversary Baby."

In looking back at my eleven years at Allegheny, I must give Ruth much of the credit for any success I may have had. Ruth was a wonderful wife, mother, homemaker, and hostess.

When we went to Allegheny, we were a family of four. Nelda was two years old, and Bill was one. Katryn was born ten years later. We lived in a house on Chestnut Street that consisted of a number of small rooms, ill-suited to entertaining. Even the living rooms were inadequate, consisting of two 12-by-12-foot rooms. This arrangement precluded entertaining large groups. Fortunately, Mrs. Arthur L. Bates, the widow of an Allegheny trustee, loved to entertain large groups, and she volunteered to help Ruth manage the big receptions and meetings with parents, trustees, faculty, and alumni by holding these gatherings in her spacious home. She was a gracious and wonderful person, and she made a contribution beyond price.

Even with the help of Mrs. Bates, we had a very busy social life. The Lafayette Hotel in Meadville was a poor excuse for a hotel, and so our guest room was in constant use. Ruth entertained our visitors admirably, making the guest room inviting with flowers and serving home-cooked meals. With board members, speakers, and guest lecturers coming to town weekly for eleven years, we were seldom without a guest, Yet, Ruth managed to make every visitor feel welcome. They, in turn, came to love and to help support Allegheny. If the College acquired important new friends during my eleven-year presidency it was in large part to Ruth's gift for friendship.

Ruth entertained our guests so well and so often that she began to find it exhausting. When we came to Syracuse, she asked, "Must we do this for the rest of our lives?"

5

MY RETURN TO SYRACUSE

When William Pratt Graham was elected Chancellor of Syracuse University in 1936, I had been among those considered for the post. When Chancellor Graham retired in 1942, I knew I would be considered again, but I was not particularly interested. Everything was going well at Allegheny, and I was full of plans for its future.

I did, however, accept an invitation from the nominating committee to go to Syracuse for an interview. The meeting was at the home of Lewis C. Ryan. All of the ten-person committee were there. Dr. Gordon Hoople was chairman; and Judge Edmund Lewis, chief justice of the New York Court of Appeals; Mrs. J. D. "Sadie" Taylor; Harold Coon; and Lewis Ryan were the most vocal members of the committee.

I was at ease with the committee, and the interview went well. I sensed that the committee had not made up its mind and that Lewis Ryan in particular was not in my corner. That did not trouble me. I would not have felt disappointed if one of the others under consideration was selected.

A week or two later Dr. Hoople came to Meadville to extend an invitation to become the seventh Chancellor of the University. I was still very much on the fence, but Dr. Hoople was most persuasive. He said, "You can say no to other colleges and universities, but you cannot say no to your alma mater. Syracuse has a first claim on your love and loyalty."

Ruth was very happy at Allegheny, and she did not want to move. She did not, however, oppose my decision to accept the offer.

I began my duties at Syracuse University on September 19,

1942. Ruth and the children did not arrive until October. By the time they came I was completely immersed in the administrative problems of the University.

When I entered Syracuse University in the fall of 1918 as a freshman, the University had some three thousand students, about one-half were in the College of Liberal Arts, and only two hundred were graduate students. When I returned as Chancellor, the University had some fifty-six hundred students evenly divided between men and women. The College of Liberal Arts was still the largest college, and there were some four hundred graduate students. The endowment was less than $5 million, and the total assets including buildings and grounds were less than $15 million. The annual budget was $3.7 million.

There was little outward evidence of World War II. To be sure, there had been a reduction in the number of upperclassmen, and the fraternities were half-empty. Even so, there were 2,160 freshmen, a surprisingly high figure; we still had varsity football; and campus activities appeared unaffected. We had 1,139 in the ROTC (Reserve Officer Training Corps) program, 100 in civilian and navy pilot programs, and another 50 in a Signal Corps program in the College of Engineering.

At the first Chancellor's reception for freshmen, the students were in a line extending from Alpha Chi Omega on Walnut Avenue around the block on Harrison Street. An electrical blackout added to student interest in the reception. Shaking hands with students by candlelight was a memorable pleasure, but standing so long was hard on the knees. Early in the fall the premier actress of America, Helen Hayes, played the leading role in the initial production of "Harriet," which later opened on Broadway. She won everyone's heart by her charm. A brilliant undergraduate, Joyce Crabtree, produced a superb musical comedy "High on the Hill," which he had written and directed.

At the first faculty reception, I was shocked by the number of faculty members over seventy. They were in sharp contrast to the young faculty I had at Allegheny. I was glad, of course, to see Perley Oakland Place, professor of classics; Raymond Piper, professor of philosophy; and Harry Hepner, professor of psychology—all former teachers; as well as Carl Bye, professor of economics; and Ross Hoople, professor of philosophy—close friends and members of my Class of 1922.

It was clear that two of the first priorities were to increase retirement benefits and raise the shockingly low salaries of faculty members. It was equally important to prepare for the exodus of our male students to military service. I immediately went to Washington, D.C., to call on the air force, the army, the marines, and the navy. To my dismay, I discovered that a letter from Chancellor William Pratt Graham was on file with each branch of the armed services saying that the University has no interest in any military training programs. I informed everyone there was new management at Syracuse and that they should disregard the letter from Chancellor Graham. I knew we could not survive without students, and that meant boys in uniform.

Fortunately, we struck up a good relationship with the air force. They said, "Don't worry. We'll send you all the men you need." In March 1943, they sent us a group of 1,050 cadets for an academic program combined with military training. Then, almost before we could digest that group, they told us a second group of 1,050 were on the way.

At the time, we had only three dormitories—Sims, Winchell, and Haven halls—a handful of cottages, and of course, the sororities and fraternities. It was obvious that we could not accommodate a large group of air force cadets, or any other armed services personnel without a great deal more housing.

We moved swiftly to buy properties around the edge of the campus. In the first month, we purchased some fifty houses and apartment houses; a large number of which were foreclosed properties that had been taken over by the Syracuse banks. We bought them at about 75 percent of their assessed real estate value. It was a good deal for the banks and a better one for the University.

The Board of Trustees was startled by the speed at which we moved, and also by the fact that we were getting into debt, but they were very supportive. Above all, the administrative officers were even more supportive. Nothing was too difficult for them.

There were many sessions of our senior administrative officers that lasted until midnight at 701 Walnut on how to solve the problems we faced. We bought new furniture and beds, and Ed Tobin gave the cadets wonderful meals, feeding them in shifts. Everything was going smoothly when I got a call from Washington telling us they had a problem. "We're in great distress," they said. "We have 550 army cadets on a train. They were due to go to another college, but the college has just informed us that it can't take care of them. Meanwhile, they're on a train. We can keep them there for two days, but we must ship them somewhere. Can you take them?"

By this time we had 2,100 air force cadets on campus, and were pushed hard to take care of them. "Look," I said, "it's half past one now. May I call you back around three this afternoon?"

I remembered that Auburn Theological Seminary in Auburn, New York, was closing its doors because of the lack of theological students. Between one-thirty and three o'clock on a Monday afternoon, we had rented the facilities of the Auburn Seminary and had put everything in the works to accommodate 550 soldiers there for dinner on Wednesday evening.

I called the Army representative back, and said "We'll take them, but you'll have to be easy on us. We must hire faculty and buy furniture, food, and supplies between now and Wednesday. We must make sure there will be enough dishes, linens, and so forth. Everything may not be in the queen's taste for a few days, but send them along."

"Dr. Tolley," he said, "if you can do this for us, you're in like Flynn. Anything you want, you'll have."

Before I assured the army representative that we would find a place for their men, we held a meeting of administrative officers at 701 Walnut. I'll never forget that session. One of our senior officers asked what kind of a village idiot did we have as Chancellor who would say yes to a request like this? It couldn't be done. Others came to my rescue and soon all warmed to the task.

George VanDyke, our treasurer, worked closely with Keith Kennedy, our registrar, who was worth his weight in gold. Kennedy was a master of detail and a fine administrator, but his talents had not been recognized. He was grateful to have responsibility and show what he could do. He had an open telephone line to Auburn, and the whole group worked effectively as a team.

What motivated us was the spirit of patriotism. The executive secretary of the University, Gordon Smith, told everyone: "Of course we can do it. We are in a war, and this is our opportunity to do our part." His optimism was contagious.

On Wednesday night, we greeted 550 men in uniform at the Auburn Theological Seminary, and Ed Tobin served them a beautiful supper. For the faculty and administration at Auburn, it was a happy solution for the use of classrooms and dormitories emptied by the war. We were able to use many of the Seminary faculty, but most of the faculty commuted to Auburn from Syracuse.

The following year, we added several hundred Women's Army Corps and two thousand Army Specialized Training Program soldiers and also launched a training program in Russian and Slavic languages in prefabricated buildings on the University farm south of the campus. In August 1943, we had a total of thirty-eight hundred men and women in uniform. We also bought many more houses near the campus.

Our military programs went smoothly. The coeds were happy to have so many men in uniform on the campus, and I recall no behavior problems. We were also fortunate in accommodating a sizable group of Japanese Americans without incident.

The shocking disaster at Pearl Harbor was followed by a wave of hatred for all things Japanese. In California, where the number of Japanese was largest, the feeling was so strong that even American-born Japanese were rounded up and put behind barbed wire in prison camps.

Soon after the air force cadets arrived at Syracuse, I received a telegram from the American Society of Friends asking if Syracuse would offer scholarships to American-born Japanese who would then be released from the prison camps. They hoped we would take at least five. I quickly returned a telegram saying that we would offer tuition free scholarships to one hundred.

We did not get the hundred we offered to take, but we did welcome some sixty-five. I knew there was a risk involved, but I felt strongly about the incarceration of loyal Americans because of racial origin.

To protect myself, I sent for Andrew O'Keefe, the editor of

the Syracuse *Daily Orange,* our student newspaper. I told Andy what I had done, and I said he was free to do as he pleased with the story. "But," I added, "if you feel as I do about the injustice to American-born Japanese, I suggest that you print nothing in the *Daily Orange* about their arrival. Let them make some friends on campus. Sit on the story for two or three weeks." To my great relief he said, "I am with you 100 percent. We think alike."

Somehow the American Legion and the Veterans of Foreign Wars learned of the arrival of the sixty-five Nisei. When they telephoned me, I counter attacked strongly. They then went to Mr. H. W. Smith, chairman of our Board of Trustees. When he sent for me I went to see him loaded for bear.

"Normally I should let you speak first, Mr. Smith," I said, "but I'll speak first this morning. My father came to America at the age of fifteen from Cornwall, England. From the time he arrived, he was no longer a Cornishman or an Englishman, he was an American. It never occurred to me as a boy that I was an immigrant's son. I too was an American. After college, I went to work on the Lower East Side dealing with recently arrived Italians, Puerto Ricans, Hungarians, and Russians. They were not yet citizens but all were loyal Americans. From the minute they got through Ellis Island, they were Americans. And of course the children born here were also loyal Americans.

"I can understand the fears of the people in California. We had the same fear about Germans during World War I. But that's no excuse, and we shall live to regret this. Mr. Smith, our campus is far enough away that no Japanese American here will be a threat to anybody. We are talking about American citizens. These young people were born in America. For heaven's sake, Mr. Smith," I said, "give them a break. What we are doing is right, and I'm relying on you to support me."

Mr. Smith let me have my say and agreed not to oppose my action.

The Japanese Americans arrived on the campus quietly and settled into classes. A few weeks after their arrival, we had an air force review with twenty-one hundred air force cadets on parade in front of the library. Part of the program included the awarding of a $100 savings bond by the American Legion for the best work of art. The winner was Frank Watanabe, a student in the School of Art, and one of the students brought in from California. I greeted Frank, said I was glad he had won, and presented him with the award.

Frank turned to me and said, "Mr. Chancellor, I have the great privilege of presenting this prize of $100 to the American Red Cross." This released the tension. Twenty-one hundred air force cadets applauded Frank's action.

We did not take military programs to make money, and I don't think they were highly profitable. They did, however, permit balanced budgets throughout the war years, and they paid for most of the cost of the houses and apartment houses we purchased. More importantly, they permitted us to make a significant contribution to the war effort.

Football was dropped in 1943. Boar's Head had presented "The Skin of Our Teeth." Freshman coeds wore orange caps (called "lids") for the first time, and the frosh coeds also took over Sims Hall, traditionally a men's dormitory. The University chorus rendition of the *Messiah* was particularly noteworthy. Over 130 inches of snow fell during the winter, a new record up to that time, although since it has been broken. The death of Dean William Powers, dean of the Chapel, was mourned by students of all faiths. Powers was not a great preacher, but he was a good organizer and he built a great deal of student interest in the religious programs. On Sunday mornings, the front pews of the Chapel were filled by delegations from fraternities and sororities listed in the printed bulletins. Between the large choir and the two or three hundred sorority women and fraternity men, the Chapel was always well filled. In looking for a successor to Dean Powers, our search was finally narrowed to two candidates. One was Harold Case, pastor of the Elm Park Methodist Church in Scranton, Pennsylvania, who later became President of Boston University. The other was Charles C. Noble, minister of the First Methodist Church in Syracuse. Harold Coon was one of the leading laymen in the First Church, a trustee of the University, and the assistant superintendent of schools in the city of Syracuse. Harold's wife, Emily, was Ruth's closest friend, and I often turned to Harold for counsel. I told him we were interested in Dr. Noble as Dean of the Chapel.

"Oh no," said Harold, "you don't want him. He is not my cup of tea. You want Dr. Radcliffe, who preceded Charlie as our minister. Dr. Radcliffe was a man of prayer. How he could pray!" he said. "Charlie Noble is not a man of prayer. You don't want him." "What do the young people think of Dr. Noble?" I asked. "The young people of our church think he is wonderful. He is great with them. But he is not my kind of minister. Radcliffe is the man you want. He is a man of prayer. Charlie is not a man of prayer."

On the way home, Ruth asked me, "What do you think?" I said that he certainly had sold me. "I am going to ask Charles Noble to become Dean of the Chapel. For students we don't need Dr. Radcliffe."

Thomas J. Van Loon, the Methodist chaplain on the Chapel staff, was an outspoken advocate of Noble's appointment. He said, "Harold Case has two or three magnificent sermons. Sunday in and Sunday out, however, no one is the equal of Charles Noble. He will fill the Chapel every Sunday." The appointment of Noble was a very happy choice. He was not only a superb preacher, but he was a wise, patient, understanding counselor of students.

Not too long after Dean Noble arrived, our organist, Mr. Leon Verese, died. Dean L. C. Dillenbeck from the College of Fine Arts appointed a committee to find a successor. I was unimpressed by the names that the committee suggested and told him so. I gave him a list of musicians who specialize in the organ and asked him to write to each of them requesting the names of the five greatest living organists regardless of age or nationality. A few weeks later, he came back with something like a sneer on his face. He threw a piece of paper on my desk saying, "I did exactly as you asked. Here is the list. There is only one person under the age of sixty-five. He is chairman of the organ department at Oberlin College. He is very happy there. And I am sure he will not consider leaving."

"Dean Dillenback," I said, "thank you very much. The ball is now in my court. I will see what I can do with Arthur Poister." I called Professor Poister and said, "I am not sure that you remember me. When I was President of Allegheny College, Professor Morten J. Luvaas introduced you to me after the close of a concert by the Allegheny Singers in Severance Hall in Cleveland. You were standing on the left-hand entrance of the stage, and you had just finished asking Luvaas to tell you the secret of the wonderful humming by the Allegheny Singers. I also knew your younger brother who was a student at Allegheny. I need counsel and help. I want you and Mrs. Poister to come to Syracuse for two or three days and let me pick your brains as we talk about the rebuilding of our organ department." "I don't think I ought to come," said Poister. "I am very happy here and I have no interest in looking at a new position." "I understand," I said. "What I want is your counsel and advice. Please come."

When he came, I showed him the organ in Crouse College and the organ in Hendricks Chapel. He told me both should be replaced. The Roosevelt organ in Crouse, he said, was originally a fine instrument but had been ruined by people who knew nothing about organs. The organ in the Chapel was a mistake from the start. He said a new organ in Crouse would cost over $100,000 and a new organ in Hendricks some $50,000. "What else do we need?" I asked him. "Well," he said, "you need three or four practice organs. They will cost about $12,000 each. If you had two new organs and the practice organs, you would have the best organ equipment in the nation." I found out what his salary was at Oberlin and offered him an increase generous enough to make it worthwhile for him to move.

In my experience the best people are cheap at any price. Certainly, this was true in Poister's case. He built one of the great organ departments in America. In addition, he was a magnificent choral director, in some ways as good as Luvaas at Allegheny or Christiansen at St. Olafs. With Dean Noble and Arthur Poister, we had an unbeatable combination in Hendricks Chapel. On Sunday morning one had to get there early to find a seat on the main floor.

One of the high points of worship in Hendricks Chapel was what happened after the benediction. Once the service was over, students and members of the choir would fill the front three or four rows, and Poister would play an impromptu recital of organ pieces by Bach. No organist of his time was so gifted an interpreter of Bach. We were as uplifted by Poister's organ recitals as we were by Charles Noble's sermons. To go to Hendricks Chapel on Sunday morning was a memorable and rewarding experience.

The war years were a time of rapid change. One of the major changes was in race relations. I discovered in my first year at Syracuse that we had no young black women in our dormitories. When Dean Eunice Hilton said she did not know how to attract them, I telephoned my friend David Jones, President of Bennett College at Greensboro, North Carolina, and offered scholarships covering tuition, board, and room to twenty Bennett College undergraduates for a year's exchange program. They were wonderful young women, and their presence created so much goodwill that thereafter our dormitories for women always had a sizable number of blacks.

I remember only one unpleasant incident. As school opened in September of 1944, a beautiful white woman in her early forties came to my office weeping. She told me she was from Mississippi and that her daughter had been assigned a roommate from Mississippi who was black. "You have come to the right man to see," I greeted her; "I am the person responsible." I told her we were looking for black coeds for our former all white women's dormitories. "I am sorry," I continued, "that better judgment was not exercised for two girls from the Deep South, but I urge you to help both girls save face by sharing the room for a few days until we can find new roommates."

By the end of the second day the two young women had become friends and they remained roommates. The black student became president of Haven Hall, was elected to Phi Beta Kappa and to the women's senior honorary society, Eta Pi Upsilon. The white student made an excellent record but would have been the first to say that her roommate's record was clearly superior to hers.

One of the problems of that period in time was the deep-seated prejudice against Jews. I found clear evidence that there were quotas for Jewish students in the medical school and in some other schools. It took several years to eliminate the old habits and attitudes. Continued pressure, however, from the Chancellor's office eventually brought a more enlightened admissions policy.

Hiring blacks as well as women in general for the faculty was another challenge. The attitude of the white male department chair was at best sullen and often close to mutinous. I found that the best approach was to say, "You find them, or I shall find them." In a few cases I brought to the attention of department chairmen outstanding candidates who, when appointed, made a distinguished record at Syracuse.

When the war ended, Governor Thomas Dewey called for a meeting of all the college presidents in Albany. He told us that with all the men in uniform coming back to college at the same time and with the generous scholarship aid under the federal bill 346, we faced a national emergency. The G.I. Bill provided a year of college for ninety days of service and one additional month for each additional month of service up to a total of forty-eight months. In addition to tuition, the G.I. Bill paid for fees, books, and supplies, and provided a small living allowance.

It was legislation born of the fear of long unemployment lines as millions of servicemen returned to the labor market. It was generous because Congress wanted to be sure that the men in uniform would take advantage of it. The head of the Veterans Administration predicted that no more than 700,000 veterans would go to college under the G.I. Bill. The feeling in Washington was that this number was too high. No one anticipated that more than two million veterans would take advantage of it.

Even those of us who had worked hard to ensure its passage underestimated the significance of the legislation. We did not see that it would transform American higher education overnight. By eliminating financial barriers, the bill leveled all the barriers of poverty, class, color, and national origin. Except for parts of the Deep South, it ushered in a new day for blacks and Hispanics. It was a revolutionary change. American higher education was no longer for the few; it was now for all the people.

Governor Dewey was one of the first to recognize the impact the G.I. Bill would have on college and university enrollment. He asked the universities of the state to double their enrollments between spring and fall. Governor Dewey was right. It was indeed an emergency. If these young people didn't have a chance to go into college at that time, they probably would never get the education they needed. It was then or never. Some universities refused to increase their enrollment. Dartmouth, for one, took the position "Dartmouth comes first. We are not going to have the quality of Dartmouth impaired by a temporary glut of returning servicemen."

Our attitude was just the opposite. We were a University in the public service. We had always been in the public service. "What we have to do, we'll do!" was our motto. In the fall of 1946, our enrollment on campus doubled to 11,937. By 1948, it was up to 15,000. At the same time, we also made the University a center for graduate study. Our graduate enrollment rose from 400 in 1942 to 1,250 in 1946 and to 8,000 by 1948.

It was a far more difficult time than the war years. Housing conditions weren't the best. Classrooms were packed to the rafters. We couldn't hire faculty fast enough. To accommodate everyone, we had to spread out into the region miles from the main campus. I remember asking a young veteran I met on campus where his dormitory was. He said, "I'm not sure where it is. It's called Baldwinsville."

My heart sank. Baldwinsville is a little town about half an hour northwest of Syracuse, and we had boys there in what had been an army camp. We also had a large number of men housed in the New York State Fair Building. I told the young man I'd come out to visit him, which later I did.

I made it my business to go to all the outposts we had and to meet as many of the students as I could. I wanted to find out what we could do to help things go from bad to better. Actually, the morale was much higher than we dared hope it would be. Most of the veterans realized that the University was doing all it could in the national interest and that this was above all a patriotic effort as the war was winding down.

While patriotic efforts are born of the spirit, they become successful by hard work. Our talented team of administrators worked long hours finding ways to accommodate the returning veterans. We bought land south of the main campus and built several hundred prefabricated buildings there and on the main campus, west of Hendricks Chapel. We also built a trailer camp for married veterans at Drumlins.

Even this enormous building program wasn't enough to accommodate the influx of veterans. We were running out of room, and so we began to turn our eyes elsewhere.

I went to Albany to see Governor Dewey and told him we had taken all the students we could. I then reminded him there was a tremendous army barracks at Sampson on Lake Geneva that was practically empty. I said I would be willing to join with some other presidents of privately endowed universities as an unpaid group to run a program for the veterans at Sampson for very little money. We could hire a faculty and direct an academic program for 20,000 or more veterans.

"This is an inspired idea. Why didn't I think of this?" he said. "Are you sure you can get some help from other university presidents?" "Yes," I said. "I've already talked to Rufus Day, President of Cornell, and Livingston Houston of Rensselaer Polytechnic Institute. They will go on the board with me, and we will get the other university presidents."

"How soon can you do it?" the governor asked. "We can do it almost overnight," I assured him. In less than six weeks we opened Sampson. It was such a success that later we opened another branch in Plattsburg on Lake Champlain in the empty barracks there and a third in abandoned army barracks in Utica.

The man who made these associated colleges such a success was Asa Knowles, who had made his mark as a Dean at Northeastern University. In planning for the opening of a college at Sampson, Rufus Day brought in Edward Charles Elliott, the retiring president of Purdue, to be interviewed for the position of running the programs. Dr. Elliott had come highly recommended, but in the interview he went through a list of all the things that could not be done. I listened for about ten minutes. Then I asked Rufus to step outside.

"Look Rufus," I said, "send Dr. Elliott home. We need a 'can do' man. I know a young man named Asa Knowles who is perfect for the job." Asa was a terrific guy, tireless, full of energy, and very bright. We brought Asa in for an interview, and he sold himself immediately. Before we were through, Asa was running all three of the associated colleges. The associated colleges never cost the state of New York a penny. We borrowed from the state enough for the start-up costs, ran the colleges out of the revenues we received, and when we closed them we returned a substantial balance to the state of New York.

Asa Knowles was an excellent financial manager as well as a fine academician. The universities helped Asa find faculty members, but he needed surprisingly little help from us. All the privately endowed universities in the state were represented by their presidents on the Board of Trustees, but President Day of Cornell and I assumed both the leadership and the responsibility. We also did most of the work. The Associated Colleges of the State of New York gave the young returning veterans the chance they deserved for a college education and the opportunity to develop the good life they'd fought so hard to defend.

When I was in my first years at Allegheny College, I used to wonder what I would do if I lost my job. Along with such lowly options as becoming a shoe salesman or running a dance orchestra, I considered starting a college in Binghamton. I knew that only 3 or 4 percent of the young people between the ages of eighteen and twenty-two were going to college in the southern tier. I suspected that even with the presence of Colgate and Hamilton, only about 4 percent of the Utica youth were going to college. Educationally speaking, the southern tier, with Binghamton at its hub, had the lowest percentage of youth going to college of any region in New York State.

During the depression of the 1930s, Syracuse developed a number of extension centers, including one at Binghamton and another at Utica. They were primarily for postgraduate work for teachers in our public schools, but they also offered some engineering and business administration courses. We had several hundred part-time students in both cities. When World War II came to an end, and we saw we could not accommodate all the veterans who wanted to come to Syracuse, I decided to establish colleges in Binghamton and Utica to take care of them.

I made a trip to New York to enlist the aid of Thomas J. Watson, President of IBM. When I told him of my desire to establish a college in Binghamton, he said, "I have a counterproposal. I think the time has come for me to establish the International Business Machines College, and I'd like you to serve as President. I don't know what your salary is, but I shall be glad to pay you several times what you are making now."

"Mr. Watson," I said, "it shouldn't be done. No one will believe that it is not completely dominated by IBM. It won't work."

We argued about it for some time. He returned to the salary question several times, and I told him that for anyone in the field of higher education money is not that important. My trustees would pay me more if I asked them.

"You people in academia are a different breed," he said. I agreed. Finally, I told him to forget about the IBM College and help us organize a branch college of Syracuse in the southern tier for the returning veterans. I emphasized the point that if the men and women returning from the armed services missed this opportunity to go to college, they would never have another opportunity to do so. Before I left, Mr. Watson agreed to give us a beautiful old mansion IBM owned at Endicott. It was called The Colonial and was centrally located in Endicott. I knew we could acquire prefabricated buildings for classrooms, library, and laboratories with federal and state funds. Since the college would serve Endicott, Binghamton, and Johnson City, we called it Triple Cities College. It opened with 934 students and was an immediate success.

When the State University of New York (SUNY) was organized, I knew that it was only a question of time before the state would either establish a college in the Binghamton area or take over Triple Cities College. I went to the SUNY officers and told them that I would give them the Colonial and all the prefabricated buildings free of charge. SUNY would be expected to take over the salaries of our employees, and pay approximately $200,000 for the library that Syracuse University had provided. They agreed that these terms would be fine. When they finally agreed to take over Triple Cities, however, they did not want to pay for the library. Some of the leading citizens of Binghamton who had given us no help in forming Triple Cities were asked to go to Tom Watson and say "Tolley's trying to get the State University to buy the Triple Cities library. You can nip that in the bud." I received a phone call from Mr. Watson just before moving up day asking me to be in his office at ten o'clock the next morning. Before I left, I asked my secretary, Miss Longbon, for copies of my correspondence with the SUNY officers.

Whenever Mr. Watson was going to dress somebody down, he would puff himself up into a towering rage. "Young man," he said to me in his most intimidating voice. "I sent for you." "I know you did," I replied. "Please hold everything, Mr. Watson. You're a very fair-minded person. Before you make a decision you will want the whole truth. Here is my first letter to the State University advising them what the terms would be should they want to take over Triple Cities College. Read it.

"Here's the second letter repeating the offer. Here's the third letter reaffirming it. We told the State University what we would do, and what we wouldn't do. The message is exactly the same in all three letters." Mr. Watson read the three letters. "I'm not a swearing man," he said, "but I could swear. They lied to me." We had no more trouble with Mr. Watson.

Since we were not charging the State University for the expense of cataloging the books, the price we were asking for the library was half of what it was worth. Nevertheless, SUNY decided against buying the library. We gave the library to Utica College, and SUNY paid more than half a million dollars to replace it.

I found the officers of the State University difficult to deal with. Everything was a one-way street. They were cheap and mean in the negotiations for Triple Cities College and even more so in the transfer of our medical college to the SUNY system.

When it became clear that there would be one SUNY medical college downstate and one upstate, we knew that Albany and the University of Buffalo would probably offer their medical colleges as sites for the SUNY medical college.

In reviewing the situation, I decided that we should offer our medical college to SUNY. We had a strong faculty. We were doing well. The medical college was not a burden to the University. It was an asset of which we were proud. Its location in the center of the state made it, however, the logical site for the Upstate Medical Center.

At the time, Alvin Eurich was President of the State University. The chairman of the committee negotiating for the SUNY trustees was a fine man named Norman Goetz. He and Earle Machold, chairman of our negotiating committee, were very close friends. Eurich, Goetz, Machold, and I spent the better part of a day negotiating for the transfer of the Syracuse University medical college to the SUNY system. At nine o'clock that night, I received a call from Dr. Eurich saying there were several things in the contract that he wanted to change. "Al," I said, "we made a deal. If you want to scrap the deal we'll return to square one. We're not going to take this package apart." "No," he said, "we've got to change it."

I called Machold and told him the situation. "Relax," he said, "I'll call Norman Goetz." When Goetz learned what had happened, he said, "Earle, we made a deal. When our clients make a deal we don't let them reopen it. I'll fix Mr. Eurich. I'll tell him if he wants to reopen it, he'll have my resignation from the SUNY board." Thanks to Goetz, the transfer went through as agreed, and the Upstate Medical Center was established at Syracuse.

Locating the Upstate Medical Center in Syracuse was a very happy choice. We gave a fine medical college to SUNY. It is a better medical college today. Given the escalation in the cost of medical education, it is a blessing that we do not have to finance it. The cost of running a medical college was not, however, a factor in our decision to give it to the State University. We did it because Syracuse was the right location for it.

The opening of the College at Utica took place the same time we opened Triple Cities College in 1946. We were familiar with Utica because of our extension program. We opened the College with no financial assistance from the community. We rented the Plymouth Congregational Church at Oneida Square and used the Sunday school rooms as classrooms. The church's minister, Gordon Gilkey, was an outstanding man in every way. I'm sure that at times he must have regretted his decision to let us use the church, but he couldn't have been more cooperative. On the day we opened the College we did not have half the chairs we needed. Dean Winton Tolles asked if I had any suggestions. "Telephone all the funeral directors," I said, "and borrow their funeral chairs." They followed my suggestion, and we managed to find all the chairs we needed.

Fortunately, it was a time when everyone was willing to put up with inconveniences. The veterans were so glad to have the chance to go to college that they did no complaining. It required heroic measures to find qualified faculty members, but we opened on schedule. With an initial enrollment of 806, every classroom was full. Eventually we purchased a number of adjoining properties and cleared land for temporary buildings. We also rented the Francis Street school building within a block of Oneida Square and installed modern science laboratories. Eventually, we were able to buy a beautiful stretch of property at Burrstone Road, which became the permanent campus.

Today, the years at Oneida Square are only a memory. They are, however, very happy memories. It was a surprisingly good college, even in the first years and it has become steadily better. We were fortunate to have the leadership of Win Tolles and Ralph B. Strebel, both men of exceptional talent. We were also blessed by great teachers like Virgil Crisafulli, Charles Samuels, Sidley Macfarland, Ralph Schmidt, Ray Simon, and Robert Willard. Once it opened, Utica's civic leaders took deep pride and interest in it. A group of civic leaders soon helped us form the Utica College Foundation, which became the fund-raising arm of the college. The foundation was headed by Moses Hubbard, a distinguished lawyer, and included among its members Boyd Golder, a trustee of the State University; Peter Karl, a local industrialist; Pearl Nathan, a newly minted graduate of the college; Richard Balch, President of Horrocks-Ibbotson, a sporting goods company; Walter Matt, President and CEO of Matts Brewery; and Rocco E. DePerno of the Teamster's Union. Scores of people deserve special credit for the success of Utica College. Most of the deans were superior people. The unsung hero of the College was, however, Clark Laurie, the business manager. Clark was the quiet and effective power behind the deans. Without his influence, it would have been a very different story.

Recently, we celebrated the fortieth anniversary of Utica College. Over the years, it has produced many distinguished graduates and is now winning sufficient financial support from its alumni to ensure its survival. Utica College remains today an integral part of Syracuse University. The members of the faculty are members of the faculty at Syracuse University. The students receive Syracuse University degrees. The time may come when the College will declare its independence of the University. There is no pressure, however, for it to achieve independent status. Its endowment is growing steadily, and the College is operating without deficits. Its relationship to the University has been an asset of incalculable value.

After I came back to S.U. and was getting reacquainted with Syracuse, one of the things that impressed me most was the relationship between town and gown. In Meadville, there was a lack of trust between college and city, despite my best efforts to cement good relations. At Syracuse, the situation was totally different. The community had a deep sense of loyalty to our athletic teams, and we had an excellent relationship with the business community, the common council, and the mayor. One evidence of this was that Chancellor Graham was elected councilor-at-large after he retired at the age of seventy-two, and he served for many years thereafter as President of the common council.

When the mayor proposed the organization of the Syracuse-Onondaga Post-War Planning Council, I was asked to serve as chairman. The purpose of the council was to marshal the forces of the city and county to begin thinking of their current and future needs, many of which had been neglected during World War II. The Syracuse Post-War Planning Council, for instance, was the first community organization to investigate ways to clean up Onondaga Lake, which had become a dumping area for Allied Chemical and for raw sewage from the villages bordering the lake. Environmentalism had not yet become a popular community issue.

The director of the council was Sergei Grimm, a professional planner employed by the city. Sergei spoke with a Russian accent, and few people understood the workings of his mind. The longer he spoke the more confused his listeners became. I understood him, however, and came to appreciate his knowledge and judgment.

Service in the Post-War Planning Council gave me the opportunity to meet all the community leaders. I became active in the Chamber of Commerce and the Manufacturers Association. It was a crash course in community relations.

I soon learned that two people ran the city. One was William Lawyer Hinds, of the Crouse Hinds Company. The other was Hurlbut W. Smith, President of L. C. Smith Corona. Hinds and Smith dominated the Republican party. They led all the fund-raising campaigns in town. Both were active trustees of the University. H. W. Smith was chairman of the Board of Trustees. They were generous men and very civic-minded. Their gifts, however, were in every case gifts from their corporations. Crouse Hinds was one of our major supporters, but I don't remember any personal gifts from W. L. Hinds. The L. C. Smith Corporation was also very generous, but H. W. Smith personally gave us very little until he eventually made a gift of $100,000. I had first met Mr. Smith in 1922, when I was a senior and was presiding at a student YMCA dinner. I remember how frightened I was at the prospect of introducing the chairman of the Board of Trustees.

If the two most visible leaders in the community were H. W. Smith and W. L. Hinds, the third person with a unique role as a civic leader was the attorney Stewart W. Hancock. Stewart was a graduate of Wesleyan University and was very active in its affairs. He was a thinking machine, with a beautiful analytic mind. Everyone turned to him for counsel. He did not push himself forward. He preferred to do his work behind the scenes. It was Stewart, for instance, who saved the floundering City Bank by arranging for the First Trust and Deposit Company to take it over. He also played a leading role in persuading Carrier Corporation to come to Syracuse and set up its headquarters here. Not surprisingly, Stewart was a driving force in the Planning Council.

The report of the Syracuse-Onondaga Post-War Planning Council received national publicity in *Fortune* magazine and other publications. It was cited as a model for other cities. Once the war was over, however, much of the detailed planning had little influence. Nevertheless, the work of the council was an important exercise. The chief value was the unity it created. Every community organization was represented, and all learned to work together in harmony. It was as if we were a village, and all knew each other as friends.

Just as the friendly relationship between the Syracusans and the University was a welcome surprise, the lively participation between the S.U. alumni and their alma mater was also very encouraging. Chancellor James Roscoe Day had taken the position that he did not need the support of alumni. He had fifteen or twenty rich friends, most of whom were former parishioners of Methodist churches he had served while living and working in New York City as a minister. He relied on these friends almost exclusively for support of the University.

When Charles Wesley Flint became Chancellor in 1922, he reversed the policy of Chancellor Day and began to cultivate alumni. Alumni organizations were set up in each of the important cities of the nation, and Flint spoke at scores of alumni meetings across the country in the course of a year.

Despite the loyalty of alumni, the Alumni Association was still largely independent of the University in 1942. Its director, J. Winifred Hughes, a wonderful person and a legend in her own time, felt that she worked for the alumni, not the University. It required a good deal of patience and tact to effect the integration of the Alumni Association into the structure of the University. Win Hughes' able associate, Charles Lee, who was field secretary for the Alumni Association, had been very helpful in accomplishing this. Charlie did wonders in building alumni associations and making the alumni fund grow. Later, he created the Lettermen of Distinction organization, which honors outstanding athletic alumni with major accomplishments in their post-college years.

The greatest strength of the University was the quality of the administrative staff, led by Vice-Chancellor Finla Goff Crawford. Dr. Crawford was an outstanding teacher and scholar in the field of political science. He had unlimited capacity for work. In addition to serving as Vice-Chancellor, he was Dean of the College of Liberal Arts from 1938 until 1950. All matters of academic organization and administration were under his control.

As Vice-Chancellor, Dr. Crawford did a beautiful job of compensating for the weak spots in Chancellor Graham's leadership. While Dr. Graham was a man of exceptional ability, he pursued a leisurely course during his six-year tenure as Chancellor. He came and went when it pleased him during the school year; and on commencement day, he and Mrs. Graham would pack their bags and travel to their summer home in the Thousand Islands. They stayed there until school reopened in September. With Chancellor Graham so often absent, Dr. Crawford stepped in to fill the void. He had all of the qualifications to be Chancellor, and he would have made a great one.

Shortly before Graham retired, Dr. Crawford was persuaded to run for mayor of Syracuse on the Democratic ticket. His loss on that ticket cost him the chancellorship at S.U. The Board of Trustees was almost exclusively Republican, and its members resisted the idea of electing such an active Democrat as Chancellor. Had he not run for mayor, he would almost certainly have been named Chancellor. The fact that he was not, was a bitter pill for Dr. Crawford to swallow.

Late in the fall of 1942 my secretary, Miss Lorena Longbon, said, "I don't think I should tell you this, but I must. Vice-Chancellor Crawford hates you."

"Thank you very much," I said. "I think this is my fault." I made it my business to win Dr. Crawford's friendship. I praised him privately and publicly. I sought his judgment and followed it. I gave him almost complete freedom. By the end of the first year, Vice-Chancellor Crawford and I were the best of friends, and we remained so as long as he lived. It took much longer to win the friendship of Mrs. Crawford. To the end of her life she was bitter about the trustees' failure to make her husband chancellor.

Dr. Crawford had one exceptional administrative strength: He could make decisions quickly. Anyone who came to him with a question or request received an immediate answer. Often, people were not happy with his decision, but they knew that it would not be reversed. He kept paperwork to a minimum, and often made difficult decisions over the telephone.

Fin was a baseball buff, and one of his favorite sayings was, "Don't judge me by the number of times I strike out or hit a home run. Judge me by my batting average." Finla Crawford was not always right, but his batting average was very high indeed. As head of the College of Liberal Arts, our largest college, he was the Dean of deans. He knew all about the programs offered by the College, and all the members of the faculty. He was the friend of all the faculty members, except for Sawyer Falk.

Sawyer Falk was head of the drama department. An outstanding teacher, he was a nationally known leader of the American theater who had directed Broadway plays. He was also a prima donna. He would walk into Vice-Chancellor Crawford's office and say, "Mr. Crawford, here are all the campus parking tickets that have been dumped on my car. Put them in your waste basket, will you?" Falk would not take any orders from Crawford. He would tell him, "I have only one boss, and that is William P. Tolley. I'll do anything he says, but I won't take orders from anyone else." The truth, however, was that Sawyer Falk did not take orders from anyone.

During my first year at Syracuse, I decided to make the goal of putting our debts behind us one of my top priorities. Chancellor Flint had paid off several million dollars of current expense deficits incurred during Chancellor Day's administration, but I found we still owed some $400,000 on the Day deficits. Executive Secretary F. Gordon Smith was a great help in doing this. Gordon had begun his fund-raising strategy by creating the Centurion Club, to which all donors who gave gifts of $100 or more were automatically admitted. He attracted several hundred such donors who annually gave $100 gifts to the University. I suggested that alumni should raise their sights, and so we created a Chancellor's Group for donors who gave $1,000 or more.

Gordon Smith was on the road constantly, and I often accompanied him. I soon discovered that if I wanted to sleep, I needed to fall asleep before he did; he was the loudest snorer I have ever heard. Although he could keep me awake at night, I valued Gordon highly. With his natural charm, he made friends easily.

Aside from snoring, Gordon had one minor social problem. Someone in his family had been an alcoholic, and as a result Gordon was afraid that he, too, would become one. He never touched a drop of liquor. In those days, I too drank nothing. It was embarrassing for two nondrinkers to call on people who could hardly wait for the 5:00 P.M. cocktail hour to come. I decided that the next man we hired to raise money would take at least a glass of wine or sherry.

To expand our alumni and fund-raising efforts, I added Newell W. Rossman to the staff as director of development. He was then in Panama getting experience in international relations. He was married to Kathleen "Kay" Walker Rossman, a delightful woman who came from a prominent Buffalo family. Newell turned out to be a jewel and eventually was named Vice-Chancellor for University Development. He was a charismatic extrovert with a great gift for making friends and holding them. He would also take a drink, which saved me from embarrassment. Later, I learned to take a glass of sherry with him.

As essential as both Smith and Rossman were to strengthening our relations with alumni and the general public, Kenneth Bartlett was equally important in developing our public relations program. The chairman of our radio and television department, Bartlett was the best public relations person I have known. I soon realized he belonged in the central administration, and I made him Dean of University College and later Vice-President and director of public affairs. Bartlett's extraordinary public relations gifts made him our ambassador to the town. He did a great deal to strengthen the relationship between the city and the University. He became President of the Syracuse Chamber of Commerce and later served in the New York State Assembly. He could have been elected mayor, but he lived outside of the city. In many ways he was Mr. Syracuse, and he built a tremendous amount of goodwill toward the University.

Bartlett was a fine teacher with a talent for teaching large classes. Many of his students remember him for founding and developing the student-run FM radio station, WAER, which won numerous awards. He also developed the strongest radio-television program of any college or university.

We had an outstanding registrar in Keith Kennedy, and a good bookstore manager in Fritz Foster, once he learned that we would not be satisfied with a break-even operation. Frank Bryant was a better than average director of admissions, but we found an even better one in John Stuart Hafer, who was known to everyone as Bill. Bill Hafer was a strikingly handsome man. Before coming to Syracuse he had played professional baseball and served as a public school teacher and principal. He was a good judge of people, and he trusted his instincts when admitting students. He introduced the highly successful Late Bloomer program which helped young people with high school records that did not match their abilities. The students in this program reported to Bill regularly so that he could look after them and ensure good study habits. Because of his interest in students, Bill developed a large

coterie of friends among the parents, many of whom gave substantial gifts to the University.

We lost Hafer after I received a call from Curry College in
New England, which was looking for a new President. I recommended Bill. He paid off their debts, restored their academic accreditation, and built a first-rate faculty.

We replaced Dean Hafer with Les Dye. A former football
player and assistant coach, Dye was also an excellent Dean of Admissions. Neither he nor Hafer, however, could have done the jobs
they did without the help of Mrs. Pauline Madey, who had been a
summa cum laude student. It was she who ran the office, and both
Hafer and Dye were smart enough to let her do so. She spoke half
a dozen languages fluently and would converse with students
from these countries as easily as she did with English-speaking
students.

I hired Florence Quast shortly after the war to replace Edward J. Tobin as director of Food Service. Whenever we asked
Miss Quast to do something, her first response was to say no.
Eventually, however, she would say yes. Once we learned to get
along with Miss Quast, we found her to be a quick learner who
could run a fine food operation. When she retired, we replaced
her with Ursula Prater, who later became Mrs. Frederick B. Pettingill. Florence Quast was an excellent director of our dining
halls, and we were sorry to lose her.

Ursula Prater Pettingill was even better. Her hobby was visiting fine restaurants and studying new menus, and her banquets
could equal the greatest. She was an excellent judge of people and
had a sharp business sense. Under her direction, we developed a
beautiful bakery and a large butcher shop, which enabled us to
eliminate the middlemen and buy directly from large producers.
There wasn't anything that Mrs. Pettingill couldn't do. Under her
supervision, the dining halls produced a sizable net income.

I had learned a great deal about managing auxiliary operations at Drew and Allegheny, but at Syracuse I needed the help
of Hugh Gregg, whom I had recruited from Iowa State to become
our new business manager in 1946. Gregg was a prodigious
worker with a fine memory and exceptional business judgment.

He had a special interest in real estate, which he knew well. We became fast friends as well as colleagues. He was supervisor of all of our auxiliary enterprises, including our large food service and housing operations, the Syracuse University Press, and the infirmary. He made a monumental contribution to the University.

While a university needs excellent business management to succeed, it should also have administrators who have faith in students and know how to give them confidence in themselves. At Syracuse, we were blessed with two men who had this gift—Frank Piskor and Eric Faigle.

I appointed Frank Piskor Dean of Men when he was thirty years old. Piskor was a graduate of Middlebury College who had come to Syracuse to pursue his doctorate at the Maxwell School of Citizenship and Public Affairs. Piskor was the best Dean of Men Syracuse ever had. He knew hundreds of students and quickly won their confidence. We gave him more and more responsibilities. When Finla Crawford retired, Frank Piskor replaced him as Vice-Chancellor.

In making Frank Piskor Vice-Chancellor, we had to disappoint Eric Faigle, who succeeded Dr. Crawford as Dean of the College of Liberal Arts. I explained to Eric, whom I loved dearly, that he and I were both "yes" men. What I needed in a Vice-Chancellor, however, was a strong "no" man. I had had one in Fin Crawford, and I expected Frank to learn to be one.

Eric Faigle's strength was his rapport with young people. Perhaps he owed this talent to the fact that as a young man he had had to examine his own life and make some important changes. A graduate of Wyoming Seminary Preparatory School, he had been a cross-country star and a natural leader. After graduating, he became a brakeman for the Delaware and Hudson Railroad and the New York, Ontario and Western Railroad for some six years. When he had saved enough money, Faigle went to the President of the railroad and told him he was going to leave to go to college. The president said, "Eric, you stay here and some day you'll be President of this railroad."

Faigle was much older than most undergraduates when he came to Syracuse in 1924 to study geography. Despite the age difference, he was a natural leader and became captain of the cross-country team. After earning his master's degree in 1930, he earned a Ph.D. from the University of Michigan in 1935. While at Michigan, he studied under the direction of Preston Everett "Jimmy" James, one of the giants in geography in the United States. After graduating from Michigan, he returned to Syracuse to teach in the geography department, which would soon be headed by his mentor, Jimmy James. Later, Dr. Faigle became Dean of the College of Liberal Arts and the School of Speech and Dramatic Art.

Eric Faigle had a great gift with students. He was a master in the art of nurturing people. Knowing that Dr. Faigle believed in him, the student could not let him down. Under Faigle's loving direction, many students who would have otherwise failed at Syracuse graduated and went on to successful careers.

Every year, I would send Faigle a list of forty to fifty students who were in need of special counseling and help. He took them all on, and they all graduated. Some were late bloomers, while others were problem children from wealthy families. Eric Faigle straightened them all out; he never lost one. He became the Mr. Chips of Syracuse and was universally loved.

Universities are judged by their academic excellence. To be outstanding, a university must have the brightest students and the best faculty. It must also have faith in and love for students. Eric Faigle had a tremendous love for people and a limitless faith in them. It was his contention that we can never overestimate how far a young person can go. All they need is somebody to give them confidence. Eric Faigle did that for all his students.

I was most fortunate not only in the services of able secretaries but in talented and hard-working assistants. Three of them went on to careers as distinguished college presidents. John Olson, a fine teacher of Bible, was a particularly useful assistant. His father, Dr. Oscar Olson of Cleveland, Ohio, had been a candidate for the presidency of Allegheny when I was selected in 1931. Olson was particularly gifted in working with faculty members. He also helped me with correspondence and the preparation of speeches. Later, he had a very successful career as President of Oklahoma City University.

Dr. C. Robert Pace was a distinguished psychologist, who left us to go to the University of California at Los Angeles.

Robert F. Oxnam was the son of Bishop G. Bromley Oxnam of New York City and a graduate of the University of Southern California. He left us to take the vice-presidency of Boston University, then served as President of Pratt Institute, and later became President of Drew University.

Dr. Louis T. Benezet was a Dartmouth graduate. An exceptionally able assistant, he left to become President of Allegheny College and then served as President of Colorado College, the Claremont College, and as President of the State University of New York at Albany. Reaching the age of retirement at Albany, he accepted the post of distinguished professor at Stony Brook and wrote one of the best books on the college presidency.

6

DEVELOPMENTS AFTER
WORLD WAR II

*A*fter the Second World War had ended, there was increased energy for new projects both at the University and in Syracuse in general. One such enterprise came as a suggestion by Hrs. H. Winfield Chapin, who was a great benefactress for the School of Music. She envisioned that Syracuse should have its own symphony orchestra. André Polah, a member of the music faculty and an excellent conductor, volunteered his services, and the Syracuse Symphony Orchestra got underway. We were able to pay only the musicians who were members of the union. A number of faculty in the School of Music played in the orchestra without compensation, along with eight or ten of their music students. We could give only a few concerts a year.

It was, however, a beginning. Mrs. Chapin supported the orchestra with gifts that rarely exceeded $5,000 a year. Her contributions were supplemented by gifts from a number of banks and corporations. Donald Pomeroy, a leading insurance man in Syracuse and a trustee of the University, served as chairman of the board of directors and the University paid the deficits at the end of each year. The University continued its support of the orchestra until there was enough community support for a purely professional symphony orchestra. Today, the Syracuse Symphony Orchestra enjoys wide recognition for the quality of its music and enjoys generous support by the Syracuse community.

It is clear that in the past thirty years there has been a complete transformation in the quality of cultural life in Syracuse and Onondaga County. To be sure, we had the Famous Artists Series,

Civic Morning Musicals, and the Syracuse Friends of Chamber
Music. Today, however, the Syracuse Symphony, the Everson Museum, Syracuse Stage, the Syracuse Opera Company, and the
quality of lectures and concerts available to the general public are
a dramatic advance in cultural offerings available to Syracusans.

Every university has a variety of educational projects that
have cultural implications not only for its own population but for
the surrounding urban community as well. Still, these academic
endeavors often flourish when fostered by an enlightened administration. President William Rainey Harper of the University of
Chicago is a prime example of this administrative influence in action. He was a strong believer in adult education and built a program of continuing education that was a model for the nation. He
also believed in the importance of a university press. Shortly after
my arrival at Syracuse, I borrowed some of President Harper's
ideas about adult education and renamed our evening sessions
for adults, held in the old medical college building, University
College.

I also began to plan for the creation of a Syracuse University Press. One day, Thomas J. Watson, President of IBM, told me,
"I have just received a letter from a publisher criticizing IBM for
the publication of two books. The books deal with machines and
measurements and were written by our people. They are very
useful indeed to our employees. Let me read the letter to you." In
the letter the publisher said he would stay out of the business of
building business machines if IBM would stay out of the publishing business. "What should I do?" asked Mr. Watson. "Let Syracuse University publish them," I replied. "We have been planning
to establish a university press, and these will be our first two
books." "Fine," said Mr. Watson, "We do not want any royalties."
The Syracuse University Press was thus launched in 1943. Instead
of going to IBM, the royalties built up a substantial scholarship
fund at the University.

The first S.U. Press director was William Miller. Several
members of the faculty formed an editorial committee, and we
began on a very modest basis. In 1955, we were able to attract
Donald Bean to Syracuse as director of the press. Bean had been
director of the university press both at Chicago and Stanford. He

transformed the press almost overnight. By the time he retired in 1960, the press was making its mark in the bibliographic field, special education, and other areas. Bean was succeeded by Richard Underwood. Underwood had a special aptitude for design, and he also was an imaginative leader of the press. He was succeeded by Arpena Mesrobian, who received her training under both Bean and Underwood. It is a source of deep satisfaction to know that a venture begun on a shoestring is now a major force among university presses.

An interesting development of the 1950s was the creation of the Goon Squad. Each fall, the sophomore men and women volunteered to welcome the incoming freshmen and carry their baggage and personal belongings to the dormitory rooms. Hundreds of sophomores participated, and the services were appreciated by the parents as well as by the incoming freshmen. Many traditions are lost after a few years. The Goon Squad, however, continues to function.

In 1947, Dean Kenneth G. Bartlett established radio station WAER. The faculty director was Professor Lawrence Myers. It was the nation's first noncommercial FM station and until very recently it was managed and directed by students. The station was originally WJIV, but its call letters were changed in July 1947 to incorporate the Alpha Epsilon Rho and its motto "Always Excellent Radio." The station earned its full broadcast license from the FCC in 1951 and increased its power from 600 to 1,000 watts. Its general format was a mix of classical music, campus and community news, sports coverage, jazz, and contemporary music. In the 1960s the station received another power increase to 6,000 watts. WAER was first housed in a campus prefab building but shortly thereafter was moved to the basement of Carnegie Library. Ted Koppel, Dick Clark, Len Berman, and Mary Elvert are but a few of the important personalities in the broadcasting industry who had their first experience and training in station WAER.

Alumni in the entertainment field include Peter Falk; Frank Langella; Sheldon Leonard; Gerald Stiller; Anthony Malara, President of CBS; Laurence Caso, director of Daytime Programming, CBS; Dick Stockton, sports announcer at CBS; Eugene

Cowen, Vice-President of ABC; Fred Silverman, President of ABC; Bob Costas, NBC sportscaster; Drew Middleton and William Safire of the *New York Times;* and Mel Elfin with *U.S. News and World Report.*

Donald Williams, our director of Audio Visual Services, was a dynamic leader in the making of motion pictures. He developed an outstanding program for services to colleges and universities in America, and also established a regional audiovisual center to service the counties in the Middle East and Africa. Williams's talents allowed us to play a leading role among American universities in the development of visual aids for higher education. Our program was worldwide, including a strong influence in China.

M. Lyle Spencer, Dean of the School of Journalism, was invited to become a visiting professor at the University of Cairo in Egypt. While he was there, he launched the first journalism program in that country. Later, Dean Wesley C. Clark took a sabbatical to direct the program in Cairo.

Another interesting development was a program initiated by the department of fine arts in the College of Liberal Arts for a semester abroad in Italy. The chosen city was Florence. The University purchased a building near the University of Florence. Other institutions, like Stanford, purchased villas outside of town; but our program was in the heart of Florence, and we required our students to live with Italian families. Most had their initial contact with the Italian language on shipboard going from the United States to Italy. They had a difficult time their first few weeks in Italy. Like children thrown into deep water, however, they escaped drowning by swimming. Unlike the French, the Italian people are very patient with those who do not speak their language. Our students in Florence became fluent in Italian before their course of study was completed. They also had a deep immersion into Italian art and art history. When the great flood came and damaged so many of the art treasures in Florence, our Syracuse students did a heroic job of salvage and restoration. One cannot put a value on the service they rendered. It was an exhilarating experience, done without thought of reward. For all, I am sure, it is still a deep source of pride.

The University also developed programs for students in France, Holland, Guatemala, Spain, and England. The programs have grown in size and influence.

No university can thrive unless it is in touch with its strongest supporters—the parents of students. I formed the Syracuse University Parents Association in 1957, following a successful Parents Weekend. In that meeting we agreed to form a Parents Association that would have four objectives: allow parents to work with the University in developing policies that would affect student life, increase and improve communication between parents and the University, help parents better understand the University's aims and policies, and function as a fund-raising arm that would increase financial support of the University.

There were between two hundred and three hundred active Parents Association members. The annual meeting was held each fall, during Parents Weekend. Members attended the School for Parents, established in 1958, which included such events as student and faculty art exhibits, campus religious services, concerts, movies, library displays, and student dramatic productions. Receptions for parents were also held in the various living centers as well as in the sororities and fraternities. I also met with the parents and students during a Saturday morning breakfast convocation. Football games were always scheduled for Parents Weekend, and we would all attend the game. Parents Weekends were planned with the help of a student committee as well as the parents' planning committee.

Through these weekends, parents could meet the faculty who taught their children, see firsthand where their children lived, and meet many of their friends. Out of these meetings grew important discussions that helped us to plan better dormitories, reorganize existing ones, and improve our counseling services. The officers of the Parents Association were very useful advisors.

Members of the Parents Association were kept informed of all new developments on campus through the *Report to Parents* newsletter. Today, the Parents Association is part of the Parents Office, the first full-time office established for the sole purpose of communicating with parents of University students.

One of the most perplexing problems in graduate education is the doctoral dissertation. Graduate students have no difficulty accumulating credits toward their doctorate degree. They do well in seminars and have little difficulty maintaining a B average in their graduate courses. While they frequently fail preliminary oral or written examinations, their real stumbling block is the writing of the doctoral dissertation. A very small percentage of those who register for the doctorate receive it. Departments differ greatly in their requirements, but when graduate students are examined as a whole, the percentage receiving a Ph.D. is surprisingly small. The world is filled with people with ABD's (All But Dissertation). This is in spite of the fact that most of these students have done first-rate original research in high-level graduate seminars.

To combat this problem, I decided to create a doctoral program with entirely new requirements. The place to begin, I thought, was the social sciences, where the level of completed doctorates was much lower than in the laboratory sciences. I discussed my ideas with Roy Price who was then head of our program for training teachers of the social sciences. His enthusiasm soon made the program his rather than mine. To distinguish it from the traditional degree of Doctor of Philosophy, we proposed a degree of Doctor of Social Science. We planned a program that could be completed within a three-year time frame for full-time students. We eliminated the requirement of a dissertation, but instead required students to conduct original research in their graduate seminars. In each of the seminars, students were expected to make a fresh and original contribution to learning, even though the seminar might focus on a problem of limited size and significance. Our aim was to teach the meaning and value of high-level inquiry and to develop habits of objective and thorough scholarship. Books might not be written in the seminars, but they would produce meaningful and well-documented chapters of books.

The program developed by Dr. Price was successful from the start. There was no problem placing the students who earned the degree of Doctor of Social Science. There was little or no criticism of the program or of the quality of the men and women who earned the Doctor of Social Science degree. What did happen surprised us. There was soon a demand throughout the entire graduate faculty that we bestow the degree of Doctor of Philosophy on the program graduates. Once this was done, the faculty also approved giving the earlier graduates holding Doctor of Social Science degrees a new diploma for the Doctor of Philosophy degree.

The weakness in graduate education may be the absence of adequate counseling. If this is true, much of it has to do with the heavy time demands on senior professors busy with their own teaching and research in addition to the burden of supervising doctoral dissertations. In both the physical sciences and engineering there are now fast tracks to the doctorate. In schools of education, the completion rate for the doctorate is somewhat lower, and the quality of the dissertations is still open to question. In the humanities and social sciences, the completion rate is still much too low, and the battlefield is covered with the bodies of ABD's.

When General Dwight Eisenhower was inaugurated President of Columbia University, I attended the inaugural ceremony. It ran behind schedule and was not particularly well organized. In the academic procession, the lady directly in front of me was weeping.

"What is wrong?" I asked.

"My petticoat shows," she said tearfully.

"Please dry your tears," I said. "I have been walking in academic processions for a quarter of a century. Nobody sees us as individuals. We are all penguins."

She smiled and said, "I will try to behave."

At the conclusion of the exercises, I had dinner with Thomas J. Watson and his wife, Jeanette. "The Columbia inauguration and commencement ceremony was very interesting," I said.

"No," remarked Mr. Watson, "it was poorly planned. We

have just come back from Europe. We attended the Oxford and Cambridge commencements and we also attended the commencement at Coimbra in Portugal. They know how to run commencements. They make them memorable pageants. When are we going to learn to do the same? We have no royal family. We have no knighthood. We do, however, give honorary degrees at college commencements, and that is a form of knighthood. We should think of a commencement exercise as a pageant, and we should put some color in it."

When I got back to Syracuse, I reported my conversation with Mr. Watson to the members of my cabinet. They were not impressed, but I persisted. I sent for our professor of design, Montague Charman, and asked, "Could you design some gowns for us?" He designed the gowns for the marshals, deans, and chancellor. Being bright orange, they required a little courage to wear at the first commencement, and not everyone was pleased with the change. One remark from a faculty member amused me: In speaking of my orange costume, he said, "Who does he think he is, a cardinal?" He did not know much about the color cardinals wear. Some years later, however, scores of universities were following the Syracuse example, and had also adopted the style of our chancellor's hat.

Under the leadership of our public relations director, Kenneth G. Bartlett, Syracuse had one of the most impressive commencements in the nation. Every detail was carefully planned. We began exactly on time. Moreover, the weatherman was almost always good to us. There were several years where we took a long chance and won.

One year, however, when Gilbert Hyatt of Columbia was our speaker and Chief Justice Earl Warren was on our list of honorary degree recipients, it began to rain. We had a canvas top over the speakers' platform, and as the downpour continued the canvas top dropped lower and lower until it was in danger of touching our heads. I stepped forward, conferred all the degrees in a single sentence, and declared the commencement adjourned. The Chief Justice got off the platform safely, but before he reached his car, he slipped and fell. The cameramen were there, and the picture of Chief Justice Earl Warren sprawled in the mud was sent all across America.

College presidents and boards of trustees are notorious for their failure to take the long view. Current financial problems control financial policy. Today's needs take precedence over long-term needs. Trustees and administrators of American colleges should spend more time visiting universities abroad. It would give them a better understanding of how permanent universities are and how essential it is to plan for the centuries ahead.

I discovered the truth of this in my first year at Syracuse when in the purchase of houses needed for men in uniform in World War II, I bought properties that had been owned by the University several times before. Some had been sold in the panic of 1893. Some had been sold after the panic of 1907, and others in the depression of the 1930s. At Allegheny, I had taken care to provide land for future expansion. I was determined to do the same at Syracuse. Although we had a difficult problem in balancing our budget, I sensed the opportunity Syracuse had to become a great university, and I had ambitious dreams for its place in the years ahead.

Shortly after coming to Syracuse, I was able to acquire eighteen acres from the Oakwood Cemetery for some $64,000. This gave us the site for the Women's Building. When an opportunity came to purchase the Williams farm south of the University farm, I bought it. The price was ridiculously low—$20,000 for two hundred acres, including a house and a barn. I bought the Jones tract of thirty acres and twenty-five acres from the Morningside Cemetery for the site now occupied by the Manley Field House for $5,000 an acre. I bought the Hookway acreage of eighty acres for $40,000. I asked Gordon Smith to go out and look at the Hookway property when it came on the market. He said, "You don't want it. It is too far from the campus." I replied, "It is really closer to the campus than the University farm, and we will eventually use not only the University farm but all the land behind it." As time went on, we were able to buy sizable acreage on Ainsley Drive and Jamesville Avenue to provide a place for our Food Service and Physical Plant operations. We also bought everything that was available on the north side of Colvin Street adjoining the University farm.

Shortly before I retired, I purchased Drumlins. I had heard a rumor that a developer wanted to buy Drumlins and its

350 acres and develop it as a site for fine homes. I like the English view of keeping properties forever green, and instinctively I felt the University should own Drumlins if only to prevent its two golf courses from becoming housing developments. I called Roger Burlingame, the owner of Drumlins, and asked him to have lunch with me at the Century Club. "Roger," I said, "how much do you want for Drumlins?" He said "$2.4 million." "How much do you have in cash in the corporation," I said. "About $400,000," he replied. "Fine." I said. "I will pay your asking price of $2.4 million. I shall expect to find $400,000 in cash and on the balance of $2 million I will pay 3 percent per year, or $60,000." Mr. Burlingame was primarily concerned about the asking price, and we shook hands on the deal before leaving the luncheon. Thus, we acquired an asset of inestimable value to the University and one that will help protect our land needs far into the future.

If we include all the properties we purchased adjoining the campus, we added between nine and ten hundred acres to our land holdings within the city limits between 1942 and 1969.

Physical planning has normally had a higher priority than the protection of land needs. This too, however, has frequently been neglected. Chancellor Day had much more vision and optimism than most university presidents. Early in his administration, he engaged the services of Frederick Law Olmsted, the designer of Central Park in New York and the most famous landscape architect of the nineteenth century, to develop a long-range plan for the campus of Syracuse University.

His successor, William Marquis, carried on his work, and we engaged him to revise the old studies of Olmsted and help us develop a new long-range plan of physical developments.

We had been using Professor Ralph Laidlaw to assist us with interior decoration, and Professor Reed Rotunno served as our landscape architect. Both made major contributions, but we needed the vision and direction of Mr. Marquis in physical planning.

Mr. Marquis was a strong leader, but he was also skilled in drawing out the best in other people. He encouraged us to appoint a special committee of students, faculty, and trustees known as the University Design Board.

The Design Board was made up of about twenty people. Its

members included Robert Cutler, a senior member of Owens Skidmore of New York; Harry King, our university architect; D. Kenneth Sargent, Dean of our School of Architecture; Gordon Hoople and Gertrude Brooks, both trustees; Reed Rotunno, and Finla Goff Crawford. Membership changed often. Students graduated, and I rotated trustees every three years or so. The only members of the board who never left were trustee Gertrude Scarrett Brooks and Dr. Hoople.

When we began to build new buildings shortly after World War II, Mrs. Brooks raised a storm. She hated the new buildings. They were barren; they had no taste.

"Gertrude," I said, "I know you want us to build colonial buildings. I've been talking to the Dean of the School of Architecture, and he tells me you can't find a school of architecture today that designs colonial buildings. The schools of architecture remind us that we have new materials. We have glass. We ought to use it. We have steel. We ought to use it. We have young people intent on developing their dreams of buildings that are unlike any that have been designed before. We should let them spread their wings."

Mrs. Brooks would not be dissuaded. The Design Board, however, gave her a forum where she would express her views.

Whenever the Design Board would consider a new building, it would send out committees to other colleges to find out what mistakes had been made in similar buildings that they had built. In this way, we profited from their mistakes. In the case of the library, sending out visiting committees was the most important thing we did. We appointed our best faculty members to the committee, including Mary Marshall, professor of English, as well as trustees and architects. They visited all of the newest campus libraries that had been built. In all, they must have looked at fifteen or twenty university libraries.

The planning committee stayed at each library for several days in order to have enough time to talk with assistant librarians as well as the people studying in the library. The committee members would ask such questions as, "What's good and what's bad about this library?" "If you were designing a new building, how would you improve it?"

We wanted to find the answers to problems with traffic, eating, access, quiet, the location of elevators, and toilets. We asked, "What rooms are used most?" and we made sure that these were put on the first floor and the basement.

There was no infighting among board members. People did become angry during discussions; but when the meeting was over, they were all good friends.

We ran the Design Board in the same way that we oversaw the University Senate. Whenever the Senate would have a close vote, such as 32-27, I would say, "The ayes have it, but this is a very important issue. I don't think it should be settled by a close vote. I suggest that we discuss this again in the next meeting in order to arrive at a consensus." We were often sharply divided on issues. If we remained divided after a second meeting, I would say, "We're still too far apart. Let's get a consensus if we can." Then we would discuss the issue in a third session. Our final vote would often be unanimous.

Harry King, our architect, used to say, "Let's make our mistakes on paper. Let's not worry about overdoing the planning stage. We can't plan carefully enough."

We may have made mistakes in physical planning, but we would have made many more without the leadership of William Marquis, the Design Board, and the visiting committees.

Academic freedom became a critical issue during the 1950s, primarily due to the senate hearings led by Joseph McCarthy. Earlier during my years at Drew and Allegheny, pacifism was an issue but there was little discussion of communism. In my undergraduate years professors were frequently fired for espousing socialistic theories, but it was not until after the end of World War II that the Communist party began to infiltrate colleges and university faculties.

Senator Joseph McCarthy was successful in securing the dismissal of literally hundreds of professors. Many were dismissed because they chose to take the Fifth Amendment when summoned to appear before the House Un-American Committee.

We had a cartographer in the geography department at Syracuse who was spending his weekends in New York City as the active head of the Communist party in New York City. When we asked the FBI what they wished us to do, they told us to do nothing. They said that he was under surveillance, and they were fully informed of his activities. A few months later, the University of Chicago appointed him a full professor without any approach to our geography department.

It came as a surprise for me to learn that William Martin, who had been chairman of our mathematics department, was an active member of the Communist party and had been one of the leading Communists in New England before coming to Syracuse. When summoned to Washington by Senator McCarthy, Professor Martin made a full disclosure of his Communist activities. In revealing the names of his fellow Communists, he said that our Professor Abe Gelbart was an active member of the Communist party. Gelbart came to my office to tell me his side of the story. As a graduate student at MIT, he had lived with the Martins in Cambridge, and he was present when active Communists visited the Martin household. "I was never a member of the Communist party," he said. "I had no interest in politics. I was a young mathematics student studying for my doctorate. There is no way, however, I can prove I was not a Communist. My only guilt, however, is that of association. I have no choice but to take the Fifth Amendment when I appear before the House Un-American Committee."

After talking to Professor Gelbart, I was inclined to agree that he should take the Fifth Amendment. The members of the math department were divided in their support, but the faculty committee appointed by Dean Faigle recommended that no action should be taken against Gelbart. I presented the case to the Board of Trustees and was greatly relieved when the trustees supported the retention of Gelbart by unanimous vote.

A year or two later I made a speech before the Syracuse Chamber of Commerce in which I said that the United States was no longer in danger of being taken over by the Communists. I had been out of the city before making the speech and was unaware that a local newspaper had just begun a syndicated series of articles on the danger of communism. The newspaper publisher thought my speech was an attack on the articles he was publishing, and he launched a violent attack against me. My response was to print a complete and accurate copy of the address and send it to all Syracuse alumni in Onondaga County. That defused the issue.

In 1954 Harold Stassen, Director of the Foreign Operations Administration, gave the commencement address. As he left he told me that in the following week he would send one of his assistants to Syracuse to tell me about a problem that was troubling him. When his assistant came to my office, he told me the problem he wanted to discuss was the Dean of the Maxwell School, Paul Appleby. He brought with him a dossier which revealed the close links between Appleby and Henry Agard Wallace and about a dozen political figures reputed to be at the extreme left of the political spectrum. It was another case of guilt by association. There was nothing in the dossier that I did not already know. My visitor told me that because of Appleby's reputation and record, the Maxwell School had been blacklisted by the federal government, and we would see a sharp drop in grants from federal agencies. "I hesitate to put it bluntly, Chancellor Tolley," he said, "but Dean Appleby must go." When he finished I said, "I thank Director Stassen for his thoughtfulness, and I appreciate very much the manner in which you have presented the problem. Thank you for coming." I stood up and shook his hand. "But," said my guest, "what are you going to do about Dean Appleby?" "Oh," I replied, "we like Dean Appleby."

I did not discuss the matter with Dean Appleby, and he never learned about it. After his death I shared the story with Mrs. Appleby. She said, "Paul would have been furious. He was never a Communist. He was never a Communist sympathizer. He was indeed a very close friend of Henry Wallace, but that does not mean that he shared all of Wallace's views." Today, I regret telling Mrs. Appleby the story. We raised her blood pressure needlessly.

With the exception of my experience with Bishop Leonard at Allegheny, I know of no other instance of attempted pressure to limit freedom at any institution I served. From time to time, trustees like Crandall Melvin would raise questions about some left-wing faculty member he particularly disliked. That, however, was the end of the matter. Except for the dismissal of Frederick Roman, mentioned earlier, I cannot recall any case at Drew, Allegheny, or Syracuse where a member of the faculty suffered because of his political opinions. In all universities, we must maintain freedom of inquiry. We need differences in political and social points of view. Where everyone thinks alike, no one thinks very much. It is the hope and belief of colleges and universities that in the open competition of ideas the truth will eventually prevail.

Just as a free flow of ideas is crucial at a university, I believe it is equally important to foster open communication between the faculty, students, and administration.

At Syracuse I kept in contact with three to four hundred students each year. I met many students by attending the services at Hendricks Chapel each Sunday morning. After the service, we would move to the front of the Chapel to listen to Arthur Poister play organ pieces by Johann Sebastian Bach, and the choir would fill the front three or four rows of the pews.

I never missed a Sunday service unless I was out of the country. Ruth often protested about this saying, "You're dead tired. You've been up late every night this week. You should stay in bed on Sunday morning." But I would tell her, "No, I need it. It's good for me." I met many other students by attending Jewish services during the High Holy Days, and Catholic masses at Crouse College.

I also met many students while walking across campus. I would fall in step with a student and ask his or her name, the name of the town from which he or she had come, the class year, and the field of study. I liked to gather as much information as I could from each student, for I found that we need a cluster of memories to help us recall something. Each bit of information supports other memories. It is also very important to get the name right the first time one hears it. In some cases, I got the name wrong and continued to call the student by that name long after he or she had graduated.

I was playing tennis one afternoon when my opponent asked if the University would be interested in a beautiful vacation property on upper Saranac Lake in the Adirondack Mountains. I answered yes. At the close of the match, I learned that the possible donor was Carl M. Loeb of Loeb Rhodes, a New York City investment firm. My tennis partner telephoned Mr. Loeb that afternoon and made an engagement for me to see him the next morning in New York City. When I completed my presentation to him, Mr. Loeb said, "I will give Syracuse University the property. Let me tell you why. I am giving it to the University because the University didn't send a deputy sheriff to ask for it."

A few weeks after our first meeting, Mr. Loeb purchased an adjoining property and presented it to us. The next year, he financed the building of an art school facility on this property and provided a small endowment for its maintenance. The Pinebrook properties, as they became known, were used as a conference center and for a summer art program.

Pinebrook proved to be a major influence in building better relationships between administrators and students. Each fall and spring a group of faculty, administrators, and I would take some fifty to sixty student leaders to spend Friday evening, all day Saturday, and Sunday with us at Pinebrook. When we later acquired Sagamore, with about 1,500 acres, our groups grew to nearly a hundred. We also acquired Minnowbrook at Blue Mountain Lake, where conferences for thirty-five people could be held.

In the early years, the student conferences tended to become gripe sessions. I remember hearing a senior coed at one of the early Pinebrook planning sessions tell her fellow students: "That's not nearly enough. Think again. See if there isn't something you don't like about your teachers, your subjects, the dormitories, the food. This is our one opportunity to complain." Fortunately, the meetings evolved from gripe sessions into conferences where both students and administrators could share their interests and concerns. We wanted students to get things off their chests, and we had no desire to shut off complaints. What we worked for were shared information, stronger bonds of respect, and increased loyalty and pride.

Our athletic activities at the Adirondack centers were particularly useful in developing mutual respect. I played tennis and pool and also bowled with students, and I took my morning dip with a few brave young people, whether the month was April or October. Saturday evening was always a time for recreation. I have dozens of happy memories of student and faculty skits and group singing around the piano. Stephen Bailey, Dean of the Maxwell School of Citizenship, was a fine pianist. He played all popular music by ear, and I added two hands to the upper octaves.

Faculty were also encouraged to vacation at Pinebrook. I made it a point to spend at least a week at Pinebrook in order to visit with the faculty who were staying there. This broke down many barriers and helped develop enduring friendships.

When Herbert Hawkes was Dean of Columbia College, he would sit at a desk outside of his office for several hours a day and talk with the students as they passed by. I did not go that far but had a rule that students did not need to make an appointment to see me. My secretaries were instructed that no student would be turned away. Even when I had as important a guest as S. I. Newhouse, they would let me know that a student was waiting, and I would excuse myself for a moment. I would take the student into an adjoining office, find out what the problem was, and either settle it right away or arrange for the student to meet with the appropriate academic officer. I don't recall any abuse of the system or any time when it was truly burdensome. I still correspond with many of the students whom I met for the first time when they called at the Chancellor's office with a question or a problem. Vice-Chancellors Crawford and Piskor also had the same open-door policy. We had a freedom of access that was rare among American colleges and universities.

In the first half of the twentieth century, most coeducational universities might be described as colleges for men open to women. Cornell is a good example. Despite its distinguished Home Economics College, women undergraduates played a minor role in undergraduate student leadership. Among small colleges, Middlebury was a notable exception. Its women were selected more carefully than its men, and they set the academic, social, and moral tone of the campus. As at Middlebury, Syracuse women students were superior to the men, and they gave impressive leadership in student organizations. The senior honorary society, Eta Pi Upsilon, has had tremendous influence among both alumni and undergraduates. In the forties and fifties, there was a

concerted effort to make Eta Pi Upsilon a part of the national society, Mortarboard. The members of Eta Pi Upsilon decided that
it made no sense to join a second-rate national organization when
Syracuse already had a unique organization for women. Tau
Theta Upsilon and Phi Kappa Alpha, the two senior honorary societies for men, also have a distinguished membership. They do
not match, however, the campus-wide influence of Eta Pi Upsilon.

In the Pinebrook and Sagamore student conferences, there
were about the same number of women students as there were
men. I was impressed by the contrast between articulate women
and inarticulate men. The men had limited vocabularies, and
their grammar often left much to be desired. The women's student organization was always well organized. The student government for men suffered by comparison. The men were clearly jeal-
ous of the influence of the women's student government.
Eventually, they destroyed it by merging the two. The change may
have been inevitable, but it was a step backward in student leadership and influence.

One of the traditions in the 1940s and 1950s was step singing in the spring. Each sorority and women's dormitory had its
own chorus. They not only went from building to building singing
during the Christmas season but repeated the experience in the
spring. A number of fraternities also had choral groups, but the
spring competition on the steps of Hendricks Chapel was primarily an activity for women.

Among the things that impressed me in the social life of undergraduates were the influence of housemothers in sororities,
fraternities, and dormitories. Dean Eunice Hilton and her successor, Dean Marjorie Smith, selected housemothers with great care.
They were excellent women, and they set the social and moral
tone of the campus.

In the athletic department, May Crandon was an institution. She was to the Department of Athletics what Winifred
Hughes was to the Alumni Office. All the coaches deferred to her,
and the athletes adored her.

Dean Eunice Hilton was easily one of the most energetic
and efficient deans of women in the nation. She developed a training program for deans of women that was unique in its effective-
ness and influence. For more than twenty years some three

hundred deans of women serving in American colleges and universities had received their training at Syracuse under Eunice Hilton.

Dean Anna Louise McCloud was a nationally known "Dean of Home Economics." She had followed one of the great women of New York State, Florence Knapp. A Vassar graduate of great social charm, Dean McCloud gave superb leadership to the College of Home Economics. She built an outstanding faculty that included Edith Nason, Anne Bourquin, Mrs. Leon Griggs, and Bernice Meredith Wright. Later, both Mrs. Griggs and Mrs. Wright served as deans with equal distinction.

The dean of the School of Nursing was Edith Smith. A brilliant scholar with a clear vision of what she wanted to achieve, she was an extraordinarily able administrator. Under her dynamic leadership, the School of Nursing became the number one nursing school in New York State, and one of the top two or three in the nation.

Another person of tremendous stature was Katharine Sibley. Katharine was the Director of Physical Education for women. She came here as an undergraduate and spent her entire life in the University. She played the old golf course on Mount Olympus. In her later years, she had a marked resemblance to Eleanor Roosevelt. She enjoyed going to New York where she often stopped traffic when mistaken for Mrs. Roosevelt. She had an unerring judgment about people. She was eventually succeeded by Lucille Verhulst, who also made an important mark on the University.

Among the women on the faculty whom I knew best was Minnie Mason Beebe. She is remembered not only as a fine history teacher but as the founder and director of the Kollege Klan.

Irene Sargent in the College of Fine Arts had tremendous influence both as a teacher and as an artist.

Mary Marshall was one of the best teachers not only in the English department but in the whole University. She made the most of her dramatic training in all of her classroom lectures. The University was wise enough to let her continue teaching at University College after the age of retirement. Although she is now in her eighties, her classes are as popular as ever.

Secretaries in college offices are unsung heroines of the universities. Lillian North in the College of Liberal Arts was an institution. Edith Little had the same influence in the College of Business Administration. Later she became Edith Little Johnson. Dorothy Hunt made herself indispensable as director of the personnel office. She was also in charge of the lost and found offices. Students enjoyed saying, "If you lose something, you can always go to Hell and Hunt." Frances Nelson was a never-ending delight both to students and to colleagues. She loved everyone.

My secretaries Lorena Longbon, Eleanor Webb, and Mary Harmand, the only secretaries I had in twenty-seven years, were not only exceptionally competent but they exemplified the best qualities one looks for in administrative officers. In retrospect, it is clear that they were all greatly underpaid. They served, however, with pride and high morale. Certainly, they played important roles in the building of the University.

Vera Nichols was one of a kind. For any limitations she might have had, she more than made up for them by her extraordinary assiduity and devotion to her job. She always arrived very early and stayed after all the others had left.

Ruth Coffin was a well organized and very efficient manager who had an influential role in the School of Education.

Nancy Fulmer was trained by the superb administrator Kenneth Bartlett. Now Nancy Fulmer Marquardt, she has become a legend in her own right. Like Bartlett, she is a perfectionist and a master of detail. No university stages better organized commencements or more perfect public dinners. Her services to the University can be described only in superlatives.

M. Helen Wigler has been with the University for thirty-seven years, the last eighteen serving as the recorder for the University Senate. She has been an important servant of the University. By unselfish dedication and hard work, Jean Crawford surmounted the handicap of being the Vice-Chancellor's daughter. As director of student housing, she never pushed herself forward or expected praise. Eleanor Ludwig made her mark on the University through deep and sincere friendships with literally thousands of our alumni. Margaret Stafford and Vernice Sill are two other staff members with a wide circle of friends among students and alumni. I worked closely with all of them.

All Syracusans are proud of the fact that the first fine arts college in America was established at Syracuse University. The S.U. College of Fine Arts consisted of three schools: the School of Architecture, the School of Music, and the School of Art. Until the mid-1960s, when heads of these schools were given the title of dean, each was run by a director who reported to the College dean.

When I arrived in Syracuse in 1942, the architecture school had an outstanding reputation, and the music and art schools were above average.

In order to bring the fine arts to as many students as possible, I established an art department within the College of Liberal Arts. This department's program of study focused on art history and appreciation and was designed for students who were interested in fine arts as part of their liberal education, rather than as a career. William Fleming from Claremont College in California, a superb lecturer and fine scholar, was appointed chairman of this new department. Fleming was also an able administrator who brought to the department such fine scholars and teachers as Abraham Veinus, Sidney Thomas, and David Tatham.

The School of Art, whose students were studying for professions in the arts, also began an impressive transformation in 1945, when we hired a new director for the school. When I reviewed the candidates that the search committee was suggesting, I realized that the faculty members were nominating their friends for the position. Because none was qualified, I began my own search. I soon found an outstanding person in Norman Rice, head of the Art Institute in Chicago. Rice was willing to consider the position because the Art Institute at that time was not a part of a university and offered no degrees.

I met with the selection committee and the entire art faculty to tell them of my decision. "This is an excellent faculty," I said, "but it is also inbred. I am going to appoint a director who will shake things up. You may not like him. I ask you, however, to give him a chance. If he proves to be an unfortunate choice, you may blame the Chancellor. The new man is Norman Rice. He is an extraordinarily able person. He will be good for the school."

My decision to override the committee's suggestions prompted the resignation of Marjorie Stuart Garfield. Garfield was a fine water colorist and an excellent teacher who had been chairman of the department of interior design for twenty years. I was sorry to see her go, but I respected the fact that she had the courage of her convictions. She left Syracuse to head the Department of Applied Arts at the University of Iowa, where she had a rewarding career.

The appointment of Norman Rice as director of the School of Art was a turning point for the school. The Department of Industrial Design—to cite but one example—made a quantum leap in its national reputation. Rice invigorated the faculty as a whole and infused it with a new point of view. With the influx of returning veterans, there was a huge expansion in enrollment. When hiring new faculty to handle the immense teaching load, Rice made certain that they represented the new ideals of personal expression associated with contemporary art which were then coming into vogue. By the time Rice left Syracuse in 1954 to become dean of the College of Fine Arts at the Carnegie Institute of Technology, he had turned around the Syracuse School of Art.

Norman Rice was succeeded by Laurence Schmeckebier. Before joining Syracuse, Schmeckebier had been chairman of the Art Department of the University of Minnesota and had headed the art program and supervised the building of a $5 million building for the Cleveland Institute of Art. Schmeckebier could be almost brutally frank. His passion for excellence caused him to drive people, whereas Rice had used a more persuasive approach. Nevertheless, both styles worked. By the time Schmeckebier retired in 1971, the art program in the Syracuse School of Art was second to none.

Schmeckebier arrived with very definite ideas. They were aimed at a deeper commitment to contemporary art and its integration into the total structure of art education. He was personally interested in the faculty: their teaching, their creative work, even their own collections. Schmeckebier visited his faculty in their studios to see their work and regularly visited their classes to see their students' progress. He believed the faculty should be productive and constantly encouraged his teachers to exhibit their work. He applied the same standard to himself in research, writing, and exhibiting his own sculpture.

Schmeckebier made significant changes in the School of Art's teaching program. In the academic year of 1955–56, just one year after becoming the school's director, Schmeckebier had replaced the school's loosely organized curriculum with a two-year core curriculum that required students to take basic courses in drawing, painting, design, English, and art history. After completing these requirements, the students could then go on to major during their junior and senior years in their specific areas of interest, including industrial, fabric, advertising, fashion design and illustration, illustration painting, sculpture, and print making. By the time they had graduated, the students had prepared substantial portfolios that allowed them to enter their trades without having to go through a low-paying apprenticeship. The revised program also included an important new feature: the Visiting Artists Program, which brought renowned artists to campus to teach for short periods of time as artists-in-residence.

We also introduced a program for a series of murals to be executed on the University campus. The idea began in 1958, when the University acquired Rico Lebrun's "Crucifixion." It was installed in the main reading room of the old Carnegie Library and is now in Heroy Hall. The mural series program was officially launched in 1960, when the distinguished French artist Jean Charlot, one of the major figures in the famous Mexican mural movement of the twenties, came to Syracuse to execute a magnificent fresco along the wall of Shaw Dormitory dining hall.

A select group of the University's best young artists worked with Charlot as apprentices. Every day these students, observed by their colleagues and teachers, would assist the master in working out drawings, transferring the designs to the wall, and painting the wet plaster, piece by piece, over the entire 9-by-45-foot area. The Syracuse film department produced a documentary of the entire process, which was shown at the dedication ceremony for the mural.

Charlot's work was the first of the mural program series, which included the famous *Sacco and Vanzetti* mural by Ben Shahn, on an exterior wall of Huntington Beard Crouse Hall, as well as murals by Adja Yunkers, Kenneth Callahan, Marion Greenwood, Robert Marx, and the distinguished Syracuse alumnus Anthony Toney. Together, these murals represent the variety of styles of that period, from abstract to realistic, which all made significant contributions to the history of American art.

In each case art students worked with these masters. The mural project was a major accomplishment. There have been other murals installed at other universities, but the integration of the educational process with mural installations by great artists was unique to Syracuse.

Schmeckebier also strove to make our art collection an essential component of our art education program. At first he hoped to make the Everson Museum part of the school's program. The Everson board members resisted, however, and it remained completely independent of the University. As a result, we decided to build our own University Art Collections.

Syracuse had already acquired a small collection of some important art objects. Progress was slow, however. By 1900, some twenty-seven gifts and purchases of art objects had been added to the University's collections. From 1900 to 1950, only 118 additional purchases were made.

Beginning in 1960, the Syracuse University Art Collections experienced an explosive growth. In less than a decade, over twelve thousand art objects were acquired. The majority of these acquisitions may be attributed to the efforts of Schmeckebier.

Among outstanding holdings of the collections is a varied group of ceramics works. The crown jewel of these is the John R. Fox collection of Korean ceramics, the largest and most varied collection of its kind. There is also an impressive collection of early twentieth-century American ceramics donated by Francis A. Wingate, Vice-President and Treasurer of the University, and Helen, his wife. A complete collection of the porcelain Boehm birds was donated by Mrs. Edward Marshall Boehm, and a unique collection of Japanese ceramics was donated by Ruth Randall.

Other holdings of the University Art Collections include the distinguished Cloud Wampler collection of European and American prints, spanning the sixteenth- to twentieth-centuries; a major collection of contemporary Scandinavian domestic houseware design, Hudson Roysher's sterling silver university mace, sculpture and drawings by Ivan Mestrovic, and a notable collection of paintings.

Among the notable paintings secured for the collections while I was Chancellor are *Briseis Restored to Achilles* by Peter Paul Rubens, *Sun, Moon, and Star* by Charles Burchfield, *The Town Beyond the River* by George Grosz, *Babette* by Bernard Karfiol, *Forbidden Fruit* by Yasuo Kuniyoshi, *Night Sea* by Irene Rice Pereira, *Portrait of Louis XIV* by Hyacinthe Rigaud, *Car Ferry Harbor* by Zoltan Sepeshy, *Apprehension II* by Moses Soyer, *Margen Vue d'Ensemble* by Maurice Utrillo, *The Picture Admirers* by Max Weber, *The Fortune Teller* by Karl Zerbe, *The Tragic Mask of Beethoven* by Emile-Antoine Bourdelle, *The Young Lincoln* by Anna Hyatt Huntington, *Monad II* by James Wines, *Circus Scene* by Jean Dufy, *Walchen See* by Adolf Dehn, *The Great Cannon* by Albrecht Durer, *The Dancing Mother* by Chaim Gross, and an exceptional painting by John Stuart Curry, *The Gospel Train.*

Some of the outstanding holdings of the Art Collections are displayed across the campus. The Class of 1951 commissioned Louise Meyers Kaish, a 1946 graduate and star pupil of Ivan Mestrovic, to execute the famous *Saltine Warrior,* which stood for many years in front of Carnegie Library before being relocated next to Bowne Hall. The Class of 1955 chose Mestrovic's *Bronze Persephone* as its class memorial. In 1961, Chi Omega sorority had Harry Bertoia execute the ten-foot bronze and steel *Syracuse Nova,* which hangs in the Huntington Beard Crouse lounge. Many other important works are also displayed across the campus, including William Zorach's *Mother and Child,* Gross's *Mother and Child,* and James Earl Fraser's *Abraham Lincoln.*

To acquire much of the Art Collections' holdings, Schmeckebier made scores of trips to the studios of leading artists to win their friendship and interest in Syracuse and the Syracuse Art Collections. Often Frank Wingate, Frank Piskor, or I would accompany him on these trips. Dr. Piskor cultivated Anna Hyatt Huntington, who donated many of her artworks to Syracuse. Martin H. Bush, an assistant to Dr. Piskor, secured important gifts from dozens of artists.

Schmeckebier did not hesitate to ask his fellow faculty members and administrators for gifts as well. Clark Ahlberg, Newell Rossman, Frank Wingate, Frank Piskor, and I were all cornered by Schmeckebier when bargains in the art field became available. No one could say no to him. Even when I could not afford it, under Schmeckebier's persuasion, I would buy an important work for the University Art Collections.

Among my gifts to the collections are a watercolor by Ruth Lee, four watercolors by Montague Charman, an oil by William Hekking, three portraits by Henry Nordhausen, an oil by Ben Shahn, an oil by Evelyn Buff Segal, the bronze sculpture, *Socrates and His Disciples,* by Mestrovic, and a watercolor by Robert Marx. I also donated to the collections the bronze bust which Mestrovic made of me.

Over the years, the many devoted supporters of the Syracuse University Art Collections came to include Theodore Newhouse, Harry and Evelyn Segal, Earl Felio, Jerome Soloman, Burch McMorran, Mr. and Mrs. H. N. Jaloneck, George Arents, Colonel Henry Crown, Arnold Grant, and Irwin Guttag.

The holdings of the Art Collections are housed in the Joseph and Emily Lowe Art Gallery, which Schmeckebier helped to plan when he first arrived in Syracuse in 1954. The gallery was created by the generosity of Joseph Lowe. I first met Joe and his brother, Myron Levy, who was also a true philanthropist, early in my administrative career at Syracuse. Myron and Joe had grown up in Syracuse and gone to New York to make their fortunes. Joe changed his name from Levy to Lowe after his invention of the JoLo ice cream stick led people to call him the Jolo man.

The Lowe Art Gallery and the Art Collections are monuments to Schmeckebier's leadership skills, as was the reputation of his revised curriculum. As Chancellor, I did not interfere with his work. My role was to give him a free hand, provide adequate financial support, and assist him in developing the Syracuse Art Collections.

I had not always been able to keep from meddling in the affairs of the School of Art, however. In 1946, shortly after hiring Rice as the school's director, I broke every rule in the book regarding new faculty appointments in order to put the great Yugoslavian sculptor Ivan Mestrovic on the faculty.

The opportunity to do this came purely by chance. Ruth and I were spending a week as the houseguests of Thomas J. Watson, President of IBM, and his wife, Jeanette Kittridge Watson. In the course of our stay, the Watsons invited us to view a bust of Tom that was being executed by "a dear friend" of theirs. This friend turned out to be the sculptor Malvina Hoffman whose book *Heads and Tales* I had read again and again. Malvina and I had met several times, and I looked forward to seeing her again. When we arrived at her studio it was obvious that she was upset about something. As soon as we had a moment alone together, I asked her what was wrong. After some hesitation, she told me.

"I am very upset," she said, "about the fate of a man who was one of my teachers. You may never have heard of him, but he is the Yugoslavian sculptor Ivan Mestrovic."

I assured her that I did indeed know of Mestrovic. I had seen his two magnificent equestrian figures of American Indians on Michigan Avenue in Chicago and had read about him in *Heads and Tales*. That book featured a photograph of the oversize statue Malvina had executed of her mentor, which was in the Brooklyn Institute. When I pointed this out to her, she laughed, saying, "You really do read my books after all, don't you?"

Then she told me her problem.

"During the war," she explained, "Ivan Mestrovic was imprisoned by the Germans. A few months ago, through the Pope's intervention, he was released and allowed to go to Italy. He is now living in Rome, but is sick with phlebitis and pneumonia. He has been unable to sell his work and is in financial trouble. I have just received a very disturbing letter from him, and it has upset me terribly. I must find a way to help him. I asked Columbia if they could hire him, but I got nowhere. They said they might be interested in him as a teacher of art, but not as a sculptor."

I assured Malvina that I understood her problem. I then proposed that we send Mestrovic the following cable: "You have appointment as professor of sculpture at Syracuse University, effective September this year. Will pay all expenses for you and family to come to States. Don't worry. Love, Malvina."

It was exhilarating to take such action, but when Ruth and I returned to Syracuse the next day, I realized that in the world of academia I had committed a sin against the Holy Ghost. Chancellors are not supposed to run universities in such an arbitrary way.

I had to cover my tracks. I first asked Norman Rice whether he had ever met Mestrovic while he was director of the Chicago Art Institute.

"I knew him well," Rice told me. "We held a one-man show of his work. He is a wonderful man, and a magnificent sculptor. Unfortunately, he's now in a prison somewhere in Europe."

"No, he's not," I told Rice. "He's free and living in Rome. But he is seriously ill and unable to sell his work. What kind of a colleague do you think he would make?"

"He'd be a wonderful colleague," Rice assured me. "He is as great a teacher as he is an artist."

I asked Rice if he'd be willing to say this to the Dean of the College of Fine Arts, L. C. Dillenback, should he ask. He assured me that he would.

I called on Bill Hekking next. Hekking was a fine marine painter and professor of painting, who had directed the Albright Gallery at Buffalo. I asked him whether he had known Mestrovic while he was at the Albright. Hekking's response was the same as that of Rice. Mestrovic had exhibited at the Albright; Hekking was convinced he was a good teacher, and "one of the greatest living sculptors."

"You know," I said, "there's a rumor that he's not too happy in Rome. I think he is available for a teaching post. Would you support him if he came here?"

"Support him? I'd do anything to help," Hekking said.

Next I called on L. C. Dillenback.

"L. C.," I said, "there's a rumor that the sculptor Ivan Mestrovic could be brought to this country. Do you want to look into this? Why don't you call Norman Rice and Bill Hekking and see what they would think of adding him to the faculty. I'll check back to see what they said."

When I called a few days later, I asked L. C. if he'd had a chance to find out anything about Mestrovic. "Oh yes," he told me, "Rice and Hekking are very enthusiastic about him." I then asked him what he would think of trying to bring him to Syracuse. "Do you know how to do it?" was his incredulous response.

"I think I do," I said.

The next call I made was to a man who had made a career out of bringing to this country artists and scholars who were political refugees. This was the great social scientist Alvin Johnson, director and professor of the New School for Social Research in New York City. I laid everything out to Johnson and told him that I knew of two Yugoslavs in New York who would help bring Mestrovic over. The three of them worked closely together, with Johnson doing all the necessary paper work free of charge. At last, everything was in order, and Mestrovic was on his way to becoming a permanent artist-in-residence at Syracuse.

Dillenback never did learn how he had been set up, and I said my prayers with extra gratitude during the next few days. I realized that I had been saved from serious embarrassment in my career as Chancellor. When I look back, however, I cannot help but feel that having had the opportunity to bring Ivan Mestrovic here, even if it did mean breaking all the rules to do so, was a kind of miracle in itself.

7

AN ACCELERATING PACE

*A*s early as 1945, we were erecting a new forestry building, constructing a dining area in Sims Hall, and completing plans for Shaw Dormitory and the Ernest I. White College of Law Building. From that time the building program moved at an even more accelerated pace. We rebuilt the Archbold Gymnasium that had been destroyed by fire, erected the Manley Field House, built the Biological Sciences Building, Huntington B. Crouse Hall, William Lawyer Hinds Hall, the Physics Building, and the two Newhouse buildings. We built the long deferred Women's Building and three large dormitories on Mount Olympus—Day, Flint, and Graham halls. We also built a long list of dormitories including Watson, DellPlain, Haven, Sadler, Brockway, Booth, Kimmel, Marion, Lawrinson, Brewster, and Boland. We were also eliminating the prefab buildings that had been so useful after the war but were now an eyesore and an embarrassment.

We did not wait for the war to end to begin our search for new faculty members. We brought an energetic new chairman of the Romance language department, Albert George, in 1943. Professor Philip Burton, probably the leading professor in advertising in the United States, returned to Syracuse in 1948. In the English department we added David H. Owen, Walter Sutton, and Mary Marshall. We brought Arthur Poister and T. V. Smith, and also added Melvin Eggers in economics, Earl Bell in sociology, Roscoe Martin in the Maxwell School, Ted Denise in philosophy, Arthur Pulos in industrial design, and Marvin Druger in science education.

Through the twenty-seven years I was Chancellor, I interviewed all candidates for faculty positions from the rank of assistant professor to that of associate professor and professor. It was time-consuming but was very rewarding. We also spent several weeks each year reviewing the growth and development of members in the faculty and working with the promotions committee of the University Senate. Vice-Chancellor Crawford and later Vice-Chancellor Piskor gave the selection of faculty members their highest priority. We recognized that the faculty was the University. Early in my experience as Chancellor, I had a long conference with Dean Herman Weiskotten of the College of Medicine in which he said, "In the selection of faculty members I try to get the best men I can for the money." This was never our philosophy. We searched long and diligently for the strongest candidates we could find. Once we located them we offered the kind of financial remuneration that would make the post attractive to them. This led to wide disparity in faculty income for a number of years following the war. Fortunately, we were able to bring up the level of all faculty salaries within a relatively short period.

For seventy-five years, Syracuse was primarily an undergraduate institution. By the time I retired in 1969, we were nationally known for our graduate and research programs.

In any account of the growth of American higher education, the role of the federal government should not be minimized. Most of it, however, was done by inadvertence. The famous G.I. Bill with its generous education benefits for veterans was designed to help keep eleven million returning soldiers out of unemployment lines.

The cold war also had a significant impact on higher education. Spurred by the realization that the Soviet Union was overtaking us in weapons, the federal government greatly increased the financial support for military, electronic, medical, and environmental research. The motive was to strengthen military defense. The result was a giant step forward for research in higher education.

If the G.I. Bill and the cold war were major factors in the explosive growth of American higher education, a third factor is the generous policy of educational benefits given to service men and women after a brief enlistment period. To make a voluntary enlistment program attractive, the armed services now offer such generous incentives that they are making a major impact on the poor and underprivileged.

The armed services are also opening doors of opportunity by the extensive educational and training programs offered during the period of active military service. The nature of military service has changed. It is now very largely a period of organized education. The men and women in uniform learn trades and profit from technical, engineering, and scientific training. This is another dramatic illustration of progress in higher education by inadvertence and indirection.

By the late fifties, more than four hundred professors and graduate students were active in scientific research, and its grant awards placed twelfth in American universities sponsored research.

Among the eminent scholars who joined the Syracuse faculty were Fred Sherman, who came to us from Brown University as chairman of the Department of Biology; Josef Zwislocki, who came to us from Harvard to found his internationally known Institute for Sensory Research; William Merrill, who came to Syracuse University from the University of Illinois as the chairman of the Department of Geology; together with Roger Harrington, known for his antenna research; and Arthur Phillips, who came from MIT to start the first germ-free animal research laboratory dedicated to studying medical problems. Phillips's research resulted in the isolation, purification, and identification of anticancer properties of the enzyme asparaginase, used in the successful treatment of lymphomatic cancer. A new metallurgical laboratory was headed by George Sachs, a nationally renowned specialist in titanium. Richard McFee's engineering work led to an accurate method for interpreting electrocardiograms. John Prucha, who came to us in geology in 1963, increased the tempo of research and recruited Ernest Muller from Cornell and Dirk deWaard from the University of California. Among the younger men in science was Donald Kennedy, now President of Stanford University.

In 1957, Dr. W. R. G. Baker, Vice-President of General Electric, persuaded us to form a new University research organization called the Syracuse University Research Corporation (SURC). Working closely with Dean Ralph Galbraith and faculty members were Glenn Glasford, professor of electrical engineering, who modeled SURC after the Stanford Research Institute and the Cornell Aeronautics Laboratory in Buffalo, New York. Unfortunately, Dr. Baker suffered a massive stroke within weeks of opening SURC. Nonetheless, he assisted us in staffing SURC with leading researchers from the University of Illinois and Carnegie Mellon University. SURC became known for electronic intelligence communications and military electronics dealing with radar and sonar. SURC also conducted research in food protection, conservation, education, social policy, and urban affairs.

During the Vietnam War, SURC became a target of antiwar sentiment. Pressure from the faculty led to the disaffiliation from the University in 1975. Even without its connection with the University, SURC has continued to flourish. Close to a dozen new industries in central New York have been created as a result of its research.

We have had many strong academic deans at Syracuse. Some that stand out are William Mosher of the Maxwell School, Ralph Kharas in law, Edith Smith in nursing, Ralph Galbraith in engineering, Kenneth Sargent in architecture, Laurence Schmeckebier in art, Eric Faigle in the College of Liberal Arts, Lyle Spencer in journalism, Clifford Winters at the University College, Harry Ganders in the School of Education, and Thomas Carroll in the College of Business Administration.

The best known school in the University was the Maxwell School of Citizenship and Public Affairs. Under the leadership of Dean William Mosher, one of the great figures in the field of public administration, it had an international reputation. Dean Mosher recruited an exceptional faculty that included Spencer Parratt, Herman Beyle, Douglas Haring, Floyd Alport, Carl Bye, William Park Hotchkiss, Jesse Burkhead, Warren Walsh, and many others.

The second Dean was Paul Appleby. He had been the editor and owner of small newspapers and was assistant director of the U.S. Bureau of the Budget before coming to Syracuse as Dean. Dean Appleby was author of a small but very important book, *Big Democracy*, which established his reputation as a philosopher in the field of government. Appleby was succeeded by the editor of

Reporter magazine, Dr. Harlan Cleveland. Dean Cleveland had a remarkable gift of simplifying complex issues. Like Appleby, he was not afraid of big government. He thought that big government was needed to counterbalance big business and big labor. The great thrust of Cleveland's leadership was in international relations. He brought in a number of senior scholars in that field and built international programs of enormous influence.

Cleveland was succeeded by Stephen Kemp Bailey. Dean Bailey was a Rhodes Scholar whom we attracted from Princeton. While still Dean, he became a member of the New York State Board of Regents. A talented public speaker, he was also a widely used consultant to federal agencies. Dr. Alan "Scotty" Campbell succeeded Dean Bailey. Like his predecessors, he was a superb teacher and administrator. Among many students of whom he was mentor was Donna Shalala, who after successful service at Hunter College became Chancellor of the University of Wisconsin at Madison. Guthrie Birkhead succeeded Dean Campbell. In a quiet and effective way, he built on the strength of his precedessors and made many outstanding faculty appointments. One assistant dean of Maxwell, Gerard Mangone, stands out in my memory. Between teaching and administrative responsibilities, Mangone did the work of several men.

One of the great teachers of the Maxwell School was Thomas Venton Smith. He was one of the most influential philosophers of our time. T. V. Smith was unquestionably the best-known professor in America. He was so sought after as a speaker that he was scheduled two to three years in advance. Before coming to Syracuse, T. V. had distinguished himself as a professor at the University of Chicago and as a congressman-at-large from the State of Illinois. When I first talked to T. V. about coming to Syracuse, my offer fell on deaf ears. Subsequently, I learned that he might be interested if we offered a divan rather than a chair. He had three great interests—poetry, philosophy, and public administration. When we offered him a professorship in all three disciplines, he accepted. Among our Syracuse alumni almost everyone who took T. V. Smith's courses looks back upon them as a high point in his or her career. We were not happy to see T. V. reach the retirement age, but we had to agree with his reason for retire ment. "I have no choice but to retire," he said. "I find myself going to sleep in the middle of my lectures."

Among the great teachers of the Maxwell School were Roscoe Martin; W. W. Kulski, a foremost author on the Soviet Union; Warren Walsh; Earl Ketcham; Stuart Gerry Brown, a magnificent teacher; Michael Sawyer, now Vice-Chancellor of the University; Ralph Ketcham; and Donald Meiklejohn, son of Alexander Meiklejohn from Amherst and Wisconsin. Like his father, Donald was a superb teacher. He was one of the most popular teachers at the University of Chicago and was equally so at Syracuse. He was also a superior tennis player who lifted the play of all his opponents, of whom I was one. The list of great teachers at Maxwell is almost too long to recite, It includes Charles K. Willie, who came to us in 1952 and left to become professor at Harvard in 1967; Irving Swerdlow; Oscar Barck; Roy Price; Guthrie Birkhead; and Dwight Waldo, the first Schweitzer Professor at Syracuse.

Within the Maxwell School, the department of geography was especially notable. Among its outstanding teachers were Preston "Jimmy" James, the leading authority on South American geography; George Cressey, an authority on the Soviet Union and China; John Thompson, author of the best book on the geography of New York State; Donald Meinig, author of *The Shaping of America,* and Robert Jensen, outstanding authority on Soviet geography. The geography department became the top recognized department in the nation during the 1950s and 1960s.

During the time I was Chancellor, schools of education in most American universities left much to be desired. At Syracuse, however, we had a very strong School of Education. Dean Harry Ganders was the best judge of talent of any of our deans, although many, like Edith Smith and Lyle Spencer, were also of unerring judgment. Dean Ganders, who was appointed Dean in 1930, transformed the Syracuse Teachers College into an all University School of Education that drew on all the resources of the University. The plan required the use of major subject matter departments like English, mathematics, economics, sociology, and political science through the appointment of dual professors who had membership in the faculties of education as well as liberal arts, journalism, business, art, and engineering.

The veterans who entered college and graduate school after World War II and the Korean War put heavy burdens on the Graduate School of Education. The maturity of the veterans and the high quality of the faculty soon attracted wide attention.

Among the many programs in which the School of Education achieved national recognition was the special education program directed by William Cruickshank, Louis DeCarlo, and later Burton Blatt; the reading and language program developed by William Sheldon; the film library, which was the largest in the East; the program in measurements and statistics under the top-ranked psychologist in the nation, Eric Gardner; the elementary education program under Clarence Hunnicutt; educational administration under Richard Lonsdale; higher education under Maurice Troyer, George Angell, and Robert Pace; developmental psychology under Raymond Kuhlen and John Shaw; audiovisual developed by Don Williams and continued by Donald Ely; and the philosophy of education under Tom Green.

Among the distinguished dual programs with academic departments outside the School of Education was the English education program directed by an extraordinarily gifted teacher, Helene Willey Hartley Alport. A second or third cousin, she was the only relative I had on the faculty. She and her husband, Floyd Alport, made a deep mark on the University. The program was later directed by Margaret Early. A joint program in social science education with the Maxwell School was under the leadership of Roy Price. Mathematics education and science education programs were directed by Myron Rosskopf and Alfred Collette. The newly formed all university psychology department developed with the School of Speech, the College of Business Administration, the School of Art, the School of Music, the School of Nursing, and the College of Home Economics. The only dual program that did not succeed was one in engineering education.

Cooperation was a way of life for faculty members in the School of Education, and an outstanding doctorate program was developed in cooperation with Alfred University. We also joined four other graduate schools in a program of educational administration with the Kellogg Foundation. Generous grants from the federal government led to a tremendous expansion in the number of outstanding research programs and particularly programs for the handicapped. Dr. Virgil Rogers succeeded Ganders in 1953. He was primarily interested in teaching and service. Dean David R. Krathwohl, who succeeded Rogers in 1965, renewed the emphasis on research and introduced a new program in higher education. Under the leadership of Vice-President Alexander Charters, Syracuse developed probably the strongest adult education in the nation. In addition to the extensive program of University College, Charters assembled the world's largest library of materials in continuing education. He also established a strong graduate program leading to the doctorate.

Syracuse has always had an excellent Department of Religion. When the department chairman, Ismar Peritz, retired, Chancellor Flint offered me the post. I was still at Drew at the time. I told him I was highly honored but was not qualified. He repeated the offer saying that they would wait for me two years if that was necessary. Again I declined with thanks. Dwight Beck was then appointed chairman of the department, and he proved to be a very wise choice indeed. He was an excellent New Testament scholar who made his subject come alive for many generations of students. He also was a superior administrator who attracted to the campus nationally known scholars of the field of religion like A. Leland Jamison, who came to us from Princeton; Huston C. Smith from MIT; Stanley R. Hopper from Drew; T. William Hall, a Danforth Scholar, from the University of Denver and the deanship at Stephens College; Gabriel Vahanian from Princeton; and James B. Wiggins, the present chairman of the department. The Department of Religion is widely recognized as one of the strongest in the nation.

Frank Piskor made a tremendous contribution to the University in the recruitment of faculty members. All the departments felt his influence, but one that stands out is the Department of English. Frank wanted us to have the best collection of poets of any department of English in the country. In addition to Philip Booth, he was instrumental in attracting W. D. Snodgrass, Donald Justice, and Sidney Schwartz. We had a tremendous group of teachers in Mary Marshall, David (C-Minus) Owen, Leonard Brown, George P. Elliott, Sanford Meech, Harlow Waite, Donald Dike, James Elson, Arthur Hoffman, and Walter Sutton.

We had several excellent directors of the College of Music during this time, beginning with Alexander Capurso, who brought the renowned violinist Louis Krasner to Syracuse to teach music and violin. Krasner stayed on the Syracuse faculty from 1949 until 1972. During his tenure, he formed his own chamber music group, the Krasner Quartet, and helped form the Syracuse Symphony and the Syracuse Friends of Chamber Music. With the addition of men like Louis Krasner and Arthur Poister, we achieved a new level of excellence throughout the school.

Capurso was succeeded by Howard Boatwright as director of the School of Music. Boatwright came to us from Yale. He was a superb violinist and with his wife, Helen, a renowned vocalist, added significantly to the reputation of the school.

In the College of Law, Ralph Kharas succeeded Paul Shipman Andrews as Dean. Kharas too made a systematic search for law professors at a higher level of scholarship and research. Robert Miller, who succeeded Kharas as Dean, continued this quest for excellence; and by the late sixties, we had a law school of distinction.

Probably the most significant achievement of the 1960s was the election of Syracuse University in 1967 to membership in the American Association of Universities. This is a proud company of universities recognized as leaders in graduate education and research. One cannot apply for membership, and before our admission the association had not added to its membership for a number of years. It included twenty state-supported universities and an equal number of privately endowed universities. Grayson Kirk, President of Columbia University, was President of the American Association of Universities at the time of our election. We had worked shoulder to shoulder in the passage of the Bundy Bill, which provided financial support to privately endowed colleges and universities, and were close friends. I suspect he was largely responsible for our election to membership.

Other important developments in the 1960s were the dedication of the two Newhouse buildings, the development of the

School of Social Work under Dean Walter Beattie, the completion of the Arnold Grant Auditorium for the Law School, the building of Heroy Hall for geology, and the ground breaking for Link Hall dedicated shortly after my retirement.

Equally important was the completion of the capital fund campaign for $76 million. We made our goal more than a year ahead of schedule. Today, this would be a very modest campaign, but I well remember the skepticism that greeted our original announcement of that goal.

Graduate study in America began for the first time in 1876 with the founding of the Johns Hopkins University. Graduate study, however, did not change the character of universities until the twentieth century. In 1900, there were only five thousand graduate students in American colleges and universities. That number climbed to fifteen thousand in 1920 and then to fifty thousand in 1930. The most recent statistics show more than one million American graduate students.

As the first university to emphasize graduate study and research, Johns Hopkins took as its model the German universities. Cornell took a different model, that of a federal land-grant institution offering not only instruction to its students in a wide variety of disciplines but also the benefits of its research and knowledge to the citizens of New York State through traveling extension agents and, later, cooperative extension centers. By the turn of the century, Cornell's reputation was overtaking that of Johns Hopkins.

The University of California at Berkeley, the University of Michigan, the University of Wisconsin, and the University of Minnesota were among the state-supported institutions that changed the face of American higher education by making a graduate and undergraduate education affordable for almost everyone.

Among privately endowed institutions, Harvard, Yale, and Columbia had become the leading American graduate universities by 1910. The University of Chicago, the California Institute of Technology, and the Massachusetts Institute of Technology took seven-league steps in the years following World War II, and Princeton also made its mark on the graduate university scene around this time.

When I came to Syracuse as Chancellor, we had an extensive graduate program in education and small but sound graduate programs in engineering, mathematics, chemistry, biology, geography, geology, physics, and English. The Maxwell School program in public administration was our best-known graduate program. From the time I arrived, it was obvious that giant steps should be taken in the development of graduate education and research at Syracuse. When I made my intentions clear to the faculty and administrators, they gave their enthusiastic approval and support.

While we would make great strides in all of our graduate programs, particularly significant gains were made in engineering and mathematics. It was clear that if our research efforts were to grow, we would need the support of local industry. Unfortunately, few of the corporations in Syracuse had any conception of what either fundamental or applied research could mean to them. Again and again, I tried to persuade H. W. Smith, the Chief Executive Officer of L. C. Smith, to let us do some research on the manufacturing of typewriters. "There is no reason," I said, "why there should not be an electric typewriter. It is a relatively simple advance, which we could help you achieve quite easily." At the time L. C. Smith had almost no quality control in its production, and the ball bearings kept dropping out of their typewriters.

I also discovered that the Niagara Mohawk Power Corporation spent nothing for research. I repeatedly talked with Earle J. Machold, the chairman of Niagara Mohawk, about forming a partnership between his company and the University's School of Applied Sciences. Despite our close friendship and his place on the Syracuse University Board of Trustees, what I had to say to him about this subject fell on deaf ears for a number of years. At that time, none of the utility companies had any interest in research. They relied on General Electric and Westinghouse to provide both fundamental and applied research because, they said, the Public Service Commission gave no tax credit for research in the fixing of rates for customers.

Louis Mitchell was Dean of the L. C. Smith College of Engineering when I came to Syracuse. He was a gentle, sweet man who cleared his desk by 9:15 each morning. So far as I know he did nothing else the rest of the day. He was also a trustful soul who was a poor judge of faculty talent. Once he recommended a candidate for a department chairmanship who had had a long succession of jobs. None had lasted more than two years. I was shocked by the interview. After talking with the candidate, I spoke to Dean Mitchell in private. "This is the poorest candidate I have ever seen," I said. "Ah," said Mitchell, "didn't you know that his brother-in-law is President of Eastman Kodak?" "Yes," I replied, "and didn't you know that the President of Eastman Kodak knows what a fool his brother-in-law is?"

Mitchell was succeeded as Dean by Ralph Galbraith. Galbraith did his undergraduate work at the University of Missouri, and took his Ph.D. from Yale. While Galbraith was Acting Dean, he submitted a budget to Vice-Chancellor Crawford and me that was clearly beyond our means. When we told him what he could have, he raised a veritable storm. "I can't live with what you have to offer," he said. "I never could face my faculty."

When Galbraith finally left my office in a huff, Crawford observed, "Well, that settles one thing. He will not be the next Dean."

"To the contrary," I replied. "He will be the Dean. I don't want yes-men to direct our schools and colleges. Ralph is a fighter. He will be difficult to deal with, but he will fight for his faculty. I think he will be a great dean."

Before coming to Syracuse, Galbraith had been chairman of the Electrical Engineering department at Georgia Tech. He was dynamic, vigorous, able, and did wonders for the college. Shortly after Galbraith became Dean, we began a search for someone to direct the Institute of Industrial Research, established in 1947. The person we selected was Ralph Montana, a Syracuse graduate teaching at the University of Minnesota.

Montana was not a hard-driving executive, but he knew his way around the federal agencies. His low-key approach won the trust of government bureaucrats, research-minded professors, and busy business executives. We soon proved the value of a partnership between industry and the University by solving problems in chemistry and mathematics for Carrier Corporation and others.

Crouse Hinds and L. C. Smith were among organizations that contributed some $880,000 to get the Institute of Industrial Research underway. During this same period, General Electric moved out of its factories at Thompson Road, where it had been conducting naval defense research. When the property was declared government surplus, Carrier and the University both put in a bid for the property. After extended negotiations we divided the facilities. Carrier paid a very modest amount for its large facility, and we moved into the other nine buildings. The federal government gave us our share at no cost. It also gave us a grant for research laboratories, classrooms, and research equipment for the College of Engineering and the Institute of Industrial Research. Because of these very generous contributions, we spent only $250,000 of the $880,000 capital funds raised to support the institute. The Thompson Road research campus provided a quantum leap in our research capability in science and engineering and had an explosive impact on the development of graduate work. The star performer was the department of electrical engineering. We attracted first-rate teachers and scholars to this department, including Wilbur A. Le Page, Glenn M. Glasford, and later, Norman Balabanian, as well as many others.

It was the mathematics department, however, that experienced the most significant change. In 1943, we brought Dr. William Martin from the Massachusetts Institute of Technology to become the new mathematics chairman. Martin attracted some of the top mathematicians of the day to our campus. Within three years, he had added Henry Scheffé, Ralph Fox, Hans Samelson, Paul Halmos, Charles Loewener, Lipman Bers, and Abe Gelbart to the department. These men were midcareer mathematicians who had already demonstrated their outstanding abilities through significant publications. Martin was able to recruit them to Syracuse by offering them good salaries, excellent working conditions, and assurances that the department was going somewhere. Martin did such a fine job of building up our mathematics faculty that three years later MIT asked him to return as chairman of its mathematics department.

Fortunately, we still had a solid group of people in the department who had good connections with other institutions.

Stewart Cairns became chairman for two years, and he added Paul Rosenbloom, a Brown graduate, and friend to three of our existing faculty—Lowener, Bers, and Donald Kibbey. Abe Gelbart brought Atle Selberg. Apparently, Syracuse suited him well, for while he was here he produced his famous elementary proof of the prime number theorem. This was considered quite an accomplishment because it had been a long-standing problem.

George Mostow, a recent Harvard Ph.D., was recommended by a friend of Kibbey. So it went. Others were attracted to Syracuse, not by friends, but by its accommodating atmosphere. Paul Erdös was a top mathematician from the Institute for Advanced Studies with rather eccentric ways. Our chief worry with Erdös was that he would be killed while crossing a busy street. When preoccupied with his own thoughts, he was oblivious to everything going on around him. To this impressive group was added Arthur Milgram, also from the Institute for Advanced Studies.

Upon leaving for MIT, Martin had remarked to Vice-Chancellor Crawford that "Donald Kibbey was a natural." We kept our eye on him, soliciting his advice on administrative matters, and found this observation to be true. In 1952, we decided to make Kibbey chairman. Having earned his degree from the renowned J. L. Doob at Illinois, Kibbey had some impressive connections among mathematicians. He was never a man to make enemies; even those who had left Syracuse remained on good terms with him, and he had other friends elsewhere who also wished him well. Between Kibbey's popularity and the most attractive research conditions possible, which included low teaching loads, good pay, private offices with blackboards, and staunch administrative support, the department began to grow.

The people Kibbey recruited during his twelve years as chairman made up an outstanding department. He brought Walter Baum from the Swiss Federal Institute and Albert Edrei from Colorado. By keeping in touch with his advisor, Doob, he also brought us Kai Lai Chung from Cornell, Guy Johnson from Rice, and the German Wolfgang Jurkat, by way of Ohio State. Irving Kaplansky came from the University of Chicago, and he and Jurkat told Kibbey about Erwin Kleinfeld and Herbert Ryser of Ohio

State. These men were already established mathematicians with reputations as producers of significant research when they came to Syracuse. Later, they attracted several young, new Ph.D.s and postdoctoral students to the faculty: Carl Kohls, Philip Church, Jack Graver, Lawrence Lardy, Mark Watkins, and Kenneth Bowen. Wolfgang Jurkat also recommended Hans Richert, and William Martin told us of Robert Davis, whose talents were going to waste at New Hampshire and whose leadership made us famous in mathematics education.

Soon after Kibbey became chairman he was approached by Ralph Galbraith with the idea that the department should move into computing. He immediately brought the proposal to me, and we launched the Computing Center with Bruce Gilchrest as director. Gilchrest was an excellent choice, and he made the center thrive. Soon he attracted the attention of IBM and left us to go there. We were able to replace him with an even more innovative director, Werner Rheinboldt of the National Bureau of Standards.

The Computing Center eventually became the College for Computer and Information Studies, a separate entity from the mathematics department. The University's international reputation in computers led to a consortium of sixteen universities, known as the Center for Applied and Software Engineering (CASE), being headquartered at Syracuse. CASE is especially regarded for its research in fourth-generation computers, which will allow computers to reason independently. The man who is the CASE research director today, J. Alan Robinson, was brought here from Rice University by Kibbey's initiative and insight.

Kibbey met Robinson at an annual meeting of mathematicians in Texas, when Robinson was President of the Association for Symbolic Logic. Kibbey was immediately struck by Robinson's brilliance and wide range of knowledge. With degrees in both philosophy and mathematics, Robinson has an outstanding combination of disciplines. He combines a love for the humanities with a keen mind for the hard sciences. Kibbey and Theodore Denise, chairman of the philosophy department, recommended that we appoint Robinson as a University professor with no departmental affiliation.

Robinson quickly established himself as the heart and soul of theoretical research in computing at Syracuse. It was our reputation in mathematics that first interested Robinson, and since then he has caused that reputation to soar.

By the 1960s Kibbey had built the mathematics department into an outstanding one. He made it happen by letting the world know that Syracuse wanted the best. He was constantly spreading the word that we wanted people who were better than anyone we had at the time. To attract such people, the department supplied good research conditions, and Kibbey worked to maintain a congenial atmosphere. It was a simple recipe for success.

By the time I returned to Syracuse as Chancellor, the University had long ago outgrown its library. Carnegie Library had been built in 1907. The director of libraries, Wharton Miller, informed me in one of his early reports that it would serve no useful purpose to increase the budget appropriation for new books when there was no space for the books we already had. I did not follow his advice, but I understood the problem.

Since we could not afford a new library building, we had to look for temporary solutions. To house our books we created an explosion of branch libraries. At various times during the 1940s, our branch libraries extended from Auburn to Baldwinsville, from Thompson Road and the State Fairgrounds to the Russian Language School at Skytop, from Endicott to Utica, from the old College of Law and University College in downtown Syracuse to more than a dozen branch libraries on campus, including the libraries at the Forestry College and the Medical College. The situation eased slightly with the addition of storage facilities at Ainsley Drive. During the 1950s we found another storage area. The Continental Can Company factory located on Erie Boulevard was closing down. As soon as I learned this, I flew to New York to ask the company President to give us the building.

"You're closing the plant because it is obsolete," I said. "You will not be able to sell it because it is so outdated. You can give it to us and make some money at the same time. We will have it appraised. Then you can give it to Syracuse University as a gift, and write off the amount of its worth from your taxes."

"We have never heard of such a thing," they said. The Continental Can Company building soon became ours, and we put hundreds of thousands of books in it before we finally were able to build a new library.

When we built new dormitories in the 1950s, we established recreational undergraduate libraries in most of these, including Flint, Day, Shaw, Watson, Brockway, and the Women's Building. We maintained all of these libraries, including the branch libraries and the main library, Carnegie, until we could break ground for the new library.

We were able to provide one of the fine libraries in the country on September 5, 1972, when the Ernest Stevenson Bird Library opened its doors to the Syracuse community. It was dedicated in April 1973.

Years of thought and research went into planning Bird Library. We wanted the building to be modern, spacious, yet easily accessible to the staff and users of the library, and easily expandable. In the end, we were able to accomplish all of these goals. Books are grouped on floors according to subject, and staff offices are centrally located on each floor so that librarians may walk quickly to any stack on the floor. Realizing that the library would ultimately use a great deal of automation, we had special "waffle" ceilings installed which allow for the running of wires and troughs in the ceilings. This arrangement has allowed the library to incorporate highly efficient computerized cataloging and reference systems. We also created an inviting interior environment. Tables of wood, rather than metal, were installed; and softly upholstered wood-frame chairs make sitting and reading a pleasure. Warm earth tones, such as orange and brown, were chosen for the color scheme. It is a library aesthetically pleasing and easy to use.

Faculty members led by Mary Marshall, Erik Hemmingsen, Harley McKee, Antonio Pace, O. T. Barck, William Park Hotchkiss, Phillips Bradley, Bruno Green, Douglas Haring, Morris Hurley, and Horace Landry were also a great help in creating Bird Library.

Libraries are the hardest institutions to support. Unlike sports, they are not highly visible. Unlike professional or academic schools, they do not produce great scholars or scientists. The people who support libraries are usually selfless, unassuming, highly intellectual, and dedicated human beings.

The first major acquisitions for the Syracuse University library were secured through the generosity of Dr. and Mrs. John Morrison Reid. Their support made it possible for Charles Wesley Bennett, University librarian and professor of history, to purchase the outstanding library of his revered teacher Leopold von Ranke in 1887. This massive collection of twenty thousand volumes focuses on early modern European history, including the history of Venice, economic history and public finance, and the history of religions.

The resourceful Bennett was replaced by Henry Orrin Sibley, and his wife, Mary J. O'Bryan Sibley, who became assistant librarian. They were incredibly dedicated. In 1894, their combined salary totaled $1,275. After her husband died, Mary Sibley took over the direction of the library, although holding only the title of assistant librarian. She also served as professor of library economy until 1913. The Sibleys' story is one of outstanding, unselfish devotion and service. They gave their lives to the library.

The library gained many friends after the turn of the century, including Andrew Carnegie, John Archbold, William J. Peck, Henry Danziger, Manly S. Hard, and James J. Belden.

Despite the dedication of the friends of the library, it would take a twenty-year campaign to make Bird Library a reality. When I was a college dean at Drew, the President of Western Reserve University, Charles Thwing, declared that patience is the quality a university president needs most. At the time, I found that difficult to believe. The process of building Bird Library, along with the time and effort needed to finance the Women's Building, taught me that Charles Thwing was right.

The biggest obstacles to building the library were financial. When I came to Syracuse there was still an unpaid current expense deficit that had been built up by James Roscoe Day. Chancellor Flint managed to pay off most of this debt, but it took me two more years to erase it entirely. To keep the University from going into debt again, we established a firm rule that we would borrow money only for revenue-producing buildings, such as dining halls and dormitories. We would not borrow for academic buildings. Living by this rule meant that we had to raise enough money to pay for the library before we could build it. To accomplish this, we had to have endless patience. I was by nature impatient. Fortunately, I was also an optimist. After a nationally known university has been built, people forget how hard the early years were and how ridiculously small were the gifts.

Bird Library was built with hundreds of modest gifts. The first major gift came from George Arents after years of cultivation. When he finally told me he would give us $1 million for the library, I rejoiced. Yet, for years to follow, we were only able to collect additional gifts of modest sums ranging from $5,000 to $10,000. At last, I approached Mr. Arents to try to persuade him to give us more. When he agreed to donate $2 million to the library, I wept with disappointment. I had asked him for $6 million. All I could think was, "I'm a failure as a fund raiser!"

George Arents and I were close friends. I recognized, however, that his primary loyalties were not with Syracuse University. They lay instead with the New York Public Library and St. Thomas Episcopal Church. George left each of these institutions $1 million in his will. The only reason that Syracuse received more than they did was because of my persistence.

Once Mr. Arents had financially committed to give the library $2 million, I decided he should be involved in planning its design. I arranged to meet him in New York and take him to see Lorimer Rich, a Brooklyn architect who had done a great deal of work for us. The three of us would discuss ideas for the building.

George Arents had inherited a fortune from his father, a cofounder of the American Tobacco Company, and he lived in a magnificent house just off Fifth Avenue, near Eightieth Street. He always rode in town in a chauffeured Bentley or Rolls Royce.

On the appointed day I picked up Mr. Arents at his house in a taxi which we left at the nearest subway entrance. On the way to the subway car, I noticed that he was acting strangely. As the subway car hurtled along toward our destination in Brooklyn, I suddenly realized that Mr. Arents had never been in a subway before. Just to be sure, I asked him. It was true. He was then seventy-one or seventy-two years old. His work in tobacco and renown as a rare-book collector had earned him honorary degrees from Syracuse and William and Mary College. He was decorated Chevalier in the French Legion of Honor, and he was a member of the American Society French Legion of Honor and the Huguenot Society. He had lived his entire life in New York, yet he had never been on a subway. We made the return trip in the safe haven of a taxi.

Despite the support of Mr. Arents, our progress in fundraising was painfully slow. His gift of $2 million grew in dividends to more than $3 million before we were ready to build the library. At last, twenty years after starting our library campaign, we received $3 million from Ernest Stevenson Bird, and his wife, Marie. We were ready to break ground in 1969.

Before we could do that, however, a site had to be agreed upon. I envisioned building the library next to the Psi Upsilon house at the corner of University Place and College Place. The University Design Board disagreed with that idea. At one point it was suggested that we put the library on the main quad, on the site of the old library, on an axis with the Physics Building. I was in favor of this plan because it would have balanced the quadrangle, which is uneven. These ideas, along with several others were voted down by the Design Board. It was Gordon Hoople who suggested the location that was ultimately settled upon, but it took several years to come to this decision.

When Bird Library was finally dedicated, we found that our work was not over. We still had to run a steady campaign to acquire and preserve books for the library. I personally solicited many of the gifts for library books by seeking out alumni who were book collectors.

The Bird Library's holdings are in excess of 2.2 million books; more than 23,000 periodicals, and more than 3 million microforms. The first million holdings were acquired over a ninety-year period, the second million in less than twenty years.

The holdings of the George Arents Research Library for Special Collections cover a vast range, but its greatest strength is in its holdings of nineteenth- and twentieth-century authors and poets. Among these important books is the great elephant folio of John James Audubon. There are extensive typographical collections, including the work of Frederick Goudy; important collections in the history of religion, including the Methodist, Shaker, and Oneida Community collections; and other materials relating largely to the nineteenth and twentieth centuries.

Syracuse University also has auxiliary libraries in medicine, geology, geography, architecture, music, science, and forestry, which are housed in the appropriate departments and colleges across the campus.

An unusual feature of the Syracuse University Library is its Audio Archives collection housed in a modern new building next to Bird, the Belfer Audio Laboratory. These holdings cover the first eighty years of commercial sound recordings and contain over 250,000 items ranging from the earliest of the Thomas Edison cylinder recordings to the most modern audio tapes. The core of the collection donated by Joseph and Max Bell contains 150,000 phonograph records and tapes dating from 1898 to 1964 of voice recordings of great figures ranging from poets and philosophers to actresses and singers and also includes rare noncommercial recordings and interviews.

8

ATHLETICS

I was twelve years old when my brother Harold went to Syracuse University as a freshman in 1912. As I followed his career, I also became interested in Syracuse athletics. I still remember the exploits of Babe White, Chris Schlacter, Joe Schwartzer, and others in football. I also followed the careers of Charlie Whiteside and Gordon Hoople in crew.

Chick Meehan of the Class of 1913 was the Syracuse coach during my own undergraduate years. He was an outstanding coach. In the Pi Kappa Alpha fraternity, we had a varsity lineman named Tommy Thomson. The only other football player in the fraternity was Lynn Waldorf. Lynn was the son of Bishop Waldorf of the Methodist Church in Ohio and had been an outstanding high school star. In Lynn's first year, Meehan had a tremendous freshman squad both in size and in quality. Despite hard work, Lynn was still on the fourth team when the freshman year was over.

As a consequence, he did not go out for the team in his sophomore year. Because Lynn was my roommate, my fraternity brothers asked me to persuade him to report for football. He said, "It's no use. I can't make the team." "Lynn," I said, "we don't care whether or not you make the team. You owe it to the fraternity, however, to go out and do your best." I put so much pressure on him that he finally agreed. In midseason, a series of injuries among the linemen gave Lynn his chance. When Meehan saw him, he said, "Where has this man been! He has the potential to be a star." Before Lynn graduated, he was an all-American.

In 1920 when the members of Pi Kappa Alpha were given the army alpha test, the man with the highest score was Lynn Waldorf. After Lynn graduated, he became known as "Pappy" Waldorf. His record as a football coach at Northwestern University and the University of California is almost without equal. His success, however, was no surprise to his fraternity brothers or his teammates at Syracuse.

Tom Keene was coach of track and cross-country. He was a great recruiter. He would come to physical education classes and take a look at students who had unusual speed. I remember that he was impressed by the quickness and speed of Ernest Stevenson Bird (who gave us the Bird Library) and my brother Harold when they were undergraduates. Unfortunately, they were working their way through college and did not have the time to go out for track. The greatest runner in my undergraduate years was Allen Woodring. He broke the world indoor record for the 300-yard run, 31.2 seconds. He equaled the world record in the 100-yard dash in ten seconds. He won a gold medal in the United States Olympics.

James TenEyck, the coach of crew, was known as "the Old Man." There have been many great coaches of crew, but the Old Man stands almost alone in his skill as a teacher and in his influence on the students who went out for crew. One of my roommates in my junior and senior years was Lester Angwin. Les was a member of the crew that won the Poughkeepsie race in 1922. This was before the days of X rays. He did not know it, but he had contracted tuberculosis and he died less than two months after the race. He must have rowed on sheer determination and intestinal fortitude.

While I was an undergraduate, Coach TenEyck, who was a widower, married for a second time. To those who knew him best, it was no surprise that on his honeymoon he rowed his new wife from Albany to New York.

Today, only a few people remember the great crew of 1920 which won the Intercollegiate Championship at Ithaca and thus received the Steward's Cup over Cornell, Pennsylvania, and Columbia. In the middle of the summer, we raced again at Duluth against the Duluth Boat Club, reputed to be the greatest crew of that time. It was a sensational race. Gus Rammi was our stroke and Ken Buckley was the commodore. The crew included George

Bush, Bernie Dawson, Ken Gallagher, Tot Hoople, R. C. Loskamp, Cap Paige, and Lowell Nicholson. Despite two broken oars, the Orange boat crossed the finish line two feet ahead of the Duluth boat.

Eddie Dollard was coach of basketball (1911–24), and Lou Carr was our baseball coach, succeeded later by wonderful Ted Kleinhans. Laurie Cox, a professor of the Forestry College was our lacrosse coach. The wrestling coach was William G. Davidson, a superior man who was also chairman of the physical education department. During my four years at Syracuse, no one in the student body could match Professor Davidson's skill in handball. I shall always be in debt to him for the counsel and help he gave me in my senior year when I was acting general secretary of the YMCA.

When I returned to Syracuse University as Chancellor in 1942, Ossie Solem was head coach of football. Solem astonished the football world in 1941 with the *Y* formation and the reverse center, both great offensive weapons. Coming here in 1937 as successor of Vic Hanson, Ossie had an exceptional record at Syracuse, even though we had to drop football in 1943 because of World War II. Solem was followed by Clarence "Biggie" Munn, who came to us in 1946 after serving as a line coach at the University of Michigan. Munn had a great staff of assistants, including Forest Evashevski, Kip Taylor, Duffy Dougherty, and Roy Simmons. He was unquestionably a great coach, as he proved later at Michigan State. He had little interest, however, in the academic side of the institution. At the end of the first semester, the faculty dropped some eighteen members of the freshman football squad for poor scholarship. This was a great shock to Biggie. He said, "I didn't know they had to go to class. In the Big Ten we didn't worry about academics." Ribs Baysinger, who had been Solem's freshman coach, succeeded Munn for two years (1947–48).

One of the greatest coaches Syracuse ever had was Roy Simmons. Simmons was coach of boxing and lacrosse, and assistant coach of football. He made a record in each field that will be difficult to match. He won national championships again and again. Recently, there was a reunion of the men who had competed in boxing under Simmons. They came from all across America and were a most exceptional group. They were high school principals, lawyers, judges, doctors, and senior officers of national corporations. The men who fought and won as members of the boxing team under Simmons also fought and won in their careers after college.

Lew Andreas succeeded Dollard as coach of basketball and served as director of athletics as well as coach of basketball. In his long career as coach of basketball, he won more than 75 percent of the games played. He had also been a successful coach of football at Syracuse. He would have been successful in any sport he coached. I remember him saying that he wished he had had an opportunity to coach crew. Lew had an exceptional mind. He was a master of organization and human relations. He was a great teacher.

He also was one of the great fishermen of our time. I remember fishing on the Chenango Canal near Hamilton, New York. Before he left to go downstream he said, "There are three or four fine trout about twenty feet downstream. Let your fly drift down on the other side of the stream. Lift the tip of your rod the instant a trout hits the fly." In a few minutes he returned, and he said "How are you doing?" I said "I almost got one. How many do you have?" I asked. "I have six or seven," he replied. At the end of a two-week fishing trip in Quebec, his guide said, "Mr. Andreas, I have been a Quebec guide for fifty years. You are the best fisherman I have ever met."

Lew Andreas was the finest director of athletics Syracuse has had. While Reeves H. Baysinger was coach, Andreas came under heavy attack from alumni. At an alumni meeting in Buffalo, Al Richie, one of our leading alumni and later a trustee, asked from the floor, "When are you going to fire Lew Andreas?" "First the trustees will have to fire me," I replied. That same year Lewis C. Ryan, a trustee, launched an attack on Andreas and persuaded the trustees to appoint a committee to investigate the state of athletics at Syracuse. He had himself appointed to the committee, and he blamed Andreas for Baysinger's failure. At a dinner meeting of the two of us at the Century Club, he made the mistake of saying, "If you don't dismiss Andreas, I shall ask for your resignation." I took a pen and a piece of blank paper out of my coat and said, "I hear you, Lew. Now it's my turn. I want your resignation as a trustee. Write it now." There was a long pause. Finally, Lew said, "You son of a bitch. You win." I had called his bluff. From that time on, we became trusted friends.

I don't know how I found the time, but I attended most of the swimming meets, the baseball games, the boxing meets, the wrestling and gymnastic meets, the crew races, the ski matches, as well as the basketball and football games. I also followed tennis closely and played against many of the members of the tennis team. I have a lot of happy memories of George Earle and the ski teams; of the Byrne brothers and Dick Prussin in boxing; of Billy Gabor, Royce Newell, Larry Crandell, Eddie Stickel, Ed Miller, Dave Bing, Vince Cohen, Andy Mogish, and others in basketball; Harold McGrath in tennis; Dick Beyer in wrestling; Carroll Coyne in baseball; Tom Kerr, Marty Hilfinger, Tip Goes, and Andy Geiger in crew; and the long procession of stars in football, including Jimmy Brown, Joe Watt, Jim Ridlon, John Mackey, Jim (Bo) Nance, John Brown, Bernie Custie, Ernie Davis, Floyd Little, Welter Mahle, Fred Mautino, and Larry Csonka.

When we were looking for a football coach at Syracuse, Lew Andreas narrowed it down to three names. All three were very young coaches. I remember when I interviewed Ben Schwartzwalder I told him who the other two candidates were. He said, "They are both excellent coaches. You couldn't go wrong with either of them."

"I note from the record," I said, "that your teams at Muhlenberg have beaten their teams three years in a row. How do you explain this if they are such good coaches?" He fired back, "You can outthink them."

After he left, I called President Levering Tyson at Muhlenberg. I had known Levering when he was at Columbia. "Lev," I said, "this is Bill Tolley. I have been talking to your football coach Mr. Schwartzwalder about a coaching job that is open here. I thought I ought to touch base with you."

"Hire him," said President Tyson. "What's wrong with him?" I asked. "Nothing," came back the reply, "but he belongs in the big time. His record here is twenty-five victories and five defeats. You have been president of Allegheny. You know the problems a small college has when football gets out of hand. Not one of our opponents wants to play us any more. I sent for Ben recently and told him unless he lost some games, I would have to fire him. He is a great coach. Hire him!"

I immediately called Lew Andreas and said "We have a new football coach." "I hope it is Ben Schwartzwalder," said Andreas. "It is," I replied. Ben Schwartzwalder was a soft-spoken hillbilly from West Virginia. As a center weighing 152 pounds, he was a tremendous overachiever. He had a distinguished war record with the rank of major and participated in scores of parachute jumps behind the enemy line. Few of his fellow officers survived. Ben had everything needed in the successful coach. He was a great recruiter, and he enlisted the help of hundreds of loyal alumni in his search for talent. He had an encyclopedic knowledge of football. He insisted on a level of conditioning our football teams had not known before. He made his players master the fundamentals. His teams were known for their defensive strength, their line play on the offensive, and the famous scissors play. Ben had an excellent staff of coaches. In addition to the incomparable Roy Simmons, he had Ted Dailey, Rocco Pirro, Bill Eschenfelder, Les Dye, Jim Shreve, and Joe Szombathy. He was loyal to his coaches, and they were loyal to him. Occasionally criticized for an offense famous for "three or four yards and a cloud of dust," Ben's philosophy was when you have the horses you use them. In the case of forward passes, two of three things can go wrong: they can be intercepted, and they can be dropped.

Ben complained bitterly about the small number of scholarships we offered at Syracuse. As I recall it, we gave about twelve scholarships a year when he came, and the number grew very slowly over a twenty-five year period. None of the scholarships involved cash. We gave a tuition scholarship and a job that provided an opportunity to earn board and room. In the matter of campus employment, athletes were treated like all other student employees.

One of the tributes to Ben that I recall with pleasure was written by Dean Charles Noble of Hendricks Chapel.

How labors now our football coach
From dawn to setting sun?
He trains his boys to run and block
Until they're number one.

Not satisfied to field a team
To rock and roll the foe:
He builds a second unit which
Can dole out equal woe.

And just in case his first two squads
Should ever ailing be,
He reaches farther down the bench
And comes up with team three.

Penn State coach would like to swap
His squad for Unit 4
And any other players whom
Ben's hid behind the door.
Oh, happy Hannukah to Ben,
And Merry Christmas, too;
On January first we'll give
The Cotton Bowl to you.

As we became a nationally known football power, we had a review of accreditation by the Middle States Association of Schools and Colleges. The committee making the accreditation study came to Syracuse convinced that there must have been sins of commission and omission. Vice-Chancellor Crawford and Director of Athletics Andreas prepared carefully for inquiries about our athletic program. We assembled in the Vice-Chancellor's office a complete record of each student athlete. We disclosed the subjects he took, the academic record he made, the jobs he held, and the record of activities other than football. We made a full and complete disclosure. When the members of the accreditation committee arrived at Vice-Chancellor Crawford's office, he said "I think we have all the records here for your examination. If, however, there is anything else you need, do not hesitate to ask us. We have no secrets to hide. We are completely at your service."

The members of the committee went through all the records with care. They were amazed at what they discovered. They said, "This has been a revelation to us. We don't understand how you maintain high academic standards, give such limited financial aid, and still have a great football team." The credit should go to Schwartzwalder and Andreas. Lew would stand for no breaking of the rules. He kept himself fully informed, and he was always in charge. He also kept me fully informed.

The only time I ever felt it necessary to rebuke Schwartzwalder was when he made a speech in Buffalo asking the alumni to write me urging an increase in the number of scholarships given to football players. I sent for Ben and asked him, "Did you say this to the alumni in Buffalo?" "Yes, I did," he said. "Ben, if you ever make a speech like that again, I will accept your resignation before you get back to Syracuse. You are always free to ask me for anything you need. In dealing with alumni, however, you owe the University and its Chancellor your complete loyalty." Ben never made that mistake again.

Several times he appealed to me for help in getting weak academic candidates admitted. I always declined. I remember several all-Americans who wanted to come to Syracuse but whose records and college boards were far below our standards.

I did intercede, however, in the cases of Jim Brown and Floyd Little. One day I received a telephone call from Holly Patterson, the county executive of Nassau County. The year before his telephone call, he had rounded up some seventy-five votes to prevent the trustees of the Forestry College from being stripped of their power by the State University. It was Holly's help that ensured our victory. Holly said, "Do I have any money in the bank?" "You certainly do," I said, "I hope, however, it is not a candidate for the medical school." "No," he said, "this is a student in the College of Liberal Arts. He is a colored boy. He has worked for me two summers. He has no father, and his mother is a charwoman. He has never had a room of his own. He is president of his class and president of the student body. I will pay his tuition for the first year if you provide tuition for the following three years." I agreed and hung up. I then called the director of admissions, Les Dye. "Take him," I said. "I have promised him admission."

In late September, John Olson, my assistant, came into my office and said, "Let's watch the freshmen play the Cornell freshmen on the main quad this afternoon." "I can't do it, John," I said. "This is a very busy day." John persisted, "Work tonight. We will only take an hour." About the time I arrived at the quad, I saw a big running back run over three defenders and score a touchdown. He did not try to avoid them. He ran over them. A few minutes later he repeated the same exploit.

"Who is that?" I asked John. "His name is Brown. He is from Manhasset, Nassau County, Long Island." A light dawned. "Don't tell me" I said, "his mother is a charwoman, he has no father, he never had a room of his own to study in, he was president of the senior class, and president of student body. Holly never said one word about his athletic ability."

Floyd Little's case was somewhat different. Floyd had lived in a poor section of his hometown in New England, and in that era of segregation he suffered from poor instruction. However, his athletic ability was so outstanding that Schwartzwalder recruited him as did Penn State and others. One afternoon Dean Eric Faigle came into my office. He reported that he had just had a distressing call from Andy Marchiano, one of our very loyal graduates. Andy was calling on Floyd Little when the postman brought in a letter from the Syracuse University admissions office advising the Littles that Floyd's application for admission had been turned down. Eric explained that Vice-Chancellor Piskor had opposed the admission of Little, but in this case Frank was clearly wrong. Eric told me what he knew about Floyd and when he completed his statement, I called the dean of admissions and asked him to telephone Floyd and say that a mistake had been made and that Floyd was being admitted. The next morning, Frank Piskor stormed into my office. "Stay where you are, Frank," I said, "you can't win them all. This case is closed."

Dr. Piskor was indeed wrong about Floyd Little. He is a man of character, intelligence, and ability who has endeared himself to Syracusans everywhere. In his senior year, Coach Schwartzwalder telephoned me to ask if I would talk with Floyd. He said, "Floyd Little has lost about twenty pounds, he is not himself, he needs medical attention, but he is afraid of doctors. Will you see him?" "Of course," I said. I sent for Floyd and when he came he had on a freshly pressed suit, a tie, and a white shirt.

"I want to talk to you about your future plans," I said. "After you get through pro football, what would you like to do?" "I want to be a lawyer," he said. "Fine," I replied. I sent for Mrs. Webb and dictated a letter stating that a three-year scholarship in the Syracuse University College of Law would be given to Floyd Little whenever he applied for admission. Tears came to his eyes and he said, "Dr. Tolley, I have leukemia. I have all the symptoms Ernie Davis had. I will never play pro football or go to law school."

"Floyd," I said, "the director of our health services, Dr. Robert Collins, has a heart as big as a barn door. I want you to see him." I called Dr. Collins on the telephone and said, "I have a frightened boy here. He thinks he has leukemia." "Let's find out," boomed the voice on the other end of the telephone. "Send him down!" Floyd did not want to go, but he went. As it turned out, he did have a deficiency in his red corpuscle blood count, but that was remedied by a few steak dinners. It took a little time to regain the lost weight, but before the season was over, Floyd was once again breaking tackles and making touchdowns for Bill Orange.

Joyce Green was a Syracuse undergraduate with a straight A average. She was a beautiful girl who earned $100 an hour as a model. She was also our May queen. She had not met Floyd Little, but she confided to a friend, "that is the man I am going to marry." She eventually managed to meet him. He fell in love with her and after their graduation, I attended the wedding.

Joyce came from a family that had moved into America's upper middle class. Both her father and mother had Ph.D.'s. Both were high-school principals. At the reception after the wedding, I said to Joyce's mother, "I have known Floyd Little for four years and I have great admiration for him. He is a very superior man." The temperature in the room dropped instantly. There was a chill in her voice as she said, "Chancellor Tolley, have you any idea what a superior girl Joyce Green is?" I realized then that from her point of view, Floyd was a boy from the wrong side of the tracks. The parents of Joyce are both dead, but I am sure they recognized long before they died that Floyd was indeed a superior boy. He was good enough even for the wonderful girl named Joyce Green.

Before I retired in 1969, I wanted to do all I could to protect the future of Ben Schwartzwalder. I knew I could not guarantee his tenure as a coach, but I thought I was protecting him by a contract giving him tenure as a professor of physical education and promising employment at a salary equal to that he received as head coach until he reached retirement age as a professor. I did not foresee that a successor would so reduce the budget for recruitment that Ben was no longer able to attract to Syracuse the number of blue-chip players required to maintain a football program of high quality. One does not have to try to have a poor football team. You do have to try to build a good one.

9

STUDENT UNREST IN THE SIXTIES

*I*t began in Berkeley, California, in 1964, and spread East. It was a national attempt to politicize colleges and universities. It was a decade of violent student unrest.

All around us, universities were being laid siege to by students. Syracuse University did not suffer violence until the year after I retired, 1970. There are those who would argue with my tactics during this turbulent decade. I maintained order by treating each student rebellion as I had Jim Brown's rebellion. When Jim was a student at Syracuse, he was on a work-study program. For several days before the Syracuse–Penn State game, however, Jim did not report to work. When his supervisor asked my advice, I told him to revoke Jim's food card. "He's just trying to see how far he can go," I said. Jim made up for lost time and showed up for work after that.

The antics of the students of the sixties were not so harmless, but they were, I believed, similarly motivated. In any case, I treated them the same way. I simply stuck to the rules. As a result, we had only a few minor sit-ins and student disruptions, none of which resulted in physical damage. Other universities—Brandeis, Cornell, Harvard, Columbia, the University of California at Berkeley, to name a few—did not hold firm and were not as lucky.

Because I was known as a hard-liner, we had few troubles on campus unless I was away. Our first sit-in occurred while I was in Albany persuading the legislative leaders to pass the Bundy Bill, which would provide financial support to privately endowed colleges and universities. When I put in a phone call to my secretary, Mrs. Webb, she said, "They have taken over your office."

"Who are *they?*" I asked.

"I don't think they're our students," she replied. "I believe many of them are from Cornell and some are from Colgate and Hobart."

"Tell them," I said, "that they are welcome to stay an extra half an hour if they like, but they'll have to be out by 5:30 P.M. or we'll have about fifty police escort them out."

Then I talked to my staff. They said I could not handle the situation in such a manner. They felt one could not solve problems like that by calling in the police.

I insisted. I knew that if the students stayed overnight, they would be there for a week. I reasoned that since most of the demonstrators were from Hobart, Cornell, or Colgate, they would not know their way around the campus and that it would be relatively easy to have them leave if we moved quickly.

I repeated my instructions to the staff. If they were not out by 5:30 P.M., the police should lead them out. While we might scare the students with the threat of police violence, I made it clear to my staff we did not want this. The police should be gentle, and only escort them off the premises without harming them.

Happily, we did not have to draw on police support, and the students left by 5:30 P.M. In those days, they were still just bluffing, trying to see what they could get away with.

Another time, I was not so fortunate. Every spring we had a Chancellor's Review of the ROTC units on the main quad. At the conclusion of the parade the American Legion, the Veterans of Foreign Wars, and others presented annual awards and medals to outstanding members of the ROTC. The parade and the presentation of awards to students attracted hundreds of parents, friends, and civic leaders. It was held each spring and was an important event.

In 1964, a handful of boys began disrupting the parade, weaving between the lines of marchers. We had security officers on patrol, but despite my orders they refused to stop the disturbance. When I realized that they would not take control of the situation, I took it upon myself to stop this nonsense. I had been struck by a car that year, and so I walked with a cane. I hobbled out of the reviewing stands into the parade, and as the boys came around, I told them to leave. They did not move.

"Look," I said, "I won't ask you again. Get out, or I will throw you out." They did not budge, so I took after them with my cane. A good back-handed stroke left one boy with a bruise on his arm for a few weeks. My tactics served to break up the disruption of the parade, but news photographers captured me hitting this boy with a cane, and the photos went all across America.

The next day, I sent for the boy and apologized for striking him. "A university chancellor has no right to lose his temper, and I lost mine," I said. "I am sorry. But tell me, why did you do it?"

"You must know, Dr. Tolley," he said. "We did it to get on national television. We wanted to be big shots, but you got all the publicity."

The students came to realize I was a hard-liner. We may not have had the warmest relationship during the sixties, but we never had a major uprising or disruption during my term as Chancellor. The closest we came was during Christmas break when the students held a sit-in for an extra week's vacation. David Kelso was president of the student body at that time. He was speaking on the steps of Hendricks Chapel to about two thousand students. I met with David and told him I wanted to speak. David was not happy about the idea, and said so. When he introduced me, he said I had not been invited to speak, but that I had invited myself.

I began my speech by saying I was ashamed of the student body. "We charge a high tuition," I said. "It is much higher than it should be, and you have to pay it. Apparently, however, you don't want your money's worth. Instead, you would rather throw it away and take an extra week's vacation. You are being children. I invite you to grow up."

This was not one of my more successful speeches. There was no applause. On the other hand, the demonstration came to an end, and the students went back to classes. This was as close as Syracuse came to any open division between students and the administration during my tenure.

Nevertheless, it was clear that the students had terrific power at their disposal. The Students for a Democratic Society (SDS), from its key chapter at Cornell, planned the strategy for rebellion and revolt in the early and midsixties. Then this SDS chapter moved to Brandeis University. Several of our left-wing students also transferred to Brandeis.

When a National Student Association (NSA) chapter was formed at Syracuse, I knew this could be the start of serious trouble. A new game was being played, and television held a leading role in it. A food riot at Dartmouth would be televised nationally, and within the next few weeks there would be twenty food riots. Each student body was waiting for another group to do something interesting so they could imitate it.

The students did not rely solely on the television for inspiration. They also relied on the NSA, which became a major conduit for national planning. The NSA leaders kept in touch with each other. A very small number of people escalated unrest on a massive scale. We were fortunate in having students who were friendly with the administration, and they reported plans for campus disruption to us. One of our sources told us that the NSA was planning a demonstration at New York University. The *New York Times* sent word to the leaders of the group that if they would transfer the operation to Columbia, three full-time reporters would cover it. The organizers were jubilant. Yet this hand-in-hand cooperation between the press and the student organizations has never been recognized. Nor has the power of these networks of student organizations been recognized.

From our student contacts, I knew about the Kent State and Columbia demonstrations before they happened. I never learned why Kent State was picked as the target, but the event was well planned. It began with the transfer of students from Ithaca and Syracuse to Brandeis University, which became the nerve center of the entire student revolution. Kent State was planned at Brandeis. The more I heard about the planned demonstration, the more convinced I was that there would be violence. The administrative officers of Kent State had plenty of warnings of impending trouble. A year before the event, students were transferring to Kent State to be in on the ground floor when it happened. I remember telling our trustees that the big news the next year would be Kent State. When it happened, the press portrayed the students as innocent kids and the military as the enemy. Nobody pointed a finger at the people who planned it.

While the students certainly had power, the colleges had power as well. But even before the tragedy of Kent State, the colleges were afraid to use their power. The destruction the students wrought at Columbia, for instance, could have been avoided if the administration had moved quickly and decisively. But they did not. The students moved into President Grayson Kirk's office, urinated and defecated on the furniture and rugs, and scratched the paintings. When he saw this, Dr. Kirk wept. What struck me most about President Kirk's report of these events was the audacity of the students. Before he left the scene, one of the students came up to President Kirk and told him his father knew Kirk and loved him dearly. "If he knew I were here," the boy said, "he would be sure to send his warmest regards."

The college and university presidents never recognized that they were up against a militant group that was determined to make trouble and would make trouble unless checked. I found the answer was quick, decisive action. I believe my philosophy worked. Across the nation, the situation was getting worse and worse. At Syracuse, however, nothing was getting worse except for a few members of the faculty.

About ten faculty members felt it was their duty to side with the handful of radical students. Anything the militant students suggested, these faculty members would support. They became intolerant of anybody on the opposite side, and soon they were trying to force the University Senate to pass any and all left-wing student requests.

While I was away on a fund-raising trip, this small group of faculty members succeeded in passing a motion in the Senate requiring the Chancellor, in the case of a student uprising, to do nothing without first consulting with a committee—a committee made up, of course, of these same faculty members. I met with the members of this special committee to discuss the issue.

"If we have a student uprising," I told them, "I shall want advice from the wisest people on the campus, and none of you qualify. I learned as a boy in the third grade that if you have 100 zeros and add all of them, you still have zero. When I add up all of you, the total is still zero." I could not disband the committee, but I am pleased to say it was never used.

One committee with which I met in my final years at Syracuse was promoting the establishment of coed dormitories. In my view, that sounded like a proposal to establish a new professional school for the world's oldest profession. When I told the student committee of my view, they did not think it was amusing.

As seemed always to be the case, the issue came to a head while I was away, and other members of my staff succumbed to the pressure. I was speaking to an alumni group in New Jersey when a call came in from Vice-Chancellor Frank Piskor saying the students had occupied the administration building and were demanding coeducational dorms. He advised me that he thought we had held the line as long as we could. He suggested we agree to a coeducational dorm using alternate floors and separate rest rooms.

"I think we are ready for this, Dr. Tolley," he said.

I argued with him, and then spoke to Newell Rossman. Newell told me he thought I had held out long enough. At last I agreed. This decision grieved me deeply. I felt if I could have talked to the students myself, I could have convinced them to wait and make this request of the new Chancellor. Fortunately, I retired before the change took place. I was relieved not to have had to live with it.

Looking back on that disruptive decade some twenty years later, I am amused to see that two of the students who viewed me as a relic from the nineteenth century have modified their views. David Kelso is now a partner in Goldman Sachs, one of the biggest stock exchange companies in New York City; and David Ifshin, who served as President of the National Student Association, is the lawyer who served as Walter Mondale's legal advisor during the 1984 presidential campaign.

Developments such as this make this old-fashioned guy smile. Perhaps the political radicalism of college undergraduates should be colored green rather than red. After testing the water of the mainstream, these students decided they liked it fine.

Having said this, let me make it clear that I am not indifferent to the great danger through which American higher education passed. For a time, a handful of students and faculty held a dagger at the throat of the most precious of our freedoms. It was a close call, much too close for comfort.

10

COLLECTING RARE BOOKS

My interest in books grew deeply during my undergraduate years at Syracuse, but the collecting of books had its birth at Drew and Allegheny. When I became Allegheny's President, Dr. Tipple gave the main address at my inauguration. Later, when we had some time alone, he told me, "As a college president you should have a good private library. I have thousands of books. I don't know what to do with them. Can you find room for some of them?"

"Yes," I said, "our garage has a second floor that will take all the books you send me." We lined the second floor of the garage from floor to ceiling with bookcases, and filled them all with the books he sent. I marvel now that the garage stood the weight of the books. There must have been three thousand of them in that small space. Many were sermons but the collection was varied. It was particularly rich in biographies, English history and literature, Greek and Roman history, theology, and Judaic literature and history. I gave many of them to Allegheny College before moving to Syracuse in 1942. After I retired from Syracuse in 1969, I was given an office next to the recreational library that I had established in Brockway Hall. I put about one thousand of Dr. Tipple's books in that library.

I began my career at Allegheny in 1930 with a salary of $8,000, part of which I sent to my parents to help support them. Consequently, I began building my personal library by buying only secondhand books that cost anywhere from one to five dollars. Whenever I was in New York, I spent my spare time browsing in secondhand book shops.

I could not afford to build a collection of rare books until after I came to Syracuse. Nevertheless, I developed a strong interest in them while I was at Allegheny. There I established a rare-book room in Reis Library, which has since been replaced by the Pellatier Library.

My first experience with an important collection of rare books was in Titusville, Pennsylvania, during the midthirties. At that time, I was paying a visit to a friend of the journalist Ida Minerva Tarbell, John Hillsdale Scheide. Ida Tarbell's father had been one of the early oil pioneers but had been ruined by Standard Oil and John D. Rockefeller. Ida made her reputation as a journalist by writing a blistering attack on Standard Oil and Mr. Rockefeller, whose monopoly of the oil business had ruined a great many people besides her father.

The Scheide family was one of the important oil families of Pennsylvania. John H. Scheide, Sr., had been a close friend of Ida's father, and Ida and his son also became friends. One day she came to tell me that John H. Scheide, Jr., was willing to pay for the writing of a history of the oil industry of western Pennsylvania and would like her to write it. She said she was far too busy to do it, and she asked whether I thought anyone on the Allegheny faculty might be willing to take on the project. I immediately nominated Paul Henry Giddens, professor of history, as a good prospect for the project, and Ida arranged for us to pay Mr. Scheide, Jr., a visit.

Our meeting not only led to a fine volume by Dr. Giddens but also to a three-hour tour of the magnificent Scheide Library housed in a modern library building adjoining his home. It was an afternoon I shall not forget; indeed, it was a turning point in my life.

I learned that Mr. Scheide had had no interest in books, much less rare books, when he was an undergraduate at Princeton. One day, on a visit to New York, he was caught in a rainstorm while strolling down Madison Avenue. Having no coat or umbrella, John sought refuge in a small shop which turned out to be a bookstore. Almost immediately a clerk approached him and said, "What books do you collect?" John was embarrassed to admit that he didn't collect any. He looked around frantically at the stacks, but had not a glimmer of how to reply. Stalling for time to gather his wits, he said, "What did you ask me?"

"I said," replied the clerk, "what books do you collect?"

"Oh," said John, "I collect Bibles."

"Well," the man said, "I just happen to have a Breeches Bible here."

Breeches Bibles were not terribly expensive. The clerk quoted John a price of $300 to $400. John said he would think about it and let the clerk know his decision in the morning. Once in his hotel room, he decided that he should collect something, and it may as well be Bibles. He returned to the store the next day and made the Breeches Bible his first rare-book purchase. Thereafter he kept buying until he eventually acquired a Gutenberg Bible.

John's father had had a distinguished library, and John continued adding to it each year as long as he lived. Ultimately, he gave the entire John Hillsdale Scheide library to Princeton, where it is one of their crown jewels.

In my visit to the Scheide Library, Mr. Scheide let me hold and examine the Gutenberg Bible. It was the first I had ever seen, and it was beautiful. There, too, were hundreds of papal bulls, completely intact with seals and signatures. It is said to be the largest collection outside of the Vatican Library. Another of his treasures was a complete manuscript of a Wagnerian opera. There were manuscripts, letters, and first editions by the thousands. When the day was over I walked out of the library on air. I didn't need any automobile to get home. I was drunk with ecstasy and excitement.

On my way home, I told myself, "I will never be able to have a great library, but from now on I will do all that I can to collect rare books." What I had seen in Titusville was far beyond my reach. Nevertheless, I vowed that some time I would have a modest collection of rare books on my own. Because of my limited means, however, I had to wait until the midforties to begin.

At Syracuse, I began collecting first editions of William James, George Santayana, Bertrand Russell, Francis Bacon, Thomas Hobbes, John Locke, George Berkeley, David Hume, Johann Gottlieb Fichte, Immanuel Kant, and Georg W. F. Hegel, all of whom were favorite philosophers of mine. Some of the early editions of Bacon and the mint copy of the *Leviathan* by Hobbes are among the most important rare books at Syracuse University today.

In the field of poetry I collected Alfred Lord Tennyson, Robert Browning, Stephen Vincent Benet, Rupert Brooks, Edna St. Vincent Millay, Edwin Arlington Robinson, Walt Whitman, T. S. Eliot, and James Whitcomb Riley among others.

As Dean of Drew University, I had once offered a professorship to Robert Frost. At Allegheny College he was a frequent visitor, sometimes coming for a week or more. At Allegheny, a young chemist named Martin Howe had an excellent Frost collection, and at Syracuse Frank Piskor was building one of the half-dozen best Frost collections. While I collected a good deal of Frost, I did it for my personal pleasure, not to compete with Martin Howe or Frank Piskor.

I also collected college histories. When I came to Syracuse and found that Dr. Piskor was also collecting histories of American colleges, I gave him all of mine, and then I concentrated on histories of colleges and universities outside of America. This led me to learn all I could of the history of higher education from Isocrates to Socrates, from Plato and Aristotle, to the medieval universities of Bologna, Salerno, Paris, Oxford, and Cambridge, and the modern universities of the late nineteenth century in Germany, France, and the British Isles.

Most people discover Lewis Carroll, A. A. Milne, Rudyard Kipling, and other authors of children's books during childhood. I had not read them as a boy, however, and did not discover them until my forties. I found special pleasure in reading and collecting first editions of these authors and sharing them with my children.

My bank balance was kept precariously low by the purchase of first editions of Stephen Crane, George Bernard Shaw, Robert Louis Stevenson, Joseph Conrad, Henry James, Henry Adams, George Ade, Arthur Conan Doyle, Thomas Hardy, J. M. Barrie, George Gissing, Sinclair Lewis, Aldous Huxley, Woodrow Wilson, William Dean Howells, Francis Bret Harte, and others. I also have a number of early editions of Martianus Capella, Macrobius, Boethius, Cassiodorus, Isidore of Seville, Calcidius, and Apuleius.

My collection owes much to the interest and help of James Drake, perhaps the foremost rare-book dealer in New York, and his brother, Colonel Marston Drake. I met Jim Drake through George Arents in the early fifties, and he soon became my close friend and mentor.

From Jim and Marston I was able to acquire a leaf from the Gutenberg Bible with the Twenty-third Psalm, the first printed copy of Lincoln's Gettysburg Address, the first printed copy of Churchill's speech calling for "blood, sweat and tears," and dozens of rare books from Colonel Drake's personal Kipling collection.

It was Marston Drake who persuaded me to collect Kipling for myself. "For the moment he is out of style," he told me in the early fifties. "I have no doubt, however, that he will be rediscovered. He is a fine poet, he is close to the level of Fitzgerald as a letter writer, and he is the greatest of the English writers of short stories. If you buy him now, you can build a Kipling collection that only the very rich will be able to afford fifty years from now." This was sound advice, and I followed it. Today, Kipling letters that I acquired for $10 to $25 are now worth from $300 to $1,000 or more.

Collecting Kipling has been a major interest for some thirty years. I remember an afternoon in a bookstore in Cambridge with Pete and Annabelle Terhune. There were more than fifty first editions of Kipling all for sale at a song. I bought all of them.

In the years since I first began my Kipling collection, I have given the Arents Library more than six hundred first editions of Kipling, and more than six hundred of his letters. It includes Kipling's mother's copy of *Echoes,* his first book, with a handwritten poem as a dedication. The collection also contains fine copies of all of Kipling's rare early editions, including *Quartet, Schoolboy Lyrics, Plain Tales from the Hills, The Jungle Book,* and the *Just So Stories for Little Children.* In addition, I acquired some sixty-six letters from Kipling to his dear friend and neighbor, Sir Henry Fielden, as well as letters from Kipling to Edward Bok, a former editor of the *Ladies Home Journal* and the *Saturday Evening Post.*

The University collection includes gifts from H. Dunscomb Colt and George Arents. In 1981 at a Christie's auction in New

York, we obtained a manuscript of an unpublished chapter of Kipling's *War in the Mountains,* which had been kept from the book out of consideration for Italian sensibilities.

Over the years I developed regular dealings with many rare-book dealers, all of whom were helpful in my search for rare books. One book dealer whom I met during one of my annual vacations abroad stands out in my memory. On this particular trip I visited a book shop in Hastings, England, for the first time.

When I entered the store, the bookshop owner looked at me keenly and said, "Aren't you Tolley of Syracuse?" When I said I was, he told me he had recently come down from Maggs Brothers in London where he had known me and that on the second floor he had put away dozens of histories of European universities and a number of Kipling items that he felt I might want. He said, "I planned to write you to see if you wanted them." After selecting a fine copy of Gilbert Chesterton's letters to his son, and a fourth folio edition of Shakespeare, I said I would be happy to have the other books he had found for me, but I did not have the means to purchase them immediately. I would gladly send him a check sometime before Christmas, and he could ship them to me then.

"No, Dr. Tolley," he said, "pay for them when you can, but we shall send them off at once." How characteristic this is of British book dealers and their trust of bibliophiles! Book collecting is a special world in which everyone is on his or her honor as a gentleman or gentlewoman.

My interest in rare books had first been sparked by my meeting with John Scheide, but in the course of my life I met two other book collectors who were most helpful: George Arents and Adrian VanSinderen. George Arents was vice-chairman of the Syracuse Board of Trustees when I came to Syracuse. Later he served as chairman. Adrian VanSinderen was President of the Brooklyn Savings Bank. He was a loyal graduate of Yale who served as a Director of the New York Telephone Company. I first met him when I became a Director of that company in 1943. We soon discovered we had similar interests and developed a lifelong friendship.

One day, Mr. VanSinderen invited me to his estate in Washington, Connecticut. There, I had yet another learning experience with rare books. Adrian VanSinderen's father-in-law, W. A. White, had been an outstanding bibliophile. The Bay Psalm Book, now in the Library of Congress, and the world's best collection of William Blake, were among the treasures of his collection, which he bequeathed to Adrian. His trust in his son-in-law was well placed. An avid collector himself, Adrian built an addition to his home where his books were shelved in an air-conditioned, fireproof building.

It was Adrian who convinced me that by forming the Syracuse University Library Associates we could greatly increase interest in and financial support for the University's rare-book collection. For years, George Arents had pushed me to form such an organization. Now that Adrian also suggested it, I agreed. Adrian became the first chairman of the Syracuse University Library Associates.

Both Mr. VanSinderen and Mr. Arents made outstanding additions to the library's collection of rare books. Adrian's first gift to the University was a collection of first editions of all of Mark Twain's work but without the first editions of *Huckleberry Finn* and *Tom Sawyer*. I remember the pleasure and pride I had in presenting these two books to the VanSinderen collection.

Mr. Arents saw to it that we had a place to house our rare books. He agreed to give us a rare-book room named for his wife Lena Richardson Arents. At the time Syracuse's rare books were scattered throughout the stacks of Carnegie Library. Some were deteriorating on the top floor of Carnegie, where they were stored in a dry and hot room without air-conditioning. The invaluable collection of books and papers of the great historian Leopold von Ranke was stored there, as were other treasures. Until I arrived, no one at Syracuse had paid much attention to rare books.

When I told our librarian, Wharton Miller, that Mr. Arents would give us a rare-book room, he said "I don't want a rare book room. It's a distraction. It costs a lot of money, and it's only of interest to a handful of scholars. I have no interest in it."

I said, "You're going to get it whether you want it or not." He fought us every step of the way. Fortunately, he was not the Chancellor of the University.

The Lena Richardson Arents Rare Book Room was small but quite handsome. It was located on the second floor of the Carnegie Library. The space which we renovated to create the rare-book room had been previously used to store magazines. In renovating this area, we created a beautiful reading room, and several rooms for stacks. Once the rooms were completed, we moved such treasures as the von Ranke collection into it. We also found room for the personal papers of Governor W. Averell Harriman.

We commissioned Lester Wells, who had gone to library school after retirement from a career with Oneida Limited, to become curator of our rare books holdings. Wells was a delightful surprise as a rare-book librarian. He loved his work, and he was full of good ideas.

The Bird Library was built in the years following my retirement. Syracuse's rare books are now housed in the George Arents Research Library on the sixth floor of Bird, which was built and dedicated to George Arents after his death.

With Jim and Marston Drake gone, I have had to find new rare-book dealers. Here too I have been fortunate. David J. Holmes of Philadelphia has been the wisest of counselors and the most trustworthy of friends. The Kipling collection owes much to his knowledge and wisdom. I owe much also to my dear friend and trustee Joseph I. Lubin, who set up a book fund in my name when I retired and came to my rescue several times to help pay bills for rare books which were beyond my reach.

I have given almost all of my books to the University and the balance will go after my death. Syracuse is where my love for books was born. The University has been my life. I want it to be as strong and as great as possible. A great university must have a great library. My modest contribution is a step in that direction.

11

FRIENDS AND CELEBRITIES

One of the benefits of being a university chancellor is the opportunity it affords to meet interesting and influential people. One's best friends are other college presidents. I knew all the presidents of Pennsylvania colleges while I was at Allegheny and all the presidents of New York State colleges while at Syracuse. I also knew the influential university presidents in the Far West, the South, the Midwest, and New England. The four university presidents with the greatest influence in my time were James Bryant Conant of Harvard, Henry Merritt Wriston of Brown, Robert Maynard Hutchins of Chicago, and Edmund Ezra Day of Cornell. I knew all of them well. Conant made a special trip to Florida to try to persuade me to take the chairmanship of the American Council on Education. Hutchins was my opponent in a well-publicized debate on the merits of a two-year bachelor of arts degree. Wriston and Day were among the closest friends I had.

In the years I spent at Syracuse, I had the honor of meeting General MacArthur, Emperor Hirohito, President Truman, Mrs. Roosevelt, Dwight Eisenhower, John Kennedy, Lyndon Johnson, Richard Nixon, and many others.

After the conclusion of World War II, no exchange of faculty or students between Japan and the United States was permitted by the Supreme Commander Allied Powers (SCAP), which ruled Japan under the leadership of General Douglas MacArthur. The United States Department of State appointed me one of five American educators to visit Tokyo to see if this rule could be changed.

When we arrived in General MacArthur's office, he asked why we were there. "The war is over," I said. "Nothing would advance peace more rapidly than an exchange of faculty and students between Japan and America. That, unfortunately, is now forbidden by SCAP."

General MacArthur answered quickly. "I was unaware that the doors are still closed," he said. "There are fools in every organization, and we must have more than our share. Of course there should be an exchange of students and faculty. How many do you suggest?"

"Why have any quota?" I said, "Why not open wide the doors?"

"That makes sense to me," he said. Thus, the business that brought us to Tokyo was completed in less than two minutes.

MacArthur insisted that we go to his house for luncheon. It proved to be a memorable experience. The luncheon table was the most magnificent I have ever seen. Each piece of silver on the table was superbly sculptured. The sugar bowls, coffee creamers, salt and pepper containers, and candelabra formed a caravan of silver animals traveling across the table. It was a museum. We were all feasting our eyes on it. The luncheon, too, was remarkable. It was a feast, with one wonderful course after another, each complemented with a vintage wine.

Mrs. MacArthur, much younger than her husband, was a magnificent hostess. She interrogated everyone at the table and kept each of us in the conversations that ensued from her questioning. She made us feel that she wanted to learn everything she could about our views on problems in higher education. General MacArthur permitted his wife to direct the conversation, but when he did speak, he put us all under his spell. I could not escape the feeling that I was in the presence of perhaps the greatest man I would ever meet. He was exactly what one would expect him to be—magnificent, magnetic, with tremendous charisma. He had everybody at the table eating out of his hand.

Before we left MacArthur's home, he asked us if we would like to meet Emperor Hirohito. "Of course," I said. The next morning a car escorted us to the Emperor's palace. We were immediately briefed by a member of the Emperor's staff on how to behave toward Emperor Hirohito, whom he called the Son of Heaven.

"The Son of Heaven can speak English," he said, "but you will speak in English, he will speak in Japanese, and there will be an interpreter. You must never turn your back on the Son of Heaven. When you leave the room, you must stand and back out. If he should leave the room, you stand, and he will turn his back and walk out."

Six assistants talked to us, one after the other, in ascending order of importance. Each gave exactly the same instructions. Finally, we met the senior secretary who, after giving us these same instructions, ushered us into Emperor Hirohito's office. We stood at attention as he announced, "The Son of Heaven will enter in exactly ten seconds." I silently counted down. At the stroke of zero, the Son of Heaven entered. He was resplendently dressed in a white linen suit, a white shirt, a white tie, a white vest, white trousers, white long underwear, which showed through his white socks, and his fly completely unbuttoned. The Son of Heaven was human!

He was a very nervous man who continually rotated his thumbs. In the course of our interview, he turned to me and said, "Chancellor Tolley, I'm so pleased to meet a Chancellor of an American university. You see, I want to send my oldest son to a university to be educated. Where should I send him?"

"I'm very happy," I said, "you asked that question. I've been authorized by the President of the United States to invite you to send your son to Harvard. That's our premier university. We think he would be very happy there. They would open all the doors for him. It would be a great experience for him, but we would no doubt get even more reward from the experience than he would."

"I have to be honest with you," the Emperor said. "My advisors will probably send him to Oxford. But I wanted your advice on where he should go should he go to the United States." Emperor Hirohito's son did indeed go to Oxford.

Emperor Hirohito was a very modest man. In the course of our meeting him it became evident that he was miscast as a ruler. A fine human being and a bright scholar, he was well trained in science. A gentle, unselfish person, he was not comfortable dealing with people, and was clearly unhappy in his role as Emperor.

He was, though, most gracious to us. "I'm so pleased to deal with scholars," he said, "How much time can you spend with me?"

We told him we could spend as much time as he would wish.

"I want to show you my laboratory first, and then my stables of horses."

Emperor Hirohito spent most of the day with us. We saw him at work in his laboratory. He was a great botanist and zoologist, and he had a fabulous collection of specimens. Although he was assisted by numerous helpers, he knew what he was talking about. As he expounded on his laboratory research, he surprised us by speaking English. After showing us his laboratory, he excused himself, saying he was tired. He wished us to see his carriages, horses, and stables, however, and turned us over to an assistant who spoke perfect English and who acted as our guide.

I have never seen such elaborate carriages. Many were very old, and elaborately carved and encrusted in gold leaf. They were magnificent. We gazed at them with our mouths open. The riding and carriage horses were also most impressive. I have seen some of the best stables in America, but never such horses as these. When we got home that night, I was walking on air. I thought, "I will never again have a day like this."

Because we were to be in Japan for two weeks, the Ministry of Education arranged for us to visit most of the major universities of Japan. First on our itinerary was the University of Tokyo, the Harvard of Japanese universities. When Japan opened its doors to the West, it borrowed the best that each of the Western nations had to offer. At that time Japan believed that Germany was the great leader in education. Consequently, all of its universities followed the German model. Many courses were actually taught in German. Among its library holdings, Tokyo University had 200,000 German books, many of which were rare and beautiful editions. As higher education continued to evolve, the Japanese began to feel that the German models were outmoded, and that British universities were the best. Oxford then became their model.

Our tour of Japanese universities included trips to the Kyoto University, Doshisha University, and the Japan International Christian University (JICU).

I had helped to organize and was a trustee of JICU, which was funded by many American Protestant denominations, including Methodists, Presbyterians, and Episcopalians, as a gesture of expiation for dropping the atomic bomb. Today, I am still an officer on the board and have received an honorary degree from JICU. In introducing the American idea of liberal education, JICU has made a unique contribution to Japanese education, which is predominantly technical, scientific, and vocational. Previous to the formation of JICU, there was no word in the Japanese language for liberal education. Located on a beautiful campus at Mitaka, just outside of Tokyo, JICU has proved to be an important success story. While its influence does not match that of the University of Tokyo, it has been an important bridge of understanding and influence between East and West.

During my visit to Japan, I was struck by the regimentation of its society. The Ministry of Education, for instance, still made all the decisions for its universities. The Ministry was consulted even about minor matters. This respect for hierarchy was seen wherever we went. People entered and left rooms according to their rank. Everyone knew his or her place in society. If you ranked fourth, you would be the fourth person to leave or enter a room. The women did not walk with their husbands. They walked behind them. Children did not talk back to their parents.

General MacArthur attempted to change this. One Japanese host told me that MacArthur was so well known for his support of women's liberation that when a neighbor of his once quarreled with her husband she said, "If you don't mend your ways, I shall tell General MacArthur about you." MacArthur's reign in Japan opened doors for Japan and for women in particular. Today, he is still venerated as a great leader and friend of Japan.

A few years after my visit to Japan, Syracuse University awarded an honorary degree to Admiral Chester William Nimitz, who had commanded the U.S. Pacific Fleet during World War II. In the course of his visit, Nimitz told me of his meeting with MacArthur on the USS *Missouri* during the time when they were conducting peace negotiations with Japan. Nimitz and MacArthur were drinking perhaps a bit more than they should. As the evening progressed, Nimitz found himself in a confessional mood. "You know," he confided to MacArthur, "I have been in the navy almost forty years and I cannot swim." To his surprise and delight, MacArthur replied, "Since we are in the mood to make confessions, let me confess that despite what the *New York Times* says, I cannot walk upon the water."

I first met S. I. Newhouse by accident, while attending a dinner at the Waldorf Astoria. Upon approaching the place assigned to me at the table, I found a man already seated there. I did not speak to him, but instead moved off into the crowd to ask who this gentleman might be. I learned he was Samuel Irving Newhouse, the newspaper publisher. I then went to the table to which he had been assigned and sat at his place. During the first course, I went to him and said, "Chancellor Tolley, I am Sam Newhouse. I own newspapers, and I've always wanted to meet a real live chancellor."

He looked up at me in shock and surprise. I looked down at the table and picked up the place card which said, "Chancellor William P. Tolley," and I handed it to him.

"My God," he said, "did I do that?"

"Yes, you did," I said, "and to my great pleasure I'm masquerading as S. I. Newhouse tonight. I'm proud of that fact." We were friends from that moment.

Sam died in 1979. As I look back on what made him the great man he was, I must say it was his exceptional mind and his unflagging willingness to work. He rose every day at five o'clock and was at work by six o'clock. When he was not attending night school, he was working evenings until ten o'clock at night, or later. His vocation was his avocation.

Sam's genius was in bringing sick newspapers back to financial health and strengthening newspapers that were already strong. He owned newspapers across the country. Despite his great success, S. I. Newhouse was a man of simple means and few words. His personal wants were minimal, his life uncluttered. He had no need or desire for the trappings of power. Not for him was the world of ocean-going yachts, jet planes, marble mansions on the Riviera, or vast estates like those of the Vanderbilts, Rockefellers, and William Randolph Hearst.

Erasmus, the great scholar and humanist, was offered a cardinal's post when he was an old man, but declined with thanks, saying "too much baggage *(impedimenta)* at the end of the journey." Sam was like Erasmus, but for him it was a lifelong policy. He was never owned by his possessions, nor kept in ignorance by too large a staff.

Sam trusted his editors and gave them great freedom. He was not interested in imposing his ideas on the newspapers he owned. He believed newspapers should serve the communities in which they were located, and not follow the social or political slant of a faraway owner. His editors had total freedom. They knew their communities; they should have the right to speak freely.

Another of Sam's policies was not to fire anybody. He kept the staff of the newspapers he purchased no matter how badly they had been doing. By building up advertising and circulation and keeping an eye on costs, a newspaper would thrive under his watchful eye.

Sam carried a little black book with him, with all the salient figures on all the newspapers he had not yet bought but was looking at. He had his eyes on the *Times-Picayune* in New Orleans for a decade before he bought it, and when he did, it was for $43 million. I remarked to him that that was a fancy price, and he said simply, "Yes, but I knew what I could do with it."

Successful as he was in business, Sam was remarkably shy and reclusive. I used to tell Ruth that I thought I could remember every sentence I ever said to Sam, and every sentence he ever said to me. These exchanges would barely fill seven pages.

Sam and his family would come up during football season and sit in our box with us. They were among the happiest hours he had all year long. His children would come with him, and while you could sit next to him for hours and barely get thirty words out of him, you could see he was enjoying himself and that he knew the fine points of the game.

To understand this quiet man, one had to know that his world centered around his family. He had started out in life in the kind of poverty we seldom see today, becoming head of the household and the chief means of support at the age of thirteen. His father's business had failed when Sam was twelve, and soon his father's health failed as well. His wonderful mother, Rose, put bread on the table by rising early each morning to travel to New York City from their home in Bayonne, New Jersey, to buy sheets, towels, pillow cases, and napkins, and then return to Bayonne to peddle them door to door, carrying this heavy load across her shoulders.

As the oldest of eight children, Sam knew he had to help. The summer he graduated from eighth grade he took a six-week course in typing, shorthand, and bookkeeping at the Gaffrey School in New York, on Eighth Avenue and Twenty-third Street. Then this tiny thirteen-year-old boy set out looking for a job. Given his youth and size, this was a difficult task. He managed to find work with Judge Hyman Lazarus in Bayonne by promising to work without wages until he could prove himself as an office boy. He had landed the job that would make him a millionaire several times over. In addition to his law practice, Judge Lazarus also owned the ailing *Bayonne Times*. At the age of fourteen, Sam was the bookkeeper and indispensable aid to the Judge. By the age of sixteen, he was office manager of the law firm and was also looking after the paper. By then, his salary was $75 a week, and he had accomplished his goal of lifting his family out of poverty.

It took less than a year for young Sam Newhouse to put the *Bayonne Times* in black instead of red ink. Soon, he had a 20-percent interest in the net income. It later became 50-percent interest, and by the time he was in his twenties, Sam Newhouse owned two papers—the *Bayonne Times* and the *Staten Island Advance*. His Horatio Alger rise was already there for all to see.

Unlike most successful men, Sam had begun his career not with riches in mind but with the simple goal of helping his family. He did not seek untold wealth and all it could buy. He simply wanted to keep the family unit together. As a boy, he was the father as well as the brother of Louis, Norman, Theodore, Ada, Naomi, Gertrude, and Estelle. As an adult, he married the incomparable Mitzi, who complemented him in so many important ways. In addition to giving him two remarkable sons, she made him at home in the new and larger worlds of arts and letters. She was the perfect wife and mother, whom he adored from the first time they met.

Mitzi protected Sam. I liked her tremendously, but she was scared to death that I would take too much money from Sam. As anyone familiar with Syracuse University and its outstanding S. I. Newhouse School of Public Communications knows, I did ask Sam for money, and he gave it.

Sam did not just give financially to Syracuse. He also gave of himself. He became a trustee, and soon Ruth and I had the opportunity to get to know his sons, Donald and S. I. They enjoyed sitting and talking with us, although S. I., junior, is more of an extrovert than his brother, Donald. Donald is like his father; he has a brilliant mind but wastes few words.

Both boys attended Syracuse, but after three years of college they decided they wanted to leave to go into business.

"Okay," Sam told his sons, "I think it's a mistake and that you'll live to regret it. But if that's what you want to do, come work for me." Both did.

Donald has since told me that he would give his right arm if he had finished his undergraduate degree, and his brother S. I. (pron. Si), a nationally known art collector, feels the same way.

Sam himself placed a high value on a university education. When he was initiated into Zeta Beta Tau, the thrill of belonging to a college fraternity and being one of the boys was priceless to him. He was also enormously proud of his honorary degree from Syracuse.

We at Syracuse are proud to have had his support and interest in us. We are deeply grateful to Sam and Mitzi for their great generosity to Syracuse University. We thank them equally for lending their name to our School of Communications.

I am certain that all who knew of Sam and his accomplishments will remember the message of his life. It is that America is still the land of unlimited opportunity; all things are possible.

Harry S Truman had retired from the presidency when I first met him. He and Mrs. Truman and their daughter, Margaret, were in town visiting the Syracuse chapter of Margaret's sorority, Pi Beta Phi. Margaret was a most attractive person with a personality that fairly bubbled over. Mrs. Truman was a reserved, motherly woman. Together with Harry Truman, they made a most attractive trio.

I gave a dinner in Truman's honor at the Century Club, a private men's club in Syracuse. Virtually everyone attending the dinner but Truman himself and Frank Dolan, a leading attorney and Syracuse trustee, was a Republican. William L. Hinds, President of the Crouse Hinds Company, sat at Truman's right side. Although Hinds was "Mr. Republican" of Onondaga County, the two of them got along famously.

After dinner, I asked Truman whether he would be willing to speak and then answer questions. He said, "Let's begin with questions," and so we did. They were wide-ranging, including concerns about foreign policy, congressional relations, and even Missouri politics. Truman had a remarkable memory. A lifelong student of American history, he could recall almost everything he had ever read. It is characteristic of America that we never forgot that he was a failed haberdasher. One frequently heard the comment, "you can walk down Main Street and meet ten people as well qualified to be President as Harry Truman." These people overlooked the fact that he had been a tremendously successful political leader in Missouri, and that he achieved success without compromising his standards or his character. These qualities led him to become a most distinguished U.S. senator.

It was difficult to bring the evening to an end at the Century Club, but at last we did so. By that time, Truman had won the hearts and minds of everyone there. It was the performance of a champion. Everyone felt not only his charm and charisma, but the strength of his mind and the breadth of his knowledge and experience. No one of us disagreed with anything Harry Truman said that night. Each left saying, "He would have my vote if he were running for President again." It was a complete conquest. Harry Truman, lifelong Democrat, won the hearts and minds of the Republicans of Syracuse and Onondaga County.

One of my happiest encounters with America's leaders came when Eleanor Roosevelt visited Syracuse. Some students told me they wished to invite her to come to the campus and that they would like me to extend the invitation.

"No," I told them, "You should write her directly. She'll say yes to any student request. Just indicate that you're president or secretary of a campus organization, and I think she'll accept your invitation."

I must admit I did not say this out of any great faith in Eleanor Roosevelt's humility and warmth. On the contrary, I thought her to be unnecessarily bossy and news-seeking. If she came, I reasoned, it would be simply to add to the publicity which I felt she sought constantly.

My distrust of her was unfounded. Not only did Mrs. Roosevelt graciously accept the students' invitation, she agreed to a schedule which was so full that I lost track of the number of speeches she made. She did have a free period, however, from one-thirty to three-thirty in the afternoon, and we brought her to 701 Walnut, the Chancellor's residence, and took her into the library.

"Mrs. Roosevelt," I said, "I don't know how you manage to keep up with this schedule, but the students are ecstatic. No one who has come here has made the kind of impression that you have made. But you must be tired, so please take advantage of our guest room upstairs and take a nap." Eleanor Roosevelt was near her sixties then, but she said, "Chancellor Tolley, I have never taken a nap in my life. I am a hyperactive person and am happiest when I'm working with students. They renew my strength. I am not tired. I'm as fresh as a daisy. You'll have to sit here and talk with me."

By then I had been charmed by her, and Ruth and I were delighted at the opportunity to visit. While we were talking our daughter Katryn rose from her nap and came into the room rubbing her eyes. She looked at Mrs. Roosevelt, then at her mother, and then at me. To our surprise she went directly to Mrs. Roosevelt and climbed up on her lap. She stayed there until Mrs. Roosevelt had to leave at three o'clock.

Mrs. Roosevelt had a magnificent way with children, and they felt this instinctively. When Mrs. Roosevelt got up to leave, she kissed Katryn and talked to her very sweetly. But she needn't have said a word. She was the same way with the students. She was simply there.

I came to know Eleanor Roosevelt better after we served on the same panel in the annual *Herald-Tribune* forum in New York City. We were each supposed to speak for twelve minutes. She came in at the last second and spoke to the man in charge, asking how long he wished her to speak.

"Twelve minutes," he said. "No more, no less."

"Fine," she answered, "after eleven minutes, forty-five seconds, raise your hand and I'll know I have fifteen seconds."

She spoke without a note to guide her, and her speech was beautifully organized. When the chairman raised his hand at the appointed time, she found just the right sentence with which to close. It was a masterpiece of public speaking, made even more so by the fact of its being televised live. She was one of the most outstanding women of her time.

I was also pleasantly surprised by the qualities I discovered in Dwight D. Eisenhower. I met President Eisenhower at the White House when I presented him with the George Washington Carver Award. When we were introduced, I found him as relaxed as an old shoe.

"Before I receive the award," he said to me, "let's talk about Syracuse football. I was present at West Point when Ribs [Reeves] Baysinger brought his team from Syracuse to play the army, and I want you to know, Chancellor Tolley, that West Point stole the game. The referees were completely wrong. I'm glad to have the opportunity to apologize and set the record straight."

Naturally, I thanked him for his concern, but he did not stop there. He must have talked about S.U. football for at least ten minutes. He mentioned Larry Csonka, Floyd Little, Jim Brown, John Mackey, and Ernie Davis, who was known as "The Elmira Express." When we left him, he said, "I've always admired Syracuse football, and I always will."

I admired President Eisenhower. I had no illusions, however, about his intellectual interests or his understanding of higher education. After he resigned from the presidency of Columbia, he called the President-elect, Grayson Kirk, to tell him he would like to give Columbia his personal library. Naturally, Kirk was delighted. He immediately went to examine the contents of the library, which was in the President's residence. First, he checked the first floor, then the second, then the third, and then the fourth—and last—floor. There he found Eisenhower's library which turned out to be a collection of between five to ten hundred Westerns.

In 1956, I had the pleasure of meeting John F. Kennedy when he came to Syracuse to give the commencement address. At that time he was still a junior senator from Massachusetts. We had a luncheon in his honor at the Hotel Syracuse, which was attended by some two hundred people. Before the luncheon began, I took him aside and said, "I am sure there will be questions. Would you be willing to answer them?"

"Chancellor Tolley," he said, "I can't speak extemporaneously, and so I'd rather not answer any questions. I know that one day I'll have to learn to do so, but as yet I'm not prepared to do so."

I could hardly believe that this handsome young man could be intimidated by this aspect of public speaking. When I went to a bank meeting the following week, I was asked what I thought of Senator Kennedy. I said I thought he would make a fine assistant professor. He was then a far cry from a charismatic leader who was perfectly at ease in fielding questions.

After this young President's untimely death, I had the privilege of meeting his successor, Lyndon Baines Johnson. Here, again, I could hardly believe what went on that day. The impression President Johnson made, however, was far less favorable than that made by Kennedy.

President Johnson came to Syracuse in 1964 to dedicate the Newhouse Communications Center. This was the first opportunity I had to entertain a U.S. President, and I had not realized how tight security would be. The Secret Service posted guards on the rooftops and everywhere else.

Sam Newhouse and I met the President at the airport, and we all rode back together. I sat in the front with one of the Secret Service men, while Sam and the President sat in the back. This was the day that LBJ would make the historic Gulf of Tonkin speech which would launch us into the Vietnam War.

"Sam," Johnson said, "you know why I'm here, don't you?" Then he came right to the point. "I need the support of the *Times-Picayune* in the next election."

Newhouse said there was no problem in New Orleans. But then the President said, "I also need to have the support of the *Oregonian,* of both the St. Louis papers, and both the Syracuse papers. Indeed, of all your papers."

Newhouse protested that he did not influence the editorial policy of any of his papers. LBJ just looked at him, and said, "Why did you think I came to dedicate the Newhouse Communications Center today?"

I could hardly believe my ears. At last Sam named some of the papers he knew favored the Democratic party. This did not satisfy Johnson.

"Look," LBJ replied, "I want all of them." Sam really began to sweat, because he did not want to call any of his editors and say, "Look, I've got to break my rule. You've got to do this for me."

At last he said, "I'll tell you what we can do, Mr. President. I'll see if we can't give you a little help with the way the headlines are written."

When we arrived on campus, Sam had had enough. I accompanied Johnson to the airport after the ceremony, but Sam did not. He had had one arm broken and was not about to have the other one broken as well.

A presidential candidate who would never have even considered such tactics, had he become president, was Adlai Stevenson. He was a gentleman in the truest sense of the word. He was also a superb orator. What set him apart from others, and especially from men like LBJ, was his unaffected humility.

I had invited him to give the Commencement address and to receive an honorary degree. After the ceremony we had a warm and informal luncheon celebration with all the guests, retired faculty, and their spouses. Everyone who had been given an honorary degree spoke, and when it was Adlai Stevenson's turn, we could see that he was dead tired. As he gathered himself for the task, he said, "Ladies and gentlemen, I can hardly wait to hear what I'm going to say." Then he held us in the hollow of his hand.

One President whom I admired was one who was the least popular of all—Richard Milhous Nixon. I had heard him speak on many occasions and had met him often. He came to Syracuse several times while I was Chancellor, and I had a good visit with him and with Mrs. Nixon each time.

In 1969, my final year at Syracuse, I knew we would be celebrating our one hundredth anniversary the next year, and so I wrote to President Nixon and invited him to be the anniversary Commencement speaker. He accepted the invitation, and I was delighted. In the spring of 1970, the student leaders said that they felt a sense of outrage that the President was coming. My successor, Chancellor Corbally, shared their sentiments. He wrote to President Nixon telling him that the invitation was withdrawn.

Later, I would be distressed by the events of Watergate and Nixon's role in them. I felt at the time, however, and I still do that Watergate was overblown and made to appear more than it was.

12

STRICTLY PERSONAL

*T*here were only fourteen months difference in age between Nelda and Bill, and as children they were inseparable. In our home at 438 Chestnut Street in Meadville, we erected a log cabin in the backyard. This was a playground for them and their friends. There was no garage at 438 Chestnut, and so the Allegheny trustees authorized the building of a new two-car garage. The garage had a very useful second floor on which we built bookcases to house the books President Tipple gave us when he retired.

Nelda, Bill, and the children in the neighborhood enjoyed the second floor of the garage as much as I did. I cannot recall, however, any conflict between their use of the garage and mine. All my life I have been able to read regardless of noise about me. I also have had the habit of reading at odd moments. This was particularly useful both during the Allegheny and the Syracuse years. Even today it's not uncommon for me to read twenty to thirty pages from one book and twenty minutes later read ten or fifteen from another. In a lifetime of administration, one moves from one problem to another. Each problem requires complete concentration. The same habits are acquired in reading. One learns to give one's full attention to the book in hand. To be sure, this habit leaves many books unfinished. On balance, however, there is much to say for a sampling process.

Nelda and Bill were good but not exceptional students. When we moved to Syracuse, they first attended the Levy School, and then the Edward Smith School and Nottingham High School. Though Bill and Nelda were happy in the public schools, we felt that they would get more personal attention at a private school.

We sent Nelda to Walnut Hill at Natick, Massachusetts; then she went to Allegheny College where she had four good years. She sang in the Allegheny Singers and was a member of Kappa Alpha Theta sorority. She received A's in graduate courses at the University of California and then went on to Syracuse where she took a master of arts' degree. Nelda is a very gifted teacher in the public schools of Hartford, Connecticut. She has two children, Jennifer and Jonathon. Jon now has two sons, Jonathon and Joel.

Both Jenny and Jon have exceptional voices. Jennifer is the chorale director and soloist in one of the largest Catholic churches in Hartford and is a public school teacher in music at Springfield, Massachusetts. In my biased view, she has the potential to be an opera singer. She had a taste of this in a brief stint in Italy between her undergraduate years at the University of Hartford and graduate study at Boston University. She has two children, Jessica and Brian.

Bill did well in high school. We sent him to Deerfield Academy for his final two years. Frank Boyden, the head of Deerfield, was a genius in his handling of students; but he did not do as much for Bill as he did for most of his students. On the basketball court when he saw Bill making a one-handed shot, he exclaimed, "Use both hands Bill, loop it! Don't throw a basketball with one hand." When Mr. Boyden interviewed Bill for admission, he asked Bill what instrument he played. "A flute," Bill replied. "A flute!" said Mr. Boyden, "ugh, ugh, ugh." That was the last time Bill ever touched the flute.

Bill wanted to go to Princeton, but Mr. Boyden thought Wesleyan would be a better place for him, so we sent him to Wesleyan. At the end of his first semester at Wesleyan, Bill transferred to Syracuse. The University was large enough for him to escape any attention on the Chancellor's son. He became a member of Phi Delta Theta fraternity, next door to our home. He majored in geology and took a master's in geology at Syracuse as well. He did additional graduate study at the University of Colorado and the University of Wisconsin. Bill has been a member of the geology faculty at Southern Connecticut University for more than twenty years. Happily married to a superior girl, Melanie Weis, Bill has three children, Neil, Sarah, and Lael.

Our youngest child, Katryn, was happy in her elementary and secondary school work at Syracuse. One of her special joys was becoming acquainted with the first editions of practically every work referred to in her English classes. I remember, for example, her borrowing Dickens in parts when her class was reading *David Copperfield* and *Great Expectations*.

We sent Katryn to Emma Willard for her final two years of high school. At the time, Emma Willard was perhaps the best girls' preparatory school in America. At the helm were two extraordinary women—Miss Wellington and Miss Lay. They were a formidable pair who did not suffer fools. They ruled with an iron hand. The reputation of the school was so good, however, that parents didn't seem to mind being intimidated. Dean Charles Noble was a great favorite at Emma Willard. The Misses Wellington and Lay had enormous respect for him, whereas until Katryn's senior year they hardly gave me the time of day. After attending several dances at Emma Willard, I finally made some headway with both Miss Wellington and Miss Lay. I greatly enjoyed dancing with them.

Katryn chose to attend Allegheny. It was a good choice. She liked her teachers, and she made a good adjustment to college. She was on the Dean's list and, like Nelda, was a member of Kappa Alpha Theta sorority. I was pleased she majored in English and was particularly happy when she decided to write her senior thesis on Kipling's short stories.

Now working as a secretary, Katryn has two boys, David and Paul. David is at Syracuse, and Paul is in high school. The boys are completely different, but are extraordinarily close to each other. Both of the boys are cross-country runners. For their grandfather, it has been a delightful experience to see them grow and mature.

I was able to take each of the children to Europe. I had two trips with Katryn, one with Bill, and one with Nelda that included the Greek Islands, Crete, and Rhodes. Each was as rewarding to me as it was to them. In 1954, Ruth and I had a memorable two-month visit without the children to Lebanon, Syria, Israel, Greece, Italy, and France. In some ways, it was the high point of many trips abroad.

In 1932 at the close of my first year at Allegheny, I spent two weeks at the Iron City Fishing Club at Georgian Bay, in Ontario, Canada, at the invitation of two trustees of Allegheny, Dr. Joseph Miles and W. Stuart Horner, who were leading members of the club. They talked about Iron City almost from the first time I met them.

The Iron City Fishing Club was organized in 1881 by a group of Methodists from Pittsburgh. When I first visited Iron City in 1932, there were between thirty and forty members, most of whom had their own cottages and boathouses. There were also a clubhouse, dining room, kitchen, tennis courts, a baseball field, and a fine sandy beach. There was a doctor in residence, and a lifeguard on duty. The club is located about twenty-eight miles south of Parry Sound and forty miles north of Midland. In the 1930s one traveled to the club by taking a four-hour boat trip on the Midland City, from Midland to Manitou Island. A small boat would meet us at Manitou and take us to the Iron City Fishing Club.

Vacationers usually stayed at Iron City for at least two or more weeks. There are some thirty thousand islands in Georgian Bay. Few places in the world are more beautiful. Until recently, the fishing has been superb and the water clear as crystal.

At the end of my second year at Allegheny, John Ritchie Schultz, the Dean of Men at Allegheny, accompanied me for a fortnight's holiday at Iron City. A great bridge player, Ritchie entered into all the activities of the club with enthusiasm and won the hearts of everyone. We had only a rowboat to use for fishing, and when we went out on our first trip together, I did the rowing. Ritchie was very critical of my rowing technique. "You're not getting your legs and back into it," he said. "You're only using your arms." When it came time to return to camp for luncheon, I suggested that Ritchie do the rowing so I could learn from observing him. He was delighted.

"See," he said, "this is how you do it. You get your back into it. You use your legs as well as your arms." "You do row much better than I do," I said. I had quietly dropped the anchor overboard, and as Ritchie rowed us to shore, he began to complain. "This boat is heavy," he said. "I'm beginning to get tired." "You're doing fine," I said. When we were about 200 feet from shore, I asked quite innocently, "Would it help if I pulled the anchor up?" The profanity that followed would have been worthy of a marine.

In the mid-nineteen thirties Ruth, the children, and I spent two summers at Lake George in a rented cottage, and one summer we had a happy month on Lake Erie, near the city of Dunkirk. We also had a brief holiday at Sheehan's Camp at Lake Panage in Ontario, Canada. I knew, however, we would eventually join the Iron City Fishing Club, where Ruth would not have to cook. We became members in the late thirties and rented cottages at the club until we were able to build our own. Bill and Nelda became devoted disciples of the seventeenth-century author Izaak Walton and his classic text *The Compleat Angler, or the Contemplative Man's Recreation.* Bill was an especially good fisherman, but he was also a sportsman. No matter how large the fish he caught, he always wanted to release it. I have watched him release small-mouth bass weighing three and a half or four pounds. One afternoon, when fishing in Lost Lake, a small pond into which we portaged our canoe, we caught a three-pound large-mouth bass, a four-pound bass, a five-pound bass, and a large-mouth bass weighing six pounds nine ounces. When we portaged our canoe back to Georgian Bay, Bill insisted on releasing all but the largest bass into the bay. "This will help the fishing," he said. We mounted our six pound nine ounce prize, and have never caught a larger one.

One week in July, I caught three muskellunges in two days, one of which I had mounted. As I caught the third one, Bill blurted out in exasperation, "That was my turn!" I couldn't help but agree.

Bill and Nelda are both expert swimmers, as was Ruth. Ruth could swim for hours. I enjoy swimming, but was never as good at it as the rest of my family.

Ruth was also an excellent equestrienne. When we were living in Meadville, I bought a horse for her named Roxy, which we kept in a riding stable about a mile north of town. I also bought a horse for Nelda, a dapple gray named Blue Bell. Ruth and Nelda rode three or four times a week from April to late November. In midwinter we rented a sleigh, bundled the children in, and had wonderful rides through the snow on unplowed back roads. I have never been happier! I rode with Ruth and Nelda occasionally, but it distressed them that I did not do it more often. When Sunday morning came, Ruth would say, "Please ride with us." I would have enjoyed doing so, but I felt obligated to go to Old Stone Church. As I look back, I wish I had ridden with them more often.

It is now fifty-six years since my first visit to the Iron City Fishing Club. Today, my daughter Katryn is a member, as is Nelda's son Jonathan Brewster Price. Katryn's two boys, David and Paul, have gone to Georgian Bay each year since their first birthdays. It has been a second home for all of us.

We seldom deserted the club for any other holiday retreat. We did, however, make an acquaintance with Eaton's Ranch near Sheraton, Wyoming, and have returned there several times. Our first visit was during my years at Allegheny, when Colonel Lewis Walker was our host. In introducing us to Alden Eaton, the owner of the ranch, he said, "Doctor Tolley is President of Allegheny College in Meadville, Pennsylvania, of which I am a trustee. You have probably never heard of Allegheny." "I think you've forgotten, Colonel," Eaton replied, "that my great grandfather Timothy Alden founded Allegheny College and was its first President."

We had only one trip to Europe during my Allegheny years. That was in 1936 and was the conventional grand tour of England, France, Germany, Norway, and Sweden.

In the years we lived in Meadville, picnics were our chief form of recreation. The children enjoyed them, and so did Ruth and I. We eventually joined the Iroquois Club on Conneaut Lake, where we would go for a swim and dinner. We almost never remembered that it was closed to women and children on Wednesday afternoon. Almost invariably when we set out for a pleasant family outing about one or two miles from the club, one of us would suddenly remember that it was Wednesday.

The schedule at Allegheny was so demanding that we liked to spend whatever spare time we had available to us as a family. We seldom invited anyone to join us either on picnics or at the Iroquois Club. After we moved to Syracuse in 1942, Gordon Smith persuaded me to buy a four-acre lot on Cazenovia Lake. We first built a tent platform for a 14-by-16-foot tent and a front porch. The tent was screened, and we had an electric light. I still recall the pleasure of sleeping in the tent during a summer shower. The sound of raindrops on canvas is the sweetest of music. We eventually built a modest two-bedroom cottage, which has served as a retreat for some forty years. I can count on the fingers of one hand the number of guests not members of the family who have stayed in our Cazenovia camp. For years we did not have a telephone, and we still do not have a post office box. The children and grandchildren stay there for weeks at a time, but Ruth and I would usually go out for a swim in the afternoon, cook our dinner on the grill, and return to Syracuse after dinner. Neither the fishing nor the swimming is the equal of Georgian Bay. Its convenience however, only a half hour from our home, is wonderful. I am sure that the camp at Cazenovia has added years to our life.

Gordon Smith also introduced me to the Hillsboro Club at Pompano Beach, Florida. We found this to be very much like the Iron City Fishing Club: simple buildings, wonderful people, wonderful food, and great tennis. For a few weeks each winter we have used the Hillsboro Club as a beachhead for fund-raising visits to alumni of Syracuse. We have been members for more than forty years.

When we came to Syracuse in 1942, Ruth was overcome by the size of the Chancellor's house. It has ten rooms on the first floor, ten on the second floor, and several on the third floor, to say nothing of several in the basement. She despaired of ever making it a home. As it turned out, her fears were groundless. Large as it was, 701 Walnut is a warm and friendly house. During the long winter months, the fireplaces in the living room and the library were almost always lit in the evening. Often we entertained groups of fifteen or twenty students, and they would gather cozily around the fire.

One of our special joys came at Christmas time when we would invite students who were serenading us to come into the house for donuts and coffee. Even with as many as fifty or sixty students at a time, we did not have to worry about where to put them. The rooms were large, and the students would sit comfortably on the oriental rugs near a log fire while we asked and answered questions.

Every year, we held receptions for the freshmen in the fall and the seniors in the spring. An average of one thousand students attended these receptions at 701 Walnut. I don't know whether the students enjoyed coming to the Chancellor's home, but Ruth and I enjoyed having them. Their visits were a high point in our lives.

Because of the number of years that Ruth and I had spent entertaining both at Drew and at Allegheny, I tried to spare her as much as I could from the burden of large-scale entertaining at Syracuse.

Shortly after we arrived in 1942, Ruth received a telephone call from Mrs. Frank Love. "Ruth," she said, "this is Winifred Love. Our American Association of University Women (AAUW) will meet at your home on October seventh."

"Mrs. Love," said Ruth, "I know that Mrs. Graham opened her house to many community groups. She had no children. We have three. We're trying to make it a home as well as the Chancellor's residence. I'm trying to select which groups to entertain, and, regretfully, I must tell you that we will not be entertaining the AAUW this year." Mrs. Love was not particularly pleased with Ruth's response, but she and Ruth were eventually the closest of friends.

We had a number of like experiences, until everyone recognized that we had the right to choose whom we could entertain. I also had an experience not unlike Ruth's when I first began taking over the management of the University. Chancellor Graham was sixty-six years old when he became Chancellor, and seventy-two when he retired. In the latter years of his term, he delegated more and more responsibility to George Hopkins Bond, a regent of the State of New York who was also our University attorney. I discovered that both the treasurer of the University and the Vice-Chancellor were referring matters to Mr. Bond instead of to me. I took Mr. Bond out to luncheon and told him that I deeply appreciated all he had done for the University, and would always lean on him for advice and counsel. I wanted him to know, however, that there was a new hand at the helm, and that I intended to be Chancellor in fact as well as in name. George's nose was out of joint for a brief time, but he knew I was right, and we soon became good friends.

At Allegheny, Ruth had not had to do much public speaking or presiding at meetings. At Syracuse, there were scores of organizations where she was not only expected to attend or to preside but was also called upon to speak. Mrs. Harold Butler, the wife of the Dean of the College of Fine Arts, had been a teacher of public speaking and knew her Roberts Rules of Order. She asked me if she could help Ruth overcome her shyness and inexperience in speaking. I assured her that Ruth would welcome it. Mrs. Butler was a fine teacher, who gave Ruth the confidence she needed.

Ruth's physical strength was limited, and she had to limit her interests. She took as her special province the College of Home Economics, in which she had been a student. She also befriended the women of the College's faculty and the wives of faculty members. At Allegheny, she had always sent birthday gifts to the faculty children. She did the same thing at Syracuse. Because of the size of the University faculty, it was not inexpensive. It was, however, most rewarding.

Ruth was gifted with an especially good memory for names and faces. She was better than I was. Many times in a reception line she would sense that I could not remember to whom I was speaking and would prompt me saying "You remember Hazel. You met her last year at our alumni meeting at Elmira," or, "You remember Joan, she and her husband, David, entertained us at their home in Albany." Little things can be very important. Everyone likes to be remembered.

Ruth's mother came to live with us in Syracuse after her seventieth birthday. We were able to offer her all the privacy and comforts of home in a delightful apartment on the second floor of 701 Walnut Avenue. This had served as the maid's quarters when the Nottingham family occupied the house. The apartment had a living room, two bedrooms, and a bath. It also had a back staircase to the kitchen.

Although her name was Florence, everyone called her "Canno" an abbreviation of Canfield, her married name. She was a most welcome addition to the Tolley household. In the ten years that she lived with us, I cannot remember a cross word or an unhappy moment. The children adored her, as did Ruth and I. She dealt firmly with the children. She was a model of tact and kindness.

Whenever Ruth and I went away, which was often, Canno would entertain the mothers of the members of the faculty living in Syracuse. She would set up the bridge tables in all the rooms of the first floor of 701. She provided cookies, coffee, and tea, and her guests would bring sandwiches and special desserts. Canno enjoyed this so much that she was always urging us to take a trip. The mothers enjoyed their evenings as much as she did.

I had business luncheons almost every day of the week while I was at Syracuse, but whenever I could I would stop home for a fifteen-minute nap before returning to the office. All my life, I have been able to fall asleep whenever my head touched a pillow. I can sleep for ten minutes and wake up completely refreshed. For anyone with my schedule, that ability can prove to be a lifesaver.

I seldom left the office until 5:30 P.M. and would usually have a dinner speech to make later that evening. Here again, 701 Walnut Avenue was a blessing. There was a gigantic bathtub on the second floor. I would fill it with hot water, jump in, and think out the speech I was going to give later that evening. Today we have whirlpool baths of the same size. They are probably the best invention since 7-Up. However, I treasure the memory of the big tub at 701 Walnut.

I retired as Chancellor of Syracuse University in September 1969. It was an ideal time to retire. The following year would bring the centennial anniversary of the University's founding, and I felt that a new Chancellor should be at the helm for the centennial celebration. I also thought the birthday celebration would be a good time to launch a new campaign for endowment and capital needs.

Ruth's health was also an important factor in my decision to retire. She was becoming increasingly forgetful, and her social burdens were harder and harder for her to face. I protected her in every way I could, but I knew that, with all the sacrifices she had made for me, she deserved an easier life. I did not know, however, that she had Alzheimer's disease and would soon need round-the-clock nursing care.

Despite my love for my work, I did not dread retirement. I was in excellent health. I was enjoying tennis more and more. I was also anxious to have a more active life of scholarship. I particularly wanted to pursue my interest in the history of medieval universities. This had been my field of study for more than twenty years. I also wanted to write a small book, *Candles in the Dark,* devoted to the handful of scholars living in the centuries following the fall of Rome. In addition, I looked forward to my book collecting, which by that time had become an addiction as well as a pleasure.

By January 1970, I was playing tennis almost daily and pursuing my reading program with renewed vigor. I read widely about the early Middle Ages and source materials about Salerno, Bologna, and the University of Paris. I reread Thucydides, Herodotus, and Xenophon. I rediscovered Isocrates, whose influence I had not fully appreciated. I reread Plato and Aristotle, Aeschylus, Euripides, Sophocles, and Aristophanes, and discovered a number of Greek and Roman authors I had not previously read. I even did some writing. I was happier than I had been in years.

My pursuit of knowledge was soon interrupted. The illness of Robert Peach forced his resignation from the presidency of Mohawk Airlines. Mr. Peach was replaced by Russell Stevenson, and I, having been a director of the airline since 1963, was named chairman of the board.

A chairman of the board who is not the chief executive officer is nothing but a fifth wheel. Nevertheless, I accepted the position. It was a long drive from Syracuse to Utica, but I did not mind it. I usually arrived just before seven o'clock in the morning. I went to the Utica offices to observe and learn, but so far as influence was concerned, my time could have been better spent reading the newspaper. By 1970, Mohawk Airlines was in a strike we could have and should have avoided. Unable to reverse labor and management policies, I did not enjoy my tenure as chairman of the board. I did, however, learn a great deal. I also found it easy to make the transition from the world of education to the world of business. In 1971, I was made chief executive officer, and this role was a challenge and an opportunity.

Under the leadership of Bob Peach, Mohawk Airlines was essentially a one-man company. Mr. Peach had been a very strong executive but he did not surround himself with officers of like strength. The company had many capable midlevel managers. Its weak spot was the quality of the officers at the top. Only after the resignation of some of the senior officers did we become profitable. By that time, however, under pressure from the Chase Bank, we had agreed to merge with Allegheny Airlines. My daily round trip to Utica smoothed my transition into retirement. Preoccupied with the situation at Mohawk, it was easy not to become too interested in what was happening in the University. Even the student uprising of 1970 did not disturb me. I refused to pass judgment on anything that happened.

Old age is not for sissies. If one lives long enough, one is bound to face problems. In my case it was Ruth's health and nursing care. With nurses twenty-four hours a day for more than four years, my life centered about her until her death in 1988. I did not particularly like doing the marketing, but the cooking was a source of pleasure and pride. I have great respect for good cooks and housekeepers. I also have great respect for nurses and nurses aids.

I was able to continue playing tennis until I passed my eighty-second birthday. My last trophy was won in 1977 in the Geritol Doubles at the Sedgwick Farms Tennis Club. My running left so much to be desired that I described my game as one of statues and runners. My partner was the runner. I was the statue.

After open-heart surgery for a new aortic valve in 1983, my exercise has been limited to walking, fishing, and swimming, and my recreation has been reading, writing, and listening to classical music. The pleasure of reading is greater than ever, but I have experienced a steady loss in my attention span. I also require more and more rest.

For a few years after retirement in 1969, I continued to serve as a director of the Colgate Palmolive Company, the New York Telephone Company, the Excelsior Insurance Company, the U.S. Air Group, the Security Mutual Life Insurance Company of New York, Key Bank of Central New York, and Key Corp of Albany, New York. In each case, I was a very active director. I still go once a month to the directors meeting of Key Bank as an advisory board member. I also meet once a year with old friends at the Christmas party of New York Telephone and the annual meetings of Security Mutual and U.S. Air.

One of my many interests has been the National Methodist Foundation for Christian Higher Education at Nashville, Tennessee. At a national meeting of Methodists at Pittsburgh, I had proposed the organization of a foundation to strengthen church ties with Methodist founded colleges and universities. In 1964, the general conference of the United Methodist Church created the foundation, and I served as its President for many years.

I had not been active in my Syracuse social fraternity after graduation in 1922, but after retiring as Chancellor, I served as President of the Pi Kappa Alpha Memorial Foundation, Memphis, Tennessee. I found it an interesting and rejuvenating experience.

For a year, I served as President of the Century Club of Syracuse, the leading social club for men. I was not a good President, being unduly stubborn in my support of an unpopular manager. I did, however, succeed in broadening admission policies to include those men formerly barred because of religion, race, or ethnic background. We also built and financed a long-needed parking facility.

I have continued my relationship to the Japan International Christian University and still serve as vice-chairman of its foundation in New York. My University interests include the Syracuse University Library Associates, the Society of Fellows, the Salzberg Program in Transportation, Orange Plus, Orange Pack, Lettermen of Distinction, the William P. Tolley Medal in Continuing Education, and Tau Theta Upsilon, which is the senior honorary society for men.

I also take an interest in the University's athletic teams. I attend most of the home games in the Carrier Dome and know the names and special skills of the men in football, basketball, and lacrosse, as well as the women in basketball, track, and tennis. With the long winters of Syracuse, the sports program of the University is as important as the Syracuse Symphony, the Library Associates, Syracuse Stage, and the Lowe and Everson museums. I have a modest apartment in St. Petersburg, Florida, but usually spend only a few weeks there. The apartment is used, however, by my children and grandchildren. I also maintain an office in the Bird Library. This has proved to be of increasing importance.

Some of my critics say that my years at Drew University and Allegheny College conditioned me to administer Syracuse University as if it were a small college. There is a good deal of truth in the charge. At Drew and at Allegheny, we were a happy family, and this was equally true at Syracuse. The members of the faculty, students, administrative staff, parents, alumni, and friends shared a common devotion to the University. We liked and trusted each other. We enjoyed doing our best, and we felt more than adequately rewarded when the University moved forward. Even when money was tightest, we had extraordinarily high morale. Genuine bonds of affection and trust enabled us to make the difficult appear easy. We were members of a winning team.

Today, I feel more like a grandfather than a father of the Syracuse family. That gives me all the pleasure without any of the responsibility. All who worked with me, however, are still members of my family. The love we share for each other and for the University is the sweetest of pleasures.

I am sure my experience is not unique. Most people who spend their lives working for a college or a university find that there is something very special about campus life. Like Norman Vincent Peale, we think positively. We are dyed-in-the-wool optimists.

If we believe in miracles, it is because we see so many before our eyes. If we believe in dreams it is because so many of them come true. We are believers in the art of becoming, which is what education is. We have a direct experience of witnessing and sharing the limitless growth of the human mind and spirit.

We stay young much longer than most people. The secret is our determination to continue to study and learn and to keep our close ties to youth of college age.

Do I recommend it to others? I do indeed! Education is a field where we are paid to do what we enjoy most. No life is a more meaningful service to others. No life is more crowded with happiness and joy. Life at the fountain of youth is life abundant, life to the full.

AT THE FOUNTAIN OF YOUTH
was composed in 11 on 13 Baskerville, on a Linotron 202
by Partners Composition;
with display type set in Baskerville Semi-Bold Italic
by Dix Type, Inc.;
printed by sheet-fed offset on 50-pound, acid-free Glatfelter Natural Hi-Bulk,
Smyth-sewn and bound over binder's boards in Holliston Roxite B,
with dust jackets printed in 2 colors,
by Braun-Brumfield, Inc.;
designed by Victoria Welch
and published by

SYRACUSE UNIVERSITY

SYRACUSE, NEW YORK 13244-1100